Thomas Aquinas

The Cardinal Virtues

Prudence, Justice, Fortitude, and Temperance

Translated and Edited, with
Introduction and Glossary, by

Richard J. Regan

Hackett Publishing Company, Inc.
Indianapolis/Cambridge

11 10 09 08 07 06 05   1   2   3   4   5   6   7

For further information, please address
Hackett Publishing Company, Inc.
P. O. Box 44937
Indianapolis, Indiana 46244–0937

www.hackettpublishing.com

Cover design by Listenberger Design & Associates

Composition by William Hartman

Printed at Sheridan Books, Inc.

Library of Congress Cataloging-in-Publication Data

Thomas, Aquinas, Saint, 1225?–1274.
    [Summa theologica. English. Selections]
    The cardinal virtues : prudence, justice, fortitude, and
temperance / Thomas Aquinas ; translated and edited with
introduction and glossary, by Richard J. Regan.
       p. cm.
    Includes bibliographical references (p.) and index.
    ISBN 0-87220-746-3 (cloth) — ISBN 0-87220-745-5 (paper)
    1. Prudence. 2. Fortitude. 3. Justice (Virtue).
4. Temperance (Virtue). 5. Christian ethics—Catholic authors.
I. Regan, Richard J. II. Title.

BJ255.T42S86213 2005
179'.9—dc22
                        2005046199

Contents

Preface

Several years ago, I translated and edited an anthology of Thomas Aquinas' texts of philosophical importance in ST I and I-II (*A Summary of Philosophy*, cited in the Select Bibliography). This work extends that effort to Aquinas' treatment of the cardinal virtues in ST II-II. The book is chiefly designed for undergraduate courses in ethics or moral theology. It complements his treatment of human acts, virtue, and law in ST I-II, which was translated amply in *Virtue: Way to Happiness* and fully in the *Treatise on Law*, both cited in the Select Bibliography. Instructors of such courses may wish to combine consideration of Aquinas' ethical views with those of other philosophers or theologians. The book will also be useful as a reader for nonacademics and a reference source for nonspecialists.

I have followed the question-and-answer format of Aquinas. The answers are in his own words, although I have edited the texts to delete almost all citations of Scripture and other philosophers and theologians. I otherwise fully provide his answers to the questions and his arguments to support his answers. I have retained only the objections and his replies to them that I deem most important. The numbering of the objections is mine, not that of Aquinas in the *Summa*. I have placed the selected objections and his replies to them after the answers to the questions. I have added italicized introductory notes to the chapter sections, and these notes aim to provide the reader with helpful guidance. The Glossary explains key terms to assist the reader, and the Select Bibliography directs the reader to important works on Aquinas' thought.

The Latin text on which I based my translation is the 1952 Marietti recension of the Leonine text. The University of Scranton Press has graciously granted permission to adapt part of the introduction to *Virtue: Way to Happiness* for use in the Introduction to this work. I am indebted to Douglas Kries of Gonzaga University for his thorough review of the manuscript and many helpful suggestions. I am also most grateful to Brian Rak of Hackett Publishing Company for his encouragement and careful attention to the manuscript.

RICHARD J. REGAN
Bronx, N.Y.

Abbreviations

ad	response to objection
A., AA.	article, articles
Cor.	Corinthians
Mt.	Matthew
NE	Aristotle, *Nicomachean Ethics*
Obj.	objection
Q., QQ.	question, questions
ST	Thomas Aquinas, *Summa Theologica*

Introduction

Thomas Aquinas flourished in the second and third quarters of the 13th century of our era (AD 1224/1225–1274). A Dominican friar, he lectured at the University of Paris and taught Dominican students at Naples. Toward the end of his life, he wrote a summary of theology, the *Summa Theologica*, to introduce beginners to the study of the discipline.

The entire *Summa* is, in effect, Aquinas' answer to the question: what is the meaning of human life? The central purpose of the *Summa* is to show why human beings exist, their destiny, and how they can achieve it. Aquinas argues that human beings exist to know God, that their destiny is to enjoy the vision of God in the next life, and that they need to act properly in this life in order to be worthy of their destiny. The *Summa* represents a major attempt to introduce the method and principles of Aristotle (384–327 BC) into the study of Christian theology.

The first part of the *Summa* (ST I) treats of God, creatures, and human nature. The first half of the second part (ST I-II) deals with the human end and the role of human acts and virtues in achieving the end. The second half of the second part (ST II-II) deals with specific virtues and the moral character of particular acts. The third part (ST III) considers the life of Christ and the role of the sacraments in the lives of the Christian faithful. In the course of summarizing Christian theology, Aquinas explicitly deals with many topics of philosophical interest and advances explicitly philosophical arguments—that is, arguments based on reason rather than Scripture or church authority. This Introduction recapitulates Aquinas' thought about the human end, human acts, virtue in general, and the natural law in ST I-II, especially in comparison with Aristotle's treatment; and outlines Aquinas' thought in ST II-II about the cardinal virtues—that is, the chief virtues related to human action: prudence, justice, fortitude, and temperance. (See Glossary, s.v. *Fortitude, Justice, Prudence, Temperance.*) This volume anthologizes that treatment of those virtues.

Aquinas' treatment of the cardinal virtues and contrary sins in the *Summa* was designed to provide a manual of moral theology for confessors and prospective confessors.[1] But it is much more. Theologians have generally regarded it as one of the most, if not the most, systematic and thorough explanations of Christian ethics, and philosophers have generally considered it a paradigm of rational analysis, whatever their view of its principles and method.

---

[1] Cf. ST, Prologue.

Aquinas, of course, was not the first thinker to develop a virtue-oriented moral system. Like most of Western philosophy, that orientation goes back to the Greeks. In particular, there were Plato (especially in the *Republic*) and Aristotle (especially in the *Nicomachean Ethics*). Aquinas was well acquainted with the latter's work, as were the arts and theological faculties of the University of Paris, and wrote a commentary on it. (See Select Bibliography.) He and his University colleagues were also acquainted with the Stoics, at least as represented in Cicero's *On Duties*.

Aquinas wrote elsewhere about morals. His monumental work was the treatise *On Evil* [*De malo*]. (See Select Bibliography.) He uses the seven capital sins as the organizing principle of that work and, in the course of discussing those sins, says much about the contrary virtues. As indicated, he wrote a commentary on the *Nicomachean Ethics*. (See Select Bibliography.) Although that work is commentary, he is evidently in general agreement with Aristotle on virtue in general and specific virtues. Aquinas also wrote two treatises on virtue: *Disputed Question on Virtue in General* and *Disputed Question on the Cardinal Virtues*. (See Select Bibliography: *Disputed Questions on Virtue*.) In addition, Aquinas' political writings offer insight, especially on political prudence. Chief among these works are the unfinished commentary on Aristotle's *Politics* and the treatise *On Kingship* [*De regno*]. (See Select Bibliography.)

The Human End

Every kind of thing has a nature that aims to achieve its specific perfection, which is its end. (See Glossary, s.v. *Nature*.) Seedlings grow into mature plants and trees capable of fully exercising vegetative functions; colts grow into mature horses capable of fully exercising animal functions; and babies grow into mature adults capable of fully exercising rational functions. Accordingly, human beings differ from other kinds of living material things (and, of course, from all nonliving material things) in that human beings have the power to understand and reason. And because the power of reason is the specific perfection of human beings, they attain their ultimate perfection, the state of happiness, by activities of reason and activities in accord with reason. Aquinas rejects any contention that human happiness consists of material goods, although material goods (e.g., a sound body and moderate wealth) are necessary for happiness in this life.[2] Rather, he holds that human happiness is a condi-

---

[2] ST I-II, Q. 2, AA. 1–5.

tion of the soul produced by activities of reason and other human activities in this life in accord with reason.[3] Aquinas is in basic agreement with Aristotle on these points.

But when Aquinas specifies the object of human happiness, he decisively parts company with Aristotle. The object of perfect happiness, says Aquinas, is the intellectual vision of God's essence, albeit not a comprehensive vision.[4] He argues that human beings will not be perfectly happy so long as there remains something more for them to know, that nature constitutes them to seek and know God, and that they cannot in this life know what God is in himself. (As presently constituted, the human intellect depends on sense images and so knows God only through his perceptible effects; that is, only as the cause of perceptible things and the possessor of the perfections of perceptible things in an infinitely superior way.)

Aristotle was satisfied with the limited, albeit daunting, goal of theoretical wisdom as the most important ingredient of human happiness. Human beings readily understand that the coming-to-be of things is due to causes, and that human beings, by the use of their reason, can discern the ultimate causes (efficient, final, formal, and material) of all changeable things. (See Glossary, s.v. *Cause*). In so doing, human beings become theoretically wise and attain the perfection of their specifically rational nature.

Aquinas does not deny that theoretical wisdom is the major ingredient of human happiness in this life. (Theoretical reason concerns the ultimate cause of things; practical wisdom concerns human action. See Glossary, s.v. *Intellectual Virtues, Prudence [Practical Wisdom]*.) Moreover, he agrees with Aristotle that human beings, in order to be happy in this life, need a body (indeed, a suitable body), external goods, and the company of friends.[5] But he insists that the happiness attainable in this life is incomplete and imperfect, a pale reflection of the perfect happiness of beholding God's essence; and that nothing material or created, including human friendship, is essential to such perfect happiness.[6]

Both Aristotle and Aquinas recognize that human happiness in this life also requires right reason to govern external actions and internal emotions, and a rightly ordered will regarding the requisite ends of human actions and emotions. Aquinas, however, goes beyond Aristotle to maintain that rectitude of the will is necessary for human happiness not only because happiness results from the proper direction of the will to act in accord with right reason,[7] but also because willing to do so entails loving

---

[3]ST I-II, Q. 2, A. 7. [4]ST I-II, Q. 3, A. 8. [5]ST I-II, Q. 4, AA. 5–8.
[6]Ibid. and Q. 2, A. 8. [7]ST I-II, Q. 4, A. 4.

as good whatever God loves and wills.[8] For Aquinas, there is no complete rectitude of the will without conformity to God's will and his commands, which reason and revelation communicate.

Thus, despite the large measure of agreement that Aristotle and Aquinas share regarding the human end, they differ sharply about the sufficiency of theoretical and practical wisdom in this life for the complete happiness of human beings. On the one hand, the pagan Aristotle does not conceive God in providential terms, and so he does not look to happiness in a future life as the final goal of human beings. On the other hand, the Christian Aquinas conceives God in such terms, and so he cannot look to the theoretical and practical wisdom accessible to human beings in this life—or even a more complete theoretical wisdom in the next life, short of the beatific vision—as the ultimate human end.

Aquinas further argues that the beatific vision is the ultimate human end because the intellect by nature desires it; that is, that the beatific vision befits human nature.[9] Philosophers and theologians will need to weigh the merit of Aquinas' argument. But his position, if accepted, raises serious problems. On the one hand, the fact that human beings have a desire from nature for the complete happiness of the beatific vision seems to suggest that God, who created human beings with such a desire, should fulfill it if human beings act in accord with right reason and his will. On the other hand, to suppose that God could have not bestowed the beatific vision on those who follow the dictates of right reason and his will seems to imply that God could have left unfulfilled the natural desire of human beings for complete happiness in the vision of himself.

Aquinas' position in this regard is that human beings can attain an incomplete and imperfect happiness in this life by their natural power to acquire intellectual and moral virtue, but that they cannot by their natural power acquire the complete and perfect happiness of the beatific vision.[10] In other words, the beatific vision is a gift that God freely deigns to bestow on those who do his will. God endows human beings with the requisite freedom and grace to carry out his will and thereby provides the requisite means for human beings to qualify for the complete and perfect happiness of the beatific vision. But however much human beings may cooperate in the dispositions of themselves for the beatific vision, the vision itself remains beyond their natural power to attain.

As a Christian, Aquinas firmly believes that God has destined worthy human beings for eternal union with himself. As a theologian, Aquinas explains the union in terms of the beatific vision and seeks to demonstrate

---

[8]E.g., ST I-II, Q. 19, A. 4; Q. 91, A. 3. [9]ST I-II, Q. 3, A. 8. [10]ST I-II, Q. 5, A. 5.

that the vision befits the rational nature of human beings. The beatific vision, although a free gift of God, complements the natural desire of human beings to know him in himself. Beyond that, Aquinas was apparently unwilling to speculate about the hypothetical possibility that God would not deign to bestow the beatific vision on worthy human beings.

But is such a state possible? The position of Aquinas and Christian tradition on the gratuity of human beings participating in God's life would seem to suggest that a state of pure nature, one in which human beings would not be destined to share in God's life, is possible. And if such were to be the case, the maximum happiness that human beings could attain would be theoretical and practical wisdom in this life, and the highest possible theoretical wisdom short of the vision of God in the next life. This happiness, of course, would be incomplete and imperfect in comparison with the beatific vision; but it would be as complete and perfect as human beings could attain by their natural power.

Some Christian theologians, especially Bonaventure (AD 1217?–1274), while agreeing that perfect human happiness is only possible in the heavenly union with God, argued that it is the love of God in such a union, not the knowledge of his essence, that makes human beings perfectly happy. The significance of this dispute may be exaggerated. On the one hand, Aquinas holds that love of God necessarily accompanies the cognitive vision of God, since the will necessarily seeks goodness, and God's essence is goodness itself. And on the other hand, Bonaventure holds that the cognitive vision of God necessarily accompanies perfect love of God, since the will is the faculty of intellectual desire and so can find perfect satisfaction only insofar as the intellect knows God. Nonetheless, there is a difference of emphasis reflecting the larger question of the relative rank of cognition and affection in the rational life of human beings.

Human Acts and Virtue in General

Aquinas theorizes precisely and systematically about the human will and human acts. He distinguishes the intellectual appetite, the will, from the sense appetites.[11] He distinguishes voluntary things from involuntary things.[12] He considers the effect of force, fear, concupiscence, and ignorance on the voluntariness of human acts.[13] The intellectually understood good is the object of the will.[14] The intellect moves the will by presenting the understood object to it;[15] emotions can dispose the will

---

[11]ST I, Q. 80, A. 2.   [12]ST I-II, Q. 6, AA. 1–3.   [13]ST I-II, Q. 6, AA. 4–8.   [14]ST I-II, Q. 8, A. 1.   [15]ST I-II, Q. 9, A. 1.

toward the object;[16] and God is the first cause of the will and its acts as such.[17] But none of these—the intellect, sense appetites, or God, unless he dispenses a special grace—causes the will to will particular means to attain happiness.[18] The intellect directs—that is, structures—what the will wills; but the will is free to choose imperfectly good things and even the perfect good thing (God) if the intellect understands that good imperfectly.[19] Practical reason deliberates about[20] and decides (judges)[21] what to do or not to do; and the will, by consenting, chooses to do or not to do it.[22] Practical reason commands sense faculties and external bodily members to carry out the will's choice.[23]

Human acts derive their moral goodness from the suitability of the acts' objects for the ultimate human end,[24] from observance of requisite circumstances,[25] and from the goodness of the ends for the sake of which one acts.[26] Conversely, human acts derive their malice from the lack of any of these things. The goodness of the will itself depends exclusively on the will's object and so on reason, which presents the object to the will as in accord or discord with right reason.[27] Since the light of human reason participates in the eternal law, the goodness or malice of the will depends even more on that law.[28] Every will that acts contrary to reason, even erroneous reason, is evil;[29] and acts of the will in accord with erroneous reason are evil if human beings will not to know, or neglect to know, what they can and should know.[30]

The most striking contrast between Aquinas' treatment of human acts and Aristotle's is the attention that Aquinas pays to the moral goodness and malice of individual human acts. Aristotle was largely concerned about the moral character of human acts in connection with the development of moral virtue—that is, with the relation of morally good and bad acts to the acquisition of morally good habits. Aquinas, although similarly concerned about the relation of morally good and bad acts to the acquisition of virtue, is also and chiefly concerned about the consequence of such acts for meriting happiness in heaven or punishment in hell.

For Aristotle, a virtuous life constitutes its own reward, and a vicious life its own punishment. For Aquinas, a virtuous life in this world does not confer complete happiness on human beings, and a vicious life in this world does not sufficiently punish human beings with unhappiness.

---

[16]ST I-II, Q. 9, A. 2.   [17]ST I-II, Q. 9, A. 6.   [18]ST I-II, Q. 9, A. 3.
[19]ST I-II, Q. 10, A. 2.   [20]ST I-II, Q. 14.   [21]ST I-II, Q. 13, A. 1, *ad* 2;
A. 3.   [22]ST I-II, Q. 15.   [23]ST I-II, Q. 17, AA. 7, 9.   [24]ST
I-II, Q. 18, A. 2.   [25]ST I-II, Q. 18, A. 3.   [26]ST I-II, Q. 18, A. 4.
[27]ST I-II, Q. 19, AA. 1–3.   [28]ST I-II, Q. 19, A. 4.   [29]ST I-II, Q. 19,
A. 5.   [30]ST I-II, Q. 19, A. 6.

Moreover, morally bad acts, in Aquinas' view, are not only contrary to the dictates of right reason and so morally bad for their perpetrators, but contrary to the dictates of God's law and so deserve fitting retribution from him. Accordingly, the morality of every human act involving serious matter is of supreme importance for human beings. For example, murder is not only contrary to the humanity of the murderer and unjust to the victim, but also a serious offense against God that deserves the punishment of hell. Conversely, just acts are not only virtuous and just to others, but they are also acts that, by God's gift of grace, merit the reward of heaven.

Aristotle held that certain emotions (e.g., spite and envy), insofar as they are subject to reason, are always morally wrong, since such emotions as such are disordered—that is, contrary to right reason and virtue.[31] He also cited acts of adultery, murder, and theft as always morally wrong, presumably because they involve injustice—against the husband of the woman in the case of adultery and against the victims in the cases of murder and theft—and so disorder the perpetrator's soul.[32] But Aquinas, going beyond Aristotle's concerns and mode of analysis, holds that some external acts are always evil because they frustrate the intrinsic ends of the acts, even if the acts are victimless; and that no larger purpose, however good, can render such acts morally good. For example, Aquinas argues that lying is always morally wrong because it frustrates the purpose of communicative speech, although much speech is not such.[33] Similarly, he argues that some sexual acts (e.g., masturbation, bestiality, homosexuality, and contraception) are always morally wrong because they are contrary to the intrinsic reproductive purpose of sex.[34]

Natural Law

For Aquinas, moral obligation is a matter of legal obligation. He defines law as the rational ordering of means to end for the good of a community by one (or more) with authority over the community, and promulgated to the community,[35] and he applies the definition to God's act of creation. In that act, God rationally orders created things, including human beings, to their specific ends and the good of the universe,[36] obviously has the authority to do so, and manifests this order in the natures of the things he creates. And because the act of creation is identical with God's eternal substance, Aquinas calls this order of created things the eternal law.[37]

---

[31]NE II, 6. 1107a9–27.   [32]Ibid.   [33]ST II-II, Q. 110, A. 1.   [34]ST II-II, Q. 154, A. 11.   [35]ST I-II, Q. 90.   [36]ST I, Q. 22, AA. 1–2.   [37]ST I-II, Q. 91, A. 1.

Irrational creatures have no freedom regarding their actions, and human beings are not free to determine their specific end or the objective rectitude of human acts.[38] But human beings are free to choose to act or not to act in ways conducive to attaining their end, and so human beings participate rationally and freely in the eternal law. If human beings rationally decide and freely choose to act in accord with their nature, they rationally and freely share in God's plan for themselves as individuals and as a community. And so Aquinas can properly call this participation in the eternal law, the natural law.[39]

Aquinas is a Christian theologian. He considers creation, and so the natural law derived from it, as one aspect of God's salvific plan for humankind. Whereas Aristotle rests content with human goodness in a self-sufficient and rightly governed community, Aquinas is concerned as well with Christian holiness and the obedience to God's commands, explicit or implicit, in his creative act and salvific will. In this regard, the natural law has a supernatural dimension: observance of the natural law can be a grace-enriched act, and failure to observe the natural law is a sinful act. In Aquinas' view, divine revelation plays a supportive role in recognizing the demands of the natural law, and divine grace an indispensable role in its consistent and substantial observance. Moreover, love of God is the guiding source of the morally virtuous activity of the Christian faithful.

But the natural law itself is accessible to reason. Reason can discern the order of nature that makes demands on human behavior. These demands derive from the order of nature, and so their observance rewards human beings with human fulfillment, and nonobservance of the demands punishes human beings with lack of human fulfillment. Nature entails this reward and punishment. From this perspective, we can say that Aquinas introduces God's creative act to provide the ontological ground for an ethic based on human nature. He brings God into the act, so to speak, to support, not supplant, such an ethic. We should strive to act in accord with right reason both because we are so constituted, and because God so constitutes us.

The first principle of practical reason—that is, the first principle of human action—is that human beings should seek things that are good for them as human beings and avoid things that are bad for them as human beings.[40] This principle is self-evident. Human beings, simply by understanding the terms *human good* and *things that human beings should seek,* and the terms *human evil* and *things human beings should avoid,* can without argument understand the necessary connection.

---

[38]ST I, Q. 82, A. 1; ST I-II, Q. 18, A. 2.   [39]ST I-II, Q. 91, A. 2.
[40]ST I-II, Q. 94, A. 2.

Because good is the end of action, human beings also understand that those things toward which human nature inclines them are human goods, and that contrary things are human evils. Aquinas, reflecting on data provided by the senses about human activity, identifies three classes of things toward which human nature inclines human beings.[41] First, nature inclines human beings, in common with all substances, to strive to preserve their being. Second, nature inclines human beings, in common with all animals, to seek sexual union and to beget and educate their offspring. Third, nature inclines human beings, precisely as rational beings, to know truths about God and his plan of creation and to live in community with other human beings. Practical reason, on understanding these things to be the objects of inclinations from nature, articulates the primary precepts of the natural law. Human beings should take reasonable means to preserve their lives, enjoy sexual union and beget offspring according to reason, know truths about God and his plan of creation, and live cooperatively in society with other human beings. As in the case of the first principle of practical reason, human beings, on understanding the precepts' terms, can assent to them without any inductive or deductive process of reasoning.

Reason, with knowledge gained from experience, enables one to draw conclusions about particular kinds of human acts by applying the primary precepts as principles; and these conclusions constitute secondary precepts of the natural law.[42] Aquinas admits that some secondary precepts may be so formulated as to be valid only for the most part. For example, one formulation of a secondary precept of the natural law prescribes that one should return property held in custody to its owner upon request for its return, but it is obviously contrary to reason that one should return a gun to an owner who has homicidal intentions. Moreover, Aquinas admits that some persons and peoples may not recognize the truth of valid secondary precepts of the natural law. For example, a secondary precept of the natural law prescribes that one should not steal the property of another; but emotions, habits, and customs may blind the reason of some persons and peoples from recognizing the precept.

Aquinas, by contrasting the conclusions of practical reason with those of theoretical reason, explains why secondary precepts of the natural law may be so formulated as not to be universally valid.[43] Theoretical reason deals with necessary things, and so its conclusions are as universally valid as its premises. But practical reason deals with contingent things, and such things can vary widely. There is an essential difference between the methods of theoretical and practical reason. Theoretical reason draws

---

[41]Ibid.   [42]ST I-II, Q. 94, A. 4.   [43]Ibid.

conclusions in a categorically deductive way in mathematics and Aristotelian natural science (see Glossary, s.v. *Science [Aristotelian]*), but practical reason (ethics) draws conclusions by relating contingent things to general principles.

The distinction within the class of secondary precepts between those that are proximate and those that are remote is as important as the distinction between primary and secondary precepts.[44] The relation of some human acts to the primary precepts is so easily understood that reason can promptly—that is, with little reflection—conclude that one, at least generally, should or should not act in a particular way. The relation of other human acts to the primary precepts is not so easily understood, and so considerable reflection is required before reason can conclude that one, at least generally, should or should not act in a particular way. The latter, remote conclusions are the province of those Aquinas calls the wise; that is, professionals practically wise and knowledgeable about the subject matter. For example, by applying the primary precept to live cooperatively in society, one can, with little reflection, conclude that one should not kill another human being without just cause; but it requires considerable reflection to decide if or when a particular cause justifies killing another (e.g., what causes, if any, justify the killing in war).

For Aquinas and Aristotle, human beings need to form a body politic in order to promote their proper human development; that is, to develop themselves intellectually and morally as well as materially. But Aquinas goes further and links human law to natural law. Human law is either a conclusion based on natural law (e.g., human laws prohibiting murder, robbery, and theft) or a further determination, or specification, of natural law (e.g., human laws regulating traffic).[45] This linkage is absolutely essential if human law is to qualify as law at all—that is, if human law is to be morally obligatory.[46]

Human laws are just if they are ordered to the common good, fall within the power of the lawmakers, and lay proportionately equal burdens on citizens. Conversely, human laws are unjust if they depart in any of these respects, and then, absolutely speaking, human beings are not morally obliged to obey them. Human beings may, however, be morally obliged to obey such unjust laws for the sake of the common good; namely, to avoid civil unrest and the breakdown of legal observance. Human laws may be unjust in another way if they command things contrary to the natural or divine law, and then human beings are morally obliged to disobey such unjust laws.[47]

---

[44]ST I-II, Q. 100, A. 1.   [45]ST I-II, Q. 95, A. 2.   [46]ST I-II, Q. 96, A. 4.
[47]Ibid.

Specific Virtues and Particular Acts

ST II-II explains the specific virtues to be cultivated in Christian life and the contrary sins to be avoided. Aquinas first considers the theological virtues of faith, hope, and charity.[48] God needs to infuse these supernatural virtues in the human soul, since human beings cannot acquire them by their own natural activity, although they can cultivate and develop them with God's grace. Some of the topics considered in Aquinas' treatment of the theological virtues are relevant to moral behavior. For example, Aquinas treats of war and insurrection in relation to charity,[49] but these subjects are also related to justice. And so this anthology, although it excludes Aquinas' treatment of the theological virtues as such, includes his treatment of war and insurrection under the virtue of justice.[50]

After treating of the theological virtues, Aquinas considers the cardinal virtues: prudence, justice, fortitude, and temperance. These are natural virtues, to which charity adds supernatural prudence and supernatural moral virtues.[51] Prudence is the first cardinal virtue.[52] Human action should be in accord with reason, and theoretical reason understands the ends of moral virtues (e.g., to be just in relations with others, brave in confronting mortal dangers and other evils, and moderate in sense desires and pleasures).[53] It is the function of prudence, or practical reason, to determine the means to achieve the ends of the moral virtues.[54] Prudence is an intellectual virtue but concerns practical, not theoretical, things.[55] It has integral—that is, constitutive—parts such as memory and understanding.[56] It has subjective parts—that is, subdivisions.[57] The principal division is between the common prudence that ordinary citizens exercise and the particular (higher) prudence that those who govern exercise.[58] It has potential—that is, related—parts: good deliberation, good judgment according to general law, and good judgment about exceptions to general law.[59] One can sin against prudence by diverging from the rules of right reason (imprudence)[60] and by lack of due care (negligence).[61]

Justice is the second cardinal virtue.[62] Since justice as a special virtue concerns one's relations to others, it is evidently the most important moral virtue.[63] Right is the object of justice.[64] Aquinas, like Aristotle, understands right as the objectively right order of social relations, not the

---

[48]ST II-II, QQ. 1–46.   [49]ST II-II, QQ. 40, 42.   [50]See below, pp. 00.
[51]ST I-II, Q. 65, A. 2.   [52]ST II-II, QQ. 47–56.   [53]ST II-II, Q. 47,
A. 6.   [54]ST II-II, Q. 47, A. 7.   [55]ST II-II, Q. 47, A. 2.   [56]ST
II-II, QQ. 48–49.   [57]ST II-II, QQ. 48, 50.   [58]ST II-II, Q. 47, AA.
12–13; Q. 48; Q. 50, AA. 1–2.   [59]ST II-II, Q. 51.   [60]ST II-II,
Q. 53.   [61]ST II-II, Q. 54.   [62]ST II-II, QQ. 57–122.   [63]ST II-
II, Q. 58, A. 12.   [64]ST II-II, Q. 57, A. 1.

subjective right of individuals. For example, it is right that human beings not deliberately kill innocent human beings. Of course, the necessary consequence of this right order is that individual, innocent human beings have a right not to be deliberately killed; but the rights of individuals are the focus of Enlightenment philosophers, not that of Aquinas. Natural, divine, and human laws prescribe the right order of social relations.[65]

Justice in general is moral virtue in general, as directed to the common good,[66] and particular justice concerns relations to other individuals.[67] Particular justice has two subjective parts: commutative justice, which concerns the quid pro quo relations between individuals; and distributive justice, which concerns the allocation of common goods to individuals in proportion to their contribution to the common good.[68] In connection with commutative justice, Aquinas considers the problem of restitution.[69]

Human beings sin against distributive justice if they give favorable treatment to particular persons irrespective of the persons' deserts.[70] Human beings sin against commutative justice by deeds against another's person (e.g., murder)[71] or property (e.g., theft).[72] Human beings sin against commutative justice by word in abuses of the criminal judicial process. In particular, Aquinas examines what justice requires of judges,[73] accusers,[74] defendants,[75] witnesses,[76] and lawyers.[77] He also considers ways in which human beings sin against commutative justice in word outside the criminal judicial process.[78] He then considers commutative justice in connection with buying and selling things and the commutative injustice of lenders exacting interest or any monetary equivalent on money lent to borrowers.[79]

There are two integral parts of justice: avoiding evil—that is, acts contrary to justice—and doing good—that is, acts required by justice.[80] Conversely, one sins against justice by transgression, acting contrary to justice, and by omission, failing to perform acts required by justice.[81] Aquinas contends that transgressions are, for the most part, more serious sins than omissions.[82]

There are potential parts of justice (e.g., acts of religion, filial devotion, and truth-telling).[83]

---

[65]ST II-II, Q. 57, A. 2.   [66]ST II-II, Q. 58, A. 6.   [67]ST II-II, Q. 58, A. 7.   [68]ST II-II, Q. 61.   [69]ST II-II, Q. 62.   [70]ST II-II, Q. 63.   [71]ST II-II, QQ. 64–65.   [72]ST II-II, Q. 66.   [73]ST II-II, Q. 67.   [74]ST II-II, Q. 68.   [75]ST II-II, Q. 69.   [76]ST II-II, Q. 70.   [77]ST II-II, Q. 71.   [78]ST II-II, QQ. 72–76. These questions are not included in this anthology.   [79]ST II-II, QQ. 77–78.   [80]ST II-II, Q. 79, A. 1.   [81]ST II-II, Q. 79, AA. 2–3.   [82]ST II-II, Q. 79, A. 4.   [83]ST II-II, QQ. 80–119. These questions are not included in this anthology.

Lastly, Aquinas relates the Aristotelian principle of equity, fundamental fairness, to justice and argues that application of legal principles to particular cases sometimes fails to effect justice.[84] In such cases, reason requires that fundamental fairness trump the letter of the law.

Fortitude, or courage, is the third cardinal virtue.[85] As a special virtue, fortitude guards the will against withdrawing from the good prescribed by reason, because of fear of the most grievous bodily harm; namely, mortal dangers.[86] The virtue disposes the will to stand firm against the fear and counterattack it with moderately bold action.[87] The former is the chief act of fortitude because it is more difficult to withstand fear than to moderate boldness.[88] The virtue of fortitude consists of the mean between too much fear (timidity) and too little fear (temerity)[89], and of the moderation of boldness by reason.[90] The corresponding sins against fortitude are timidity, temerity, and excessive boldness.

Fortitude has integral and potential parts but no subjective parts.[91] The integral parts in relation to standing fast are patience and perseverance.[92] The integral parts in relation to counterattacking fear are mental confidence, which Aquinas equates to magnanimity, and bold action, which he equates to magnificence.[93] Fortitude has potential parts insofar as human beings courageously withstand and overcome fear of things other than mortal bodily harm (e.g., fear of losing one's job unless one commits sin).

Temperance is the fourth cardinal virtue.[94] As a special virtue, temperance guards the will against choosing sense desires and pleasures contrary to the good of reason,[95] and one sins against temperance when one chooses such things.[96] The subjective parts of temperance regard food (moderate abstinence),[97] alcoholic drink (sobriety),[98] and sex (chastity).[99] The integral parts involve a sense of shame regarding intemperate acts, and a sense of honor.[100] The potential parts are continence, humility, meekness, mercy, good order, proper attire, parsimony (self-sufficiency), and moderation (simplicity).[101]

---

[84]ST II-II, Q. 120.   [85]ST II-II, QQ. 123–40.   [86]ST II-II, Q. 123, A. 4.   [87]ST II-II, Q. 123, A. 3.   [88]ST II-II, Q. 123, A. 6.
[89]ST II-II, QQ. 125–26.   [90]ST II-II, Q. 127.   [91]ST II-II, Q. 128.
[92]ST II-II, QQ. 136–38. These questions are not included in this anthology.
[93]ST II-II, QQ. 129–35. These questions are not included in this anthology.
[94]ST II-II, QQ. 141–70.   [95]ST II-II, Q. 141, AA. 2–3.   [96]ST II-II, Q. 142.   [97]ST II-II, QQ. 143, 146–48.   [98]ST II-II, QQ. 143, 149–50.   [99]ST II-II, Q. 143, 151–54.   [100]ST II-II, QQ. 143–45.
[101]ST II-II, QQ. 143, 156–70. These parts are not included in this anthology.

1

Prudence

In Itself

According to Thomas, prudence is an intellectual virtue. (See Glossary, s.v. Intellectual Virtues, Prudence, Virtue). *Unlike theoretical intellectual virtues, which concern necessary things, practical intellectual virtues concern contingent things. Unlike skills—practical intellectual virtues that concern making things—prudence concerns doing things; that is, the characteristically right disposition about what one should do or not do to achieve the proper ends of human action. Prudence applies knowledge to human action, and so a prudent person needs to know both universal principles and the individual things involved in action.*

Since one applies right reason to action only if one has right desire, prudence shares the character of virtue that moral virtues (e.g., justice, fortitude, temperance) have. But the different subjects in which prudence and moral virtues reside (prudence in the intellect, moral virtues in the will) distinguish prudence from moral virtues. Self-evident principles regarding the ends of moral virtues (e.g., just, brave, moderate actions) preexist in practical reason, and prudence does not prescribe these ends. Rather, prudence disposes regarding means to those ends. The end of moral virtues is the mean of reason (e.g., the mean between timidity and temerity, and the mean between too much and too little eating or drinking).

Prudence involves three acts of reason: deliberating well, judging rightly, and commanding what one should do or not do. Commanding what one should do or not do, since it is closer to the end of practical reason (i.e., proper human action), is the chief act of prudence. A prudent person needs to be solicitous; that is, shrewd about and quick to do what one ought to do. Prudence regards both the private good of the individual and the common good of a community, and these goods constitute specifically different ends. Prudence belongs preeminently to rulers, but also to subjects insofar as they share in ruling by their rational decisions to obey their rulers.

Prudence is true prudence if reason disposes fitting ways to achieve a good end, and false prudence if reason disposes fitting ways to achieve an evil end (e.g., to be a good robber). True prudence is imperfect if the good end is that of a special occupation (e.g., to be a good businessman), or if the command of prudence is ineffective. One who habitually loves God and neighbor has prudence. All human beings by nature know the universal first principles of prudence and the ends of

1

human life; some human beings are by nature disposed toward certain moral virtues, but no human being is by nature disposed toward the means to achieve moral virtues. Forgetfulness can hinder prudence, and emotions can destroy it.

1. Does prudence belong to the intellect or the will?[1]

We call a person prudent who sees ahead, as it were, since such a person is perspicacious and sees the outcomes of uncertain things. But seeing belongs to a cognitive, not an appetitive, power. Therefore, it is evident that prudence belongs directly to a cognitive power. But prudence does not belong to a sense power, since sense powers know only things that are at hand and present themselves to the senses. And knowing future things from present or past things, which belongs to prudence, is in the proper sense a function of reason, since prudence makes comparisons. And so we conclude that prudence in the proper sense belongs to reason.

Objection. Choosing wisely belongs to prudence. But choice is an act of the will. Therefore, prudence belongs to the will, not the intellect.

Reply Obj. The prudent person considers remote things insofar as the things are related to helping or hindering other things to be done at present. And so prudence evidently considers things ordered to other things as ends. But regarding means to ends, reason deliberates, and the will chooses. And deliberation more strictly belongs to prudence. But because choice presupposes deliberation, so we can also ascribe choosing to prudence; namely, insofar as deliberation directs choice.

2. Does prudence belong to theoretical as well as practical reason?[2]

It belongs to the prudent person to be able to deliberate well. But deliberation concerns things that we should do in relation to an end. And the reason that concerns things to be done for the sake of the end is practical reason. And so it is evident that prudence consists solely of practical reason.

Objection. Prudence is engaged in the search for truth and infuses a desire for fuller knowledge. But this belongs to theoretical reason. Therefore, prudence also consists of theoretical reason.

Reply Obj. To say that prudence is engaged in the search for truth and infuses a desire for fuller knowledge is to use the word *prudence* more broadly to mean any human knowledge, both theoretical and practical. Nevertheless, we can say that the very act of theoretical reasoning, insofar as it is voluntary, falls under choice and deliberation as to its exercise and so under

---

[1]ST II-II, Q. 47, A. 1.   [2]Ibid., A. 2.

the order of prudence. But as to its species, as it is related to its object, which is necessary truth, it does not fall under deliberation or prudence.

3. Does prudence know individual things?[3]

Both the consideration of reason and its application to action, which is the end of practical reason, belong to prudence. But no one can suitably apply something to something else unless one should know each thing; namely, both what is to be applied and that to which it is to be applied. And actions regard individual things. And so a prudent person needs to know both the universal principles of reason and the individual things that are the objects of human actions.

Objection. Prudence belongs to reason. But universal things are the object of reason. Therefore, prudence knows only universal things.

Reply Obj. Universal things are first and chiefly the object of reason, but reason can apply universal considerations to particular things. (This is why there are particular as well as universal conclusions of syllogisms.) Reason can apply universal considerations to particular things because the intellect can reach the matter of particular things by returning to the sensory sources of the intellect's activity.

4. Is prudence a virtue?[4]

Virtue makes its possessor good and the possessor's actions good. And we can speak of good in two ways: in one way, materially, meaning the thing that is good; in the second way, formally, regarding the aspect of goodness. But good as such is the object of the will. And so any habits, if they produce the right consideration of reason without respect to rectitude of the will and direct reason to something materially good (i.e., to something good but not under the aspect of goodness), have less of the character of virtue. And those habits that regard rectitude of the will have more of the character of virtue, since they regard good both materially and formally (i.e., the good thing under the aspect of its goodness). But the application of right reason to actions belongs to prudence, and one performs this only with right desire. And so prudence has both the character of virtue that other intellectual virtues have and the character of virtue that moral virtues have, and we also list prudence with the latter virtues.

5. Is prudence a special virtue?[5]

Acts and habits receive their species from their objects. Therefore, a habit for which there is a corresponding special object needs to be a special habit, and the special habit is a special virtue if the habit is good. And we call

---

[3]Ibid., A. 3.   [4]Ibid., A. 4.   [5]Ibid., A. 5.

an object special by reason of its formal, not its material, aspect, since one and the same thing in different respects is the object of the acts of different habits and powers. But the difference in the object needs to be greater to distinguish powers than to distinguish habits, since several habits belong to the same power. Therefore, the aspect in an object that distinguishes a power differs much more that the aspect that distinguishes a habit.

Therefore, we should say that prudence, since it belongs to reason, differs from other intellectual virtues by the material difference of their objects. For theoretical wisdom, scientific knowledge, and understanding regard necessary things, and skills and prudence regard contingent things. Skills regard things to be made (e.g., houses, knives, and the like), namely, things constituted in external matter; and prudence regards things to be done, namely, things constituted in the one who acts. But we distinguish prudence from moral virtues by the distinctive formal aspect of the powers; namely, the intellect, in which prudence resides, and the will, in which moral virtue resides. And so prudence is evidently a special virtue distinct from all other virtues.

6. Does prudence prescribe the ends of moral virtues?[6]

The end of moral virtue is the human good. But the good of the human soul is to be in accord with reason. And so the ends of moral virtues need to preexist in reason. But theoretical reason knows some things by nature, things we understand, and knows other things through them: namely, conclusions, things we know by demonstration. Just so, there preexist in practical reason some things as principles we know by nature, and such things are the ends of moral virtues, since ends are related to things to be done as first principles are to theoretical things. And practical reason knows other things as conclusions, and such things are means to the ends, things that we adduce from the very ends. And prudence, applying universal principles to particular conclusions about things to be done, concerns these means. And so it belongs to prudence only to dispose regarding means to the ends of moral virtues, not to prescribe the ends.

Objection. It belongs to the virtue or skill or power to which an end belongs to command the other virtues or skills to which means to the end belong. But prudence disposes regarding other moral virtues and commands them. Therefore, it prescribes their ends.

Reply Obj. Ends do not belong to moral virtues as if the latter prescribe their own ends, but because they tend toward the ends prescribed by natural reason. And prudence, which prepares the way for them, helps them by disposing means to the ends. And so we conclude that prudence is more excel-

---

[6]Ibid., A. 6.

lent than moral virtues and causes them. But *synderesis* causes prudence, just as understanding first principles causes scientific knowledge.

7. Does it belong to prudence to find the mean in moral virtues?[7]

Being conformed to right reason is itself the proper end of any moral virtue. For example, the aim of temperance is that human beings not turn away from reason because of inordinate sense desires. Likewise, the aim of fortitude is that human beings not turn away from the right judgment of reason because of timidity or temerity. And natural reason prescribes these ends for human beings, since natural reason dictates to each that each act in accord with reason. But it belongs to the disposition of prudence how and by what things human beings attain the mean of reason in their actions. For although attaining the mean is the end of a moral virtue, the mean is found through the right disposition of things ordered to the end.

8. Is commanding the chief act of prudence?[8]

Prudence is right reason about things to be done. And so the chief act of reason about things to be done is necessarily the chief act of prudence. And there are three acts of reason about things to be done. The first of these is to deliberate, which belongs to discovery, since to deliberate is to inquire. The second act is to judge about the things discovered, and this consists of theoretical reason. But practical reason, which is ordered to action, goes further; and the third act of practical reason is to command, which act consists of applying the objects of our deliberation and judgment to our actions. And this act, because it is closer to the end of practical reason, is the chief act of practical reason and so of prudence.

And the fact that the perfection of a skill consists of judging, not commanding, illustrates this point. That is why, regarding skills, we consider an artisan who judges correctly and errs intentionally superior to one who seems to judge incorrectly and errs unintentionally. But the converse is true about prudence, since one who errs intentionally, failing, as it were, in its chief act (i.e., commanding), is more imprudent than one who errs unintentionally.

9. Does solicitude belong to prudence?[9]

We call one solicitous who is shrewd and quick; namely, insofar as one with shrewdness of mind is quick to do the things that one ought to do. But this belongs to prudence, the chief act of which concerns commanding the things to be done, regarding the things already deliberated about and

---

[7]Ibid., A. 7. [8]Ibid., A. 8. [9]Ibid., A. 9.

judged. And so one needs to deliberate slowly but act quickly. And so solicitude, in the proper sense, belongs to prudence.

10. Does prudence extend to governance of a community?[10]

Some held that prudence extends only to one's own good, not the common good. And they said this because they thought that human beings should seek only their own good. But this opinion is contrary to charity, which does not seek one's own benefit (1 Cor. 13:5). The opinion is also contrary to right reason, which judges that the common good is superior to the good of an individual.

Therefore, since it belongs to prudence to deliberate, judge, and command rightly regarding the means to attain our requisite end, prudence is evidently related both to the private good of individuals and to the common good of a community.

Objection 1. The prudent seem to seek good and act for themselves. But those who seek common goods frequently neglect their own. Therefore, they are not prudent.

Reply Obj. 1. Those who seek the common good of a community consequently also seek their own good. This is true for two reasons. First, it is because there cannot be a good of one's own apart from the common good, whether of a family or a city or a kingdom. Second, it is because human beings, since they are parts of households and political communities, need to consider what is good for themselves by what is prudent regarding the good of these communities. For we understand the right disposition of parts by their relation to the whole.

Objection 2. We distinguish prudence from temperance and fortitude in the same genus. But we seem to speak of temperance and fortitude only in relation to one's own good. Therefore, we should also speak thus of prudence.

Reply Obj. 2. We can relate even temperance and fortitude to the common good. And so also precepts of the law are laid down regarding acts of temperance and fortitude. But prudence and justice, which belong to the rational part of the soul, relate more to the common good; and universal things belong directly to that part of the soul, just as individual things belong to the sensory part of the soul.

11. Is prudence regarding one's own good specifically the same as prudence reaching the common good?[11]

We distinguish species of habits by differences we note regarding the formal aspect of the habits' objects. But we note the formal aspect of

---

[10]Ibid., A. 10.   [11]Ibid., A. 11.

every means in relation to its end. And so relations to different ends necessarily distinguish species of habits. But the proper good of individuals and the good of families and the good of a city or kingdom are different ends. And so these different ends of necessity also specifically distinguish different kinds of prudence. One kind is prudence in an absolute sense, which is ordered to one's own good. And the second kind is domestic prudence, which is ordered to the common good of a household or family. And the third kind is political prudence, which is ordered to the common good of a city or kingdom.

Objection. Aristotle says that "the virtue of a good person and that of a good ruler are the same."[12] But political prudence belongs especially to the ruler, in whom it is like that of a master builder. Therefore, since prudence is the virtue of a good person, it seems that prudence and political prudence are the same characteristic disposition.

Reply Obj. Aristotle says in the same place that "the ability to rule well and the ability to be ruled well belong to the same person."[13] And so even the virtue of a ruler is included in the virtue of a good person. But the virtue of a ruler and that of a subject differ specifically, as do the virtue of a man and that of a woman.

12. Does prudence belong to subjects or only to rulers?[14]

Prudence belongs to reason. But ruling and governing belong properly to reason. And so it belongs to one to have reason and prudence insofar as one shares in ruling and governing. But it is evident that being ruled and governed, not ruling and governing, belongs to a subject as such and a slave as such. And so prudence is not the virtue of a slave as such or a subject as such. But since human beings, as rational, share in some governance by their rational decisions, it belongs to them to have prudence to that degree. And so it is evident that prudence belongs to a ruler like a master builder's skill and to subjects like a manual worker's skill.

13. Can prudence belong to sinners?[15]

We speak of prudence in three ways. There is a false prudence, that is, one by analogy. For as a prudent person is one who well disposes things to be done for the sake of a good end, a person who, for an evil end, disposes things befitting that end has a false prudence, since what the latter takes as an end is good by analogy and not truly good. Just so, we speak of a good robber, since we can thus, by analogy, call prudent a robber who devises fitting ways to rob.

---

[12]*Politics* III, 4 (1277a20–21).   [13]Ibid. (1277b13–15).   [14]ST II-II, Q. 47, A. 12.   [15]Ibid., A. 13.

And the second kind of prudence is true prudence, since it devises fitting ways for a truly good end but is imperfect in two ways. It is imperfect in one way because the good that one takes as an end is the end of a special occupation, not the common end of human life as a whole. For example, we call a businessman or sailor prudent when such a one devises fitting ways to carry on business or go about sailing. It is imperfect in a second way because it is deficient in the chief act of prudence. For example, such is the case when one deliberates well and judges rightly even about things that belong to life as a whole, but does not command effectively.

And there is a third kind of prudence, both true and perfect, which rightly deliberates, judges, and commands in relation to the good end of life as a whole. And we call only this kind prudence in an absolute sense.

The third kind of prudence cannot belong to sinners. And the first kind of prudence belongs only to sinners. And imperfect prudence is common to the good and the wicked, in particular the prudence that is imperfect because of a special end. For the prudence that is imperfect because of the deficiency of its chief act also belongs only to the wicked.

14. Does prudence belong to all who possess grace?[16]

Virtues are necessarily connected, so that those who have one have all of them. But whoever has grace has charity. And so anyone with charity necessarily has all the other virtues. And so, since prudence is a virtue, one with grace necessarily has prudence.

15. Is prudence in us by nature?[17]

Prudence includes knowledge of both universal things and the individual things to be done, to which the prudent apply the universal principles. Therefore, regarding universal knowledge, reason with respect to prudence is the same as reason with respect to theoretical scientific knowledge, since we by nature know the universal first principles of both, except that the universal first principles of prudence are more connatural to human beings. But we possess other, derivative universal principles, whether of theoretical or practical reason, by discovery through experience or by instruction, not by nature.

And again, we should distinguish regarding particular knowledge of the things of which actions consist, since actions consist of particular things, whether as regards the ends or as regards the means. But the right ends of human life are fixed. And so there can be a natural inclination

---

[16]Ibid., A. 14.   [17]Ibid., A. 15.

regarding these ends, as, for example, some persons by natural disposition have certain virtues that incline them to right ends and so, also by nature, have right judgment about such ends. But the means to ends in human affairs are not fixed. Rather, they differ in many ways because persons and occupations differ. And so, since a natural inclination is always to something fixed, such knowledge of particulars cannot be in human beings by nature, although one person is by natural disposition more fit than another to discern such things. This is also true regarding the conclusions of theoretical scientific knowledge. Therefore, since prudence concerns means, not ends, prudence is accordingly not in us by nature.

16. Can prudence be lost by forgetfulness?[18]

Forgetfulness regards knowledge alone. And so one can by forgetfulness totally lose skills and scientific knowledge, which consist of reason. But prudence consists not only of knowledge but also of desire, since the chief act of prudence commands, that is, applies the knowledge possessed to desiring and acting. And so forgetfulness does not directly take away prudence. Rather, emotions destroy it. Nonetheless, forgetfulness can hinder prudence, since the command of prudence is the product of some knowledge, which forgetfulness can take away.

Parts

Thomas next enumerates the integral, subjective, and potential parts of prudence. The integral parts are the constitutive parts of perfect acts of prudence. Five of these belong to prudence as cognitive: memory, understanding, disposition to learn, keenness, and reason. Three belong to prudence as commanding: providence, circumspection, and caution. The subjective parts are the different species of prudence. One species is the prudence by which one governs oneself, and the other is the prudence by which one governs many people. The latter is subdivided according to the different kinds of multitude governed: military prudence in commanders, who govern armies; domestic prudence in the heads of households, who govern households; kingly prudence in rulers, who govern political communities; and political prudence in subjects, who obey their rulers. The potential parts of prudence are connected virtues relating to secondary acts or subject matters, which do not possess the whole power of prudence. The potential acts of prudence are good deliberation, judgment about things that happen regularly, and higher judgment about things regarding which one sometimes needs to depart from the general law.

---

[18]Ibid., A. 16.

1. Do we suitably assign parts of prudence?[19]

There are three kinds of parts: integral parts, such as the walls, roof, and foundation of a house; subjective parts, such as cattle and lions of animal; and potential parts, such as the nutritive and sensory parts of the soul.

We can assign things necessary to constitute the complete act of a virtue as the **integral parts** of the virtue. Five things belong to prudence as cognitive. Regarding knowledge itself, there is **memory**, which is knowledge of past things, and **understanding**, which is knowledge of present things, whether contingent or necessary. And regarding the acquisition of knowledge, this is either by instruction, to which the **disposition to learn** belongs, or by discovery, to which **keenness** (i.e., the quick estimation of the middle term of a syllogism) belongs. And regarding the use of knowledge, there is **reason**, which goes from known things to knowing or judging other things. Three things belong to prudence as it commands action by applying knowledge. Reason adopts suitable means to ends, which belongs to **providence**, considers the circumstances of an action, which belongs to **circumspection**, and avoids obstacles, which belongs to **caution**.

The different species of a virtue are its subjective parts. The **subjective parts** of prudence in the strict sense are the **prudence by which one governs oneself**, and the **prudence by which a multitude is governed**. The latter prudence is subdivided according to different kinds of multitude. One kind of multitude is united for a special task (e.g., an army is united to wage war, and the prudence governing this multitude is military). Another kind of multitude is united for life as a whole. Such are the multitude of a household or family, whose governing prudence is domestic, and the multitude of a city or kingdom, whose governing prudence is kingly in the ruler and political, absolutely speaking, in the ruler's subjects.

But if we should understand prudence broadly, insofar as it includes theoretical knowledge, then we also posit **probable reasoning, rhetoric,** and **physics** as parts of prudence according to the three ways of proceeding scientifically. One way causes sure knowledge by demonstrative syllogisms, and this belongs to physics, under which we may understand all demonstrative sciences. Another way causes probable knowledge from probable premises, and this belongs to probable reasoning. A third way uses some conjectures to induce hypothetical propositions or in some way to persuade, and this belongs to rhetoric. We can nonetheless say that these three things belong in the strict sense to prudence, which reasons

---

[19]ST II-II, Q. 48, A. 1.

sometimes from necessary premises, sometimes from probable premises, and sometimes from certain conjectures.

The potential parts of a chief virtue are connected virtues. The latter are directed to secondary acts or subject matters, which do not possess the whole power of the chief virtue, as it were. The **potential parts** of prudence are **good deliberation, judgment about things that happen regularly,** and **judgment regarding which it is sometimes necessary to depart from general law.** But prudence concerns the chief act, that is, commanding.

Integral Parts

1. Is memory part of prudence?[20]

Prudence concerns contingent things to be done. But in these matters, things true for the most part rather than things absolutely and necessarily true are able to direct human beings, since first principles need to be related to conclusions, and human beings need to reach such-and-such conclusions from such-and-such things. And human beings need to consider by experience what is true in most cases. And so experience and time generate and increase intellectual power. But experience comes from memory of many things. And so memory of many things is required for prudence. And so we appropriately posit memory as a part of prudence.

Objection. We acquire and perfect prudence by practice. But we have memory from nature. Therefore, memory is not part of prudence.

Reply Obj. As prudence has an aptitude from nature but is perfected by practice or grace, so also memory arises from nature but has a good deal of skill and diligence. And there are four things whereby human beings progress in remembering well. The first of these is that human beings appropriate certain suitable but somewhat unusual images of the things they wish to remember, since we wonder more at unusual things; and so the mind is more and more strongly engaged in their regard. And this is why we remember more of the things we saw in childhood. And so we need to devise such likenesses and images. This is because simple and immaterial impressions slip rather easily out of our minds unless they are linked, as it were, to some material images; and human knowledge is more powerful regarding sensibly perceptible things. And so we also posit power of memory in the sensory part of the soul.

Second, human beings need to consider and dispose in an orderly way the things they wish to hold in their memory, so that they easily advance from one remembered thing to another.

---

[20]ST II-II, Q. 49, A. 1.

Third, human beings need to be solicitous and determined about the things they wish to remember, since the more something has been impressed on the mind, the less does it slip out of it.

Fourth, we need to think often of the things we wish to remember. And so reflection preserves memories, since customary behavior is quasi-natural. And so we quickly remember things we understand often, progressing from one thing to another by a quasi-natural order.

2. Is understanding part of prudence?[21]

We do not here take understanding to mean the power of the intellect. Rather, we here take understanding to signify a right estimation of a self-evident first principle, just as we speak of understanding the first principles of scientific demonstrations. But every deduction of reason comes from some things that we understand as first principles. And so every process of reason needs to come from some understanding. Therefore, since prudence is right reason about things to be done, so every process of prudence needs to derive from understanding. And so we posit understanding as part of prudence.

Objection. One of two contraries is not part of the other. But we divide intellectual power into two contraries: understanding and prudence. Therefore, we ought not posit understanding as part of prudence.

Reply Obj. The reasoning of prudence arrives at a conclusion about a particular thing to be done, to which prudence applies universal knowledge. But a syllogism reaches a particular conclusion from a universal proposition and a particular proposition. And so the reasoning of prudence needs to come from two kinds of understanding. And one kind of understanding knows universal things. And this belongs to the understanding we posit as intellectual power, since we by nature know both universal theoretical principles and universal practical principles (e.g., *do evil to no one*).

And the other understanding knows the last thing; that is, the first particular and contingent thing to be done: namely, the minor premise, which needs to be particular in a prudential syllogism. But the first particular thing to be done is a particular end. And so the understanding we posit as part of prudence is the right estimation of a particular end.

3. Should we posit the disposition to learn as part of prudence?[22]

Prudence concerns particular things to be done. But since there is an almost infinite variety in such things, one human being cannot sufficiently consider all things or consider them in a short span of time. And so,

---

[21]Ibid., A. 2.   [22]Ibid., A. 3.

regarding things belonging to prudence, human beings especially need to learn from others, and especially from elders, who have obtained sound understanding of the ends of things to be done. And it belongs to the disposition to learn that one receive instruction well. And so we appropriately posit the disposition to learn as part of prudence.

4. Is keenness part of prudence?[23]

It belongs to a prudent person to estimate rightly about things to be done. And we acquire right estimation or opinion in practical as well as theoretical things in two ways. We acquire right estimation in one way by discovering it by ourselves, and we acquire it in another way by learning it from someone else. And as the disposition to learn belongs to human beings who are well disposed to acquire right opinion from other human beings, so keenness belongs to human beings who are well disposed to acquire right estimation by themselves. And keenness is the easy and ready estimation regarding discovery of the middle term. And so keenness is the habit produced by quickly discovering what is fitting.

5. Should we posit reason as part of prudence?[24]

A prudent person needs to deliberate well. But deliberation is an inquiry progressing from some known things to other known things, and this is the work of reason. And so it is necessary for prudence that human beings should reason well. And since we call things necessary for the perfection of prudence necessary or integral, as it were, parts of prudence, we ought to include reason with the parts of prudence.

Objection. We should not posit something common to many things as part of any one of them, or if we should posit something common to many things as part of one of them, we ought to posit the common thing as part of that to which it most belongs. But reason is necessary in all the intellectual powers and chiefly in theoretical wisdom and scientific knowledge, which use demonstrative reason. Therefore, we ought not posit reason as part of prudence.

Reply Obj. The certitude of reason is from the intellect, but the need for reason is from the deficiency of the intellect. For things in which intellectual power is completely active do not need reason. Rather, such things (e.g., God and angels) understand truth by their pure intuition. But particular things to be done, regarding which prudence directs, are very remote from the condition of intelligibility; and the less certain or fixed they are, the more remote they are from intelligibility. For example,

---

[23]Ibid., A. 4.   [24]Ibid., A. 5.

things proper to skills, although particular things, are nonetheless more fixed and certain; and so there is no deliberation about most of the things proper to skills, since the things are certain. And so, although there is more certain reason in other intellectual virtues than in prudence, human beings need especially to reason well about what they should do or not do, so that they can rightly apply universal principles to particular things, which are various and uncertain.

6. Should we posit providence as part of prudence?[25]

Prudence, properly speaking, concerns the means to an end, and it belongs properly to the function of prudence that the means should be directed to the end. And although some things necessary for the sake of an end are things subject to divine providence, only contingent practical things that human beings can do for the sake of an end are subject to human providence. And past things have a certain necessity, since what has happened cannot now be otherwise. Likewise, present things as such have a certain necessity, since Socrates is necessarily seated as long as he is sitting. And so future contingent things, insofar as human beings can order them to the end of human life, belong to prudence. And the word *providence* signifies both of these things, since providence signifies foresight of something remote, to which present things should be ordered. And so providence is part of prudence.

7. Should we posit circumspection as part of prudence?[26]

It chiefly belongs to prudence to direct something to an end rightly. And one does this rightly only if the end is good, and the means directed to the end are good and suitable to the end. But because prudence concerns particular practical things, regarding which there are many circumstances, the circumstances may render something as such good and suitable for an end either evil or unsuitable for it. For example, showing signs of love for a person, insofar as they are such, seems to be suitable to draw that person's soul to love; but if there should be pride or suspicion of flattery in that person's soul, showing the signs of love will not be suitable to the end. And so circumspection is necessary for prudence; namely, so that human beings also relate the means to circumstances.

8. Should we posit caution as part of prudence?[27]

The things that prudence concerns are contingent practical things regarding which evil can be mixed with good, just as falsehood can be mixed with truth. This is because of the complexity of such practical

---

[25]Ibid., A. 6.   [26]Ibid., A. 7.   [27]Ibid., A. 8.

things, in which evil things often prevent good things but appear to be good. And so caution is necessary for prudence, so that we undertake good things in such a way that we avoid evil things.

Subjective Parts

1. Should we posit kingly prudence as a species of prudence?[28]

Ruling and commanding belong to prudence. And so there is a special character of prudence in which there is a special character of governance and command in human actions. But there is clearly a special and perfect character of governance in those empowered to rule both themselves and the perfect community of a city or kingdom, since the more universal the governance, extending to more things and achieving a further end, the more perfect it is. And so prudence in its special and most perfect character belongs to kings, who have authority to rule a city or kingdom. And so we posit kingly prudence as a species of prudence.

Objection. A kingdom is one of six kinds of regime. But we do not understand species of prudence in the other five kinds of regimes: namely, aristocracy, polity (also called timocracy), tyranny, oligarchy, and democracy. Therefore, neither should we understand kingly prudence regarding a kingdom as a species of prudence.

Reply Obj. A kingdom is the best regime. And so we should designate a species of prudence from kingdoms rather than other regimes. But we should include under kingly prudence all the other good regimes, though not the bad ones, which are contrary to virtue and so do not belong to prudence.

2. Do we appropriately posit political prudence as a species of prudence?[29]

Masters cause slaves to act, and rulers their subjects, by their commands, but in a different way than causes induce irrational and inanimate things to act. For other things cause inanimate and irrational things to act, and the latter do not cause themselves to act, since they do not have mastery of their actions by free choice. And so their right governance resides only in the things causing their actions, not in themselves. But the commands of other human beings cause slaves or any subjects to act in such a way that the slaves or subjects, by free choice, cause themselves to act. And so they need to have right governance whereby they direct themselves in obeying those who govern them. And the species of prudence that we call political belongs to this.

---

[28]ST II-II, Q. 50, A. 1.   [29]Ibid., A. 2.

Objection 1. Kingly prudence is part of political prudence. But we should not distinguish parts from the whole genus of which they are parts. Therefore, we should not posit political prudence as another species of prudence.

Reply Obj. 1. Kingly prudence is the most perfect species of prudence. And so the prudence of subjects, which falls short of kingly prudence in governance, keeps the general name *political*. Just so, in logic, convertible terms that do not signify the essence of something keep the general name *property*.

Obj. 2. Different objects distinguish different species of habits. But rulers command and subjects execute the same things. Therefore, we should not posit political prudence, insofar as it belongs to subjects, as a species of prudence different from kingly prudence.

Reply Obj. 2. Different aspects of an object specifically distinguish habits. But a king indeed considers the same things to be done but regarding an aspect more universal than the aspect that subjects, who obey the king, do, since many subjects obey the same king in different tasks. And so we relate kingly prudence to the political prudence about which we are speaking, as we relate the skill of a master builder to the skills of manual workers.

3. Should we posit domestic prudence as a species of prudence?[30]

Different universal and particular, or whole and partial, aspects of an object distinguish skills and virtues, by which difference one skill or virtue is chief regarding another. But a household is clearly in between an individual person and a city or kingdom. For, as an individual person is part of a household, so a household is part of a city or kingdom. And so, as we distinguish prudence in general, which governs an individual, from political prudence, so we need to distinguish domestic prudence from both.

Objection. Prudence is ordered to living well in general. But domestic prudence is directed to a particular end; namely, wealth. Therefore, domestic prudence is not a species of prudence.

Reply Obj. Wealth is related to domestic prudence as a means, not as its ultimate end. And the ultimate end of domestic prudence is living well in general with respect to life in the household.

4. Should we posit military prudence as a species of prudence?[31]

Things done by skills and reason should be conformed to things in accord with nature, which divine reason established. But nature strives for

---

[30]Ibid., A. 3.   [31]Ibid., A. 4.

two things: that each thing govern itself, and that each thing resist external hostile and destructive forces. And so nature bestows on animals both concupiscible powers, which cause them to seek things suitable for their well-being, and irascible powers, by which they resist hostile forces. And so also regarding things in accord with reason, there should be not only political prudence, which suitably disposes things proper to the common good, but also military prudence, which repels hostile attacks.

Objection. As the military occupation is included in the political, so also are many other occupations (e.g., those of merchants, craftsmen, and the like). But we do not understand the other occupations in a political community as species of prudence. Therefore, neither should we understand the military occupation as a species of prudence.

Reply Obj. Other occupations in the political community are directed to particular benefits, but the military occupation is directed to preserving the entire common good.

Potential Parts

1. Is good deliberation a virtue?[32]

It belongs to the nature of human virtue to make human acts good. And deliberation is one of the acts of human beings proper to them, since deliberation signifies an inquiry of reason about things to be done. But human life consists of such practical things, since a purely contemplative life is beyond human beings. And so good deliberation is clearly a human virtue.

Objection. A virtue is a perfection. But right deliberation signifies doubt and inquiry, and both of these belong to imperfection. Therefore, good deliberation is not a virtue.

Reply Obj. Although a virtue is essentially a perfection, not everything that is the subject matter of a virtue needs to signify perfection. For virtues need to perfect all human things, regarding both acts of reason, including deliberation, and the emotions of sense appetites—and emotions are much more imperfect.

Or we can say that a human virtue is a perfection in the manner of human beings, who cannot with certitude understand the truth about things by pure intuition, especially in practical matters, which are contingent.

---

[32]ST II-II, Q. 51, A. 1. Thomas uses the Greek words for good deliberation, right judgment, and higher power of judgment: *euboulia, synesis,* and *gnome.* He takes these words from Aristotle (NE VI).

2. Is good deliberation a virtue distinct from prudence?[33]

Virtues in the proper sense are directed to acts, which they render good. And so different kinds of acts need to distinguish virtues, especially if a different kind of goodness should belong to the acts. For if the same kind of goodness were to belong to different acts, the acts would belong to the same virtue. For example, the goodness of love, desire, and joy depend on the same thing, and so all these things belong to the same virtue of charity.

But different acts of reason are directed to action, and they do not have the same kind of goodness. For different things cause human beings to deliberate well, judge well, and command well, and this is apparent from the fact that these things are sometimes distinct from one another. And so there needs to be one virtue of good deliberation, by which human beings deliberate well, and another virtue of prudence, by which human beings command well. And as deliberating is directed to commanding as the chief thing, so also good deliberation is directed to prudence as the chief virtue, without which there would not be virtue. Just so, there would be no moral virtues without prudence, nor other virtues[34] without charity.

Objection. Ends specify human acts, to which human virtues are directed. But good deliberation and prudence are directed to the same end—that is, the general end of one's whole life—not each to a particular end. Therefore, good deliberation is not a virtue distinct from prudence.

Reply Obj. Different kinds of acts are directed to the ultimate end—namely, living well in general—in a certain order. For deliberation is first, judgment is second, and command is last. And the latter is immediately related to the ultimate end, while the other two acts are remotely related to it. But the other two acts have proximate ends: deliberation has discovery of the things that should be done, and judgment certainty. And so this shows that good deliberation is subordinate to prudence as a secondary virtue to the chief one, not that good deliberation and prudence are the same virtue.

3. Is right judgment a virtue?[35]

Right judgment concerns particular matters of action, regarding which there is also prudence, not theoretical matters. But there also need to be different virtues regarding different acts not traceable to the same cause. And the goodness of deliberation and the goodness of judgment are clearly not traceable to the same cause, since many who deliberate well do

---

[33]Ibid., A. 2.   [34]These are the supernatural moral virtues infused with charity.   [35]ST II-II, Q. 51, A. 3.

not have good sense—that is, good judgment, as it were. Just so, in theoretical things, some persons inquire well, since their reason is quick at reasoning from one known thing to another. And this seems to come from a disposition of the power of imagination easily to form different sense images. And yet such persons do not have good judgment, and this is due to a defect of their intellect, which especially results from the wrong disposition of their unifying sense. And so, in addition to good deliberation, there needs to be another virtue: the virtue of judging well. And we call this virtue right judgment.

Objection. Virtues are not innate in us. But right judgment is innate in some persons. Therefore, right judgment is not a virtue.

Reply Obj. Right judgment consists of the intellect understanding things as they are in themselves. And this indeed comes from the right disposition of the intellect. Just so, the true forms of material things are accurately impressed on a well-constructed mirror, but the images on a poorly constructed mirror appear distorted and warped. And that the intellect is well disposed to receive things as they are results radically from nature but perfectly from practice or the gift of grace. And such a perfect disposition of the intellect results in two ways. It results in one way directly regarding the intellect itself: for instance, by imbuing the intellect with true and correct, not false, concepts; and this belongs to right judgment as a special virtue. It results in a second way indirectly from the good disposition of the will, as a result of which human beings judge rightly about desirable things. And so good judgment about virtue results from the habits of moral virtues; but such judgment concerns the ends of the moral virtues, while right judgment concerns the means to those ends.

4. Is higher power of judgment a special virtue?[36]

We distinguish intellectual habits by their higher or lower principles. For example, in theoretical things, wisdom contemplates higher principles than scientific knowledge does, and so we distinguish wisdom from scientific knowledge. And so also does this need to be the case in practical things.

And it is clear that we sometimes trace things outside the order of a lower principle or cause to the order of a higher principle. For example, monstrous births of animals are outside the order of the causal power in the animals' semen but fall within the order of a higher principle: namely, a heavenly body or, higher still, divine providence. And so, if one were to

---

[36]Ibid., A. 4.

consider the causal power in animals' semen, one could not judge certainly about such monstrosities; but one can judge about them by considering divine providence.

And it sometimes happens that one should do something outside the general rules about things that human beings should do or not do, as, for instance, when one should not return something held on deposit to an enemy of one's country, or the like. And so one needs to judge about such things by some principles higher than the general rules of right judgment. And regarding those higher principles, one needs a higher power of judging, which means discernment of judgment.

Objection. Right judgment means that one judges well. But we cannot say that one judges well unless one judges well in all things. Therefore, right judgment extends to judging all things. Therefore, there is not another virtue of judging well called higher power of judgment.

Reply Obj. Right judgment judges truly about all things done according to general rules. But there are other things that one should judge outside the general rules.

Imprudence and Negligence

Thomas here considers the sins contrary to prudence; namely, sins resulting from lack of prudence or of things necessary for prudence: imprudence itself, precipitateness, lack of reflection, inconstancy, sexual lust as the sins' most frequent cause, and negligence (lack of solicitude).

1. Is imprudence a sin?[37]

We can understand imprudence in two ways: in one way, as a privation; in a second way, as a contrary. But we cannot in the strict sense speak of imprudence as a negation; namely, signifying only lack of prudence, for one can lack prudence without sin.

We speak of imprudence as a privation insofar as one lacks the prudence with which nature has endowed human beings, and they ought to have. And imprudence in this sense is a sin by reason of negligence, in not applying oneself earnestly to possess prudence.

And we can understand imprudence as a contrary insofar as reason is moved or acts in a way contrary to prudence. For example, whereas the right reason of prudence acts by deliberating, the imprudent person spurns deliberation, and acts similarly regarding the other things to be observed in the actions of a prudent person. And imprudence in this

---

[37]ST II–II, Q. 53, A. 1.

sense is a sin by the proper nature of prudence. For human beings can act contrary to prudence only if they turn away from the rules that make the reason of prudence right reason. And so there is mortal sin if this should happen by turning away from God's laws. For example, such is the case if one who, as it were, contemns and rejects God's teachings acts precipitously. But there is venial sin if one should act contrary to God's laws without contempt or detriment to things necessary for salvation.

2. Is imprudence a special sin?[38]

We can call a vice or sin general in two ways: in one way, absolutely—namely, because it is general with regard to all sins; in the second way, because it is general with regard to the particular sins that are its species. And regarding the first way, we can call a sin general in two ways. A sin is absolutely general in one way by reason of its nature; namely, because it is predicated of all sins. And imprudence is not sin in general in this way, just as prudence is not virtue in general, since imprudence and prudence concern special acts: namely, the very acts of reason. And a sin is absolutely general, in a second way, by participation. And imprudence is a general sin in this way. For as all virtues somehow partake of prudence, since prudence directs them, so also all vices and sins partake of imprudence, since there can be sin only if there should be a defect in the act of reason directing the actions of human beings; and this belongs to imprudence.

But if we should call imprudence a general sin in a qualified sense in relation to a genus of sin—namely, because it includes many species of sin in the genus—then imprudence is a general sin. For imprudence includes different species of sin in three ways. Different species belong to imprudence, in one way, as contrary to the subjective parts of prudence. For as we distinguish prudence into individual prudence, which governs one person, and other species of prudence, which govern many people, so also do we distinguish imprudence.

Different species belong to imprudence in a second way, regarding the potential parts, as it were, of prudence, which are connected virtues; and we understand them by their different acts of reason. And accordingly, regarding lack of deliberation, there is **precipitateness**, or **temerity**, as a species of imprudence. And regarding deficiency of judgment, there is **lack of reflection**. And regarding command itself, which is the proper act of prudence, there are **inconstancy** and **negligence**.

We can understand different species in imprudence in a third way, as contrary to things required for prudence, which are integral parts, as it

---

[38]Ibid., A. 2.

were, of prudence. But because all these things are ordered to direct the aforementioned three acts of reason, we trace all contrary defects to precipitateness, lack of reflection, inconstancy, and negligence. For lack of caution or of circumspection is included in lack of reflection. And lack of disposition to learn, defective memory, or defective reason belongs to precipitateness. And lack of providence, defective understanding, or defective solicitude belongs to negligence and inconstancy.

3. Is precipitateness a special sin of imprudence?[39]

We speak metaphorically of precipitateness in acts of the soul by an analogy taken from the motion of material bodies. And regarding such motion, we say that a body falling from the summit to the base of a precipice by the force of the body's own motion or by an external force, not descending step-by-step in an orderly way, falls precipitously. And the summit of the soul is reason itself, and the base is the activity performed by the body. And the middle steps, by which one needs to descend in an orderly way, are memory of past things, understanding of present things, keenness in considering future outcomes, reason relating one thing to another, and the disposition to learn (whereby one relies on the opinions of the learned). And by all these steps, one descends in an orderly way by deliberating rightly. But if, without such steps being taken, an impulse of the will or an emotional impulse should move one to act, there will be precipitateness. Therefore, since disorder in deliberating belongs to imprudence, the sin of precipitateness is evidently a species of imprudence.

Objection. Precipitateness seems to belong to rashness. But rashness signifies presumption, which belongs to pride. Therefore, precipitateness is not a special sin of imprudence.

Reply Obj. We say that things not ruled by reason are done rashly. And this can happen in two ways. It happens in one way from an impulse of the will or an emotional impulse. It happens in a second way from contempt of the governing rule, and rashness in the proper sense signifies this. And so rashness seems to come radically from pride, which shuns being subject to the rule of another. But precipitateness is disposed to both ways. And so rashness is included in precipitateness, although precipitateness more concerns the first way.

4. Is lack of reflection a special sin of imprudence?[40]

Reflection signifies an act of the intellect contemplating the truth about a thing. But as inquiry belongs to reason, so judgment belongs to

[39]Ibid., A. 3.   [40]Ibid., A. 4.

the intellect. And so also, in theoretical things, we say that demonstrative science judges, since we say it judges about the things investigated by analyzing them into intelligible first principles. And so reflection most belongs to judgment.

And so also failure to judge rightly belongs to the sin of failure to reflect; namely, as one fails to judge rightly because one contemns or neglects paying attention to the things leading to right judgment. And so lack of reflection is clearly a sin.

Objection. Whoever deliberates needs to reflect about many things. But precipitateness results from lack of deliberation and so from lack of reflection. Therefore, precipitateness is included in lack of reflection, and lack of reflection is not a special sin.

Reply Obj. The whole contemplation of the things about which we reflect in deliberation is directed to judging rightly. And so judgment completes reflection. And so lack of reflection is most contrary to right judgment.

5. Is inconstancy a special sin of imprudence?[41]

Inconstancy signifies retreating from a definite good purpose. And such a retreat derives from the will, since one retreats from a prior good purpose only because of something that pleases one inordinately. But this retreat is achieved only through a failure of reason, which mistakenly rejects what it had rightly accepted. And if reason should fail to resist an emotional impulse when it can, this is due to the weakness of reason, which does not hold firmly to the good it has conceived. And so inconstancy, as to its complete character, belongs to a defect of reason. But as the entire rectitude of practical reason belongs in some way to prudence, so every defect of reason belongs to imprudence. And so inconstancy, as to its complete character, belongs to imprudence. And as precipitateness results from a defect regarding the act of deliberation, and lack of reflection concerns the act of judgment, so inconstancy concerns the act of command. For we say that one is inconstant because reason fails to command the things that one deliberates about and judges.

Objection. Inconstancy seems to consist of the fact that a human being does not persist in regard to something difficult. But persisting in difficult things belongs to fortitude. Therefore, inconstancy belongs to fortitude rather than prudence.

Reply Obj. All the moral virtues share in the good of prudence, and persisting in good accordingly belongs to all the moral virtues, but especially to fortitude, which is subject to a greater impulse to the contrary.

---

[41]Ibid., A. 5.

6. Do the aforementioned sins arise out of sexual lust?[42]

Pleasure most corrupts the evaluation of prudence, and chiefly the pleasure in sexual matters, which absorbs the whole soul and draws human beings to sense pleasure. But the perfection of prudence and of any intellectual virtue consists of drawing one away from sensibly perceptible things. And so, since the aforementioned sins belong to deficiency of prudence and practical reason, the sins consequently arise most from sexual lust.

Objection. The aforementioned sins belong to the failure of reason. But spiritual sins are closer to reason than carnal sins are. Therefore, the aforementioned sins arise from spiritual rather than carnal sins.

Reply Obj. The farther carnal sins lead one away from reason, the more they destroy the judgment of reason.

7. Is negligence a special sin?[43]

Negligence signifies lack of due solicitude. But every lack of a required act has the nature of sin. And so negligence evidently has the nature of sin and is necessarily a special sin in the same way in which solicitude is the act of a special virtue. For some sins are special because they concern a special subject matter. For example, sexual lust regards sexual matters. And some sins are special because of a special kind of act that covers every kind of subject matter. But all the sins that concern an act of reason about things to be done are special in this sense, since any such act of reason covers any kind of moral subject matter. And so, since solicitude is a special act of reason, negligence, which signifies lack of solicitude, is a special sin.

8. Is negligence contrary to prudence?[44]

Negligence is directly contrary to solicitude. But solicitude belongs to reason, and right solicitude to prudence. And so, by contrast, negligence belongs to imprudence. And this is also evident from the very word, since we call a negligent [*negligens*] person one who does not choose [*nec eligens*], as it were. But the right choice of means to an end belongs to prudence. And so negligence belongs to imprudence.

Objection. Imprudence concerns an act of reason. But negligence does not signify a defect regarding deliberation, which is precipitateness; or a defect regarding judgment, which is lack of reflection; or a defect regarding command, which is lack of constancy. Therefore, negligence does not belong to imprudence.

---

[42]Ibid., A. 6.   [43]ST II-II, Q. 54, A. 1.   [44]Ibid., A. 2.

Reply Obj. Negligence concerns the act of commanding, to which solicitude also belongs. But one who is negligent fails regarding this act in one way, and one who is inconstant fails in another way. For one who is inconstant fails in commanding by something preventing it, as it were; but one who is negligent fails by lacking a ready will.

9. Can negligence be a mortal sin?[45]

Negligence comes from the will being remiss, in reason not being solicitous to command the things that it ought to command, or to command in the way that it ought to command. Therefore, negligence may be a mortal sin in two ways. It may be in one way regarding what is omitted through negligence. And this will be a mortal sin if it should concern something necessary for salvation, whether an act or a circumstance. It happens in a second way regarding the cause. For if the will should be so remiss about things that belong to God that it totally falls away from love of him, such negligence is a mortal sin. And this chiefly happens when negligence results from contempt. Otherwise, negligence is a venial sin if the negligence should consist of omitting an act or circumstance unnecessary for salvation; or if one should not do something out of a lack of fervor, which a venial sin sometimes prevents, rather than out of contempt.

Sins Contrary to but Resembling Prudence

Thomas here considers sins contrary to but resembling prudence, and their chief cause: prudence of the flesh, craftiness, guile, fraud, inordinate solicitude about temporal things, and covetousness as their most frequent cause. (In the following selections, the words lawful *and* unlawful *refer primarily to the natural law.)*

1. Is prudence of the flesh a sin?[46]

Prudence concerns means to the end of life as a whole. And so we speak in the proper sense of prudence of the flesh insofar as one considers goods of the flesh to be the ultimate end of one's life. But this is clearly a sin, since one is thereby disordered regarding one's ultimate end, which does not consist of goods of the flesh. And so prudence of the flesh is a sin.

Objection. Acting prudently for an end that one lawfully loves is not a sin. But one lawfully loves one's flesh. Therefore, prudence of the flesh is not a sin.

Reply Obj. The flesh is for the sake of the soul, just as matter is for the sake of form and an instrumental cause for the sake of a chief cause. And

---

[45]Ibid., A. 3.   [46]ST II-II, Q. 55, A. 1.

so one lawfully loves one's flesh, in that it is directed to the soul's good as its end. But if one should constitute the very good of the flesh one's ultimate end, there will be inordinate and illicit love of the flesh. And prudence of the flesh is directed to love of the flesh in the latter way.

2. Is prudence of the flesh a mortal sin?[47]

We call someone prudent in two ways: in one way, absolutely—namely, in relation to the end of life as a whole; in the second way, in some respect—namely, in relation to a particular end, as, for example, we call someone prudent in business or some such thing. Therefore, if we should understand prudence of the flesh by the absolute character of prudence—namely, so that one makes care of the flesh the ultimate end of one's life as a whole—then prudence of the flesh is a mortal sin. This is because a human being thereby turns away from God, since there cannot be more than one ultimate end.

And if we should understand prudence of the flesh by the aspect of a particular prudence, then prudence of the flesh is a venial sin. For one may sometimes be inordinately drawn to a pleasure of the flesh without being turned away from God by mortal sin. And so the person does not constitute pleasure of the flesh the ultimate end of the person's life as a whole. And so desiring to acquire this pleasure is a venial sin, and it belongs to prudence of the flesh.

But we do not call it prudence of the flesh if one should relate care of the flesh to a worthy end, as, for example, if one strives for food in order to sustain one's body, since a human being then uses care of the flesh as a means to that end.

3. Is craftiness a special sin?[48]

Prudence is right reason about things that can be done, as scientific knowledge is right reason about things that can be known. But one may err in two ways against the rectitude of scientific knowledge in theoretical things. A person may err in one way when reason leads the person to a false conclusion that seems to be true. One may err in a second way because reason proceeds from false premises that seem to be true, whether the premises lead to a true or false conclusion. So also a sin resembling prudence can be contrary to it in two ways. A sin resembling prudence can be contrary to it in one way because reason's desire is directed to an apparent but not truly good end, and this belongs to prudence of the flesh. A sin resembling prudence can be contrary to it in a

---

[47]Ibid., A. 2.   [48]Ibid., A. 3.

second way because one, in order to gain an end, whether a good or evil end, employs counterfeit and illusory, not true, means; and this belongs to the sin of craftiness. And so there is a sin contrary to prudence that is distinct from prudence of the flesh.

4. Is guile a sin belonging to craftiness?[49]

It belongs to craftiness to adopt counterfeit and illusory, not true, means to attain an end, whether the end be good or evil. But we can consider the adoption of such means in two ways. We can consider the adoption of such means in one way in the very devising of them, and this belongs in the strict sense to craftiness, just as devising right means to a requisite end belongs to prudence. We can consider the adoption of such means in a second way regarding execution of the planned action, and adoption of means in this way belongs to guile. And so guile signifies an execution of craftiness, and guile belongs to craftiness.

5. Does fraud belong to craftiness?[50]

As guile consists of executing craftiness, so also does fraud. But they differ in that guile seems to belong generally to executing craftiness, whether by words or deeds, and fraud more properly to executing craftiness as one does so by deeds.

6. Is it lawful to be solicitous about temporal things?[51]

Solicitude signifies an endeavor to obtain something. But one clearly uses greater effort where there is fear of failure, and so there is less solicitude where success is sure. Therefore, solicitude about temporal things can be unlawful in three ways. It is unlawful in one way regarding the matter about which we are solicitous; namely, if we should seek temporal things as our end.

Solicitude about temporal things can be illicit in a second way because of excessive striving to procure temporal things, for the sake of which one withdraws from spiritual things, to which one ought to be chiefly devoted.

Solicitude about temporal things can be unlawful in a third way regarding excessive fear; namely, when human beings fear lest they, by doing what they ought to do, lack necessary things. And the Lord in Mt. 6:25–33 gives three reasons for excluding such fear. First, because of the greater benefits God bestows on human beings: namely, their bodies and souls, which are more important than the things about which they are

---

[49]Ibid., A. 4.   [50]Ibid., A. 5.   [51]Ibid., A. 6.

solicitous. Second, because of the assistance that God gives to animals and plants, as befitting their nature and apart from human effort. Third, because of divine providence, which the pagans do not know and are, on that account, chiefly solicitous about seeking temporal goods. And so he concludes that we ought to have solicitude chiefly about spiritual goods and hope that even temporal goods will come to us according to our needs if we have done what we ought to do.

Objection. Each one is solicitous about the end for the sake of which one labors. But it is lawful for human beings to labor for the sake of temporal things, with which human beings sustain their life. Therefore, it is lawful for them to be solicitous about temporal things.

Reply Obj. The solicitude of those who acquire their livelihood by their labor is moderate, not excessive.

7. Should one be solicitous about the future?[52]

An act can be virtuous only in the proper circumstances, one of which is the proper time. And this is true regarding both external deeds and internal solicitude. For to each time there belongs a proper solicitude. For example, solicitude about harvesting grain is proper in summer, and solicitude about harvesting grapes is proper in autumn. Therefore, if one were to be solicitous about harvesting grapes in summer, one would unnecessarily anticipate the solicitude proper to a later time.

Objection. Solicitude belongs to prudence. But prudence chiefly concerns future things, since its chief part is providence about future things. Therefore, it is virtuous to be solicitous about future things.

Reply Obj. Due providence about future things belongs to prudence. But there would be inordinate providence or solicitude about future things if one were to seek temporal things, regarding which we speak of the past and the future, as ends; or if one were to seek superfluous things beyond the needs of the present life; or if one were to anticipate the time to be solicitous.

8. Do such sins arise out of covetousness?[53]

Prudence of the flesh and craftiness, as well as guile and fraud, resemble prudence in a certain use of reason. But of the moral virtues, the use of right reason is most evident in justice, which belongs to the rational appetite. And so the improper use of reason is also most evident in sins contrary to justice. But covetousness is most contrary to justice. And so the aforementioned sins arise most from covetousness.

---

[52]Ibid., A. 7.   [53]Ibid., A. 8.

Objection. Sexual lust most causes reason to lack rectitude. But the aforementioned sins are contrary to right reason; namely, prudence. Therefore, such sins arise most from sexual lust.

Reply Obj. Sexual lust, because of the vehemence of pleasure and desire, completely overwhelms reason. But in the aforementioned sins, there is a use of reason, albeit an inordinate use. And so the aforementioned sins do not arise directly from sexual lust.

2

Justice

Right

Right is the object of justice. Other moral virtues (those of temperance and fortitude) perfect human beings only in relation to themselves, and so the acts of those virtues are right only in relation to the human beings who perform the acts. For example, acts of sobriety perfect the human being who practices the virtue. But justice directs human beings in their relations to other human beings, and so the acts of justice are right if they are rightly related to other human beings—that is, if the acts observe the right objective order of human relations. (See Glossary, s.v. Right, Virtue.)

Natural right order consists of things equivalent by their nature (e.g., the quid pro quo in exchanges). Positive right order consists of things equivalent by private or public agreement (e.g., the terms of a contract and the use of money as a medium of exchange). Divine right order consists of the decrees promulgated by God, and some of these coincide with natural right order. The common right of peoples (the classical jus gentium*) consists of things equivalent to other things when natural reason considers consequences (e.g., the right of private property). Paternal right order and master-slave right order consist of things equivalent to other things insofar as some persons belong to other persons (namely, children to parents, and slaves to masters). Since law establishes right, law and right are correlative. Thus natural law corresponds to natural right, positive law to positive right, and so forth. (See Glossary, s.v. Law.)*

1. Is right the object of justice?[1]

In contrast to other virtues, it is proper to justice to direct human beings in their relations to other human beings. For justice signifies an equality, as the very word shows, since we commonly speak of equal things being exactly right, and things have equality in relation to other things. But other virtues perfect human beings only in relation to things that befit them in their own regard.

Therefore, we understand what is right in the acts of other virtues, for which the other virtues strive as their proper object, only in relation to the

---

[1]ST II-II, Q. 57, A. 1. The Latin word *jus* means law or right. In at least this article, Thomas seems to use *jus* in the latter sense. In subsequent articles in this section, I have continued to translate *jus* as "right," but "law" would seem to fit the contexts just as well or even better.

human beings causing the acts. But besides the relation of deeds to the human beings performing the deeds, the relation of deeds to other human beings constitutes what is right in acts of justice. For we call our deeds just if they return quid pro quo to others (e.g., the payment of wages due for services rendered).

Therefore, we call the object of a just act something just, possessing the rectitude of justice, as it were, even without considering how the human agent performs the act. But in other virtues, we specify things as right only if the human agent performs the act in a certain way. And so we specify right intrinsically as the object of justice beyond the rectitude of other virtues, and we call the object just, which means right. And so right is clearly the object of justice.

2. Do we appropriately divide right into natural right and positive right?[2]

Right, or justice, consists of deeds equivalent to other things in some measure of equality. And things can be equivalent to other things in two ways. They are equivalent in one way by the very nature of the things, as, for example, when one gives so much in order to receive so much. And we call this natural right.

Things are equivalent to, or commensurate with, other things in a second way by agreement, or mutual consent; namely, when one deems oneself content to receive so much. This can happen in two ways. It happens in one way by private agreement, as, for example, the things established by a contract between private persons. It happens in a second way by public agreement, as, for example, when the whole people agrees that things should be equivalent to, or commensurate with, other things, as it were; or when a ruler in charge of the people and acting in their person so ordains.

Objection 1. We call things proceeding from the human will positive things. But nothing is just simply because it proceeds from a human will; otherwise, the will of a human being could not be unjust. Therefore, since just is the same as right, it seems that there is no positive right.

Reply Obj. 1. The human will can, by common agreement, make something just in the case of things intrinsically compatible with natural justice, and positive right plays a role in such things. But if something should be intrinsically incompatible with natural justice, the human will cannot make it just, as, for example, if laws decree that it is lawful to steal or commit adultery.

Obj. 2. Divine right is not natural right, since divine right surpasses human nature. Likewise, divine right is not positive right, since divine

---

[2]Ibid., A. 2.

right depends on divine, not human, authority. Therefore, we inappropriately divide right into natural right and positive right.

Reply Obj. 2. We call decrees promulgated by God divine right. And divine right partially concerns things that are naturally just, although their justice is concealed from human beings, and partially concerns things that are just by divine institution. And so also we can distinguish divine law by these two kinds of things, just as we distinguish human right. For the divine law commands some things because they are good or prohibits some things because they are evil, while other things are good because divine law commands them or evil because divine law prohibits them.

3. Is the common right of peoples the same as natural right?[3]

Natural right, or natural justice, consists of things that are by their nature equivalent to, or commensurate with, other things, and this can happen in two ways. It can happen in one way as we consider things absolutely, as, for example, men are by their nature commensurate with women in the begetting of children, and parents with children in rearing the latter.

Things are by nature commensurate with other things in a second way, as we consider what results from them (e.g., the ownership of property), not as we consider them absolutely. For if we should consider a particular plot of farmland absolutely, there is no reason why it should belong to one person rather than another. But if we should consider the plot as to its suitable cultivation and peaceful use, the plot in this respect belongs commensurately to one person rather than another.

Absolutely possessing things belongs both to human beings and to other animals, and so the right called natural in the first way is common to us and other animals. But the common right of peoples is distinct from the right called natural in that sense, and considering things in relation to their consequences belongs to reason. And so such consideration is natural to human beings as regards their natural reason, which dictates it. And so all peoples protect what natural reason establishes among human beings, and we call this the common right of peoples.

4. Should we distinguish paternal right and master-slave right as special kinds of right?[4]

We speak of right or justice by the equivalence of some thing with other things, and we can speak of things being other in two ways. We can

---

[3]Ibid., A. 3. This article concerns the *jus gentium*, the customary law common to the peoples of the Roman world. Its relationship to the natural law was disputed, and, as Thomas indicates, resolution of the dispute depends on what one means by "natural."   [4]Ibid., A. 4.

speak of things being other in one way as absolutely other, as altogether distinct. Such is the case of two human beings, neither of whom is subject to the other, although both are subject to the ruler of a political community. And among such, there is justice without qualification.

We speak of things being other in a second way, not as absolutely other but as one thing belongs to another, as it were. But in human society, children belong to their fathers in this way, since children are, in one respect, parts of their fathers; and slaves belong to their masters, since slaves are instruments of their masters. And so fathers are not related to their children as absolutely other, and the paternal relationship has a certain justice—namely, paternal justice—but not justice absolutely. And by the same argument, the master-slave relationship has a certain justice—namely master-slave justice—but not justice absolutely.

And wives, although they belong to their husbands, are nonetheless more distinct from their husbands than children are from their fathers, or slaves from their masters, since wives share in the common life of marriage. And so there is more of the character of justice between husbands and wives than there is between fathers and their children, or between masters and slaves. But husbands and wives have an immediate relation to a domestic community. Therefore, there is between them domestic justice rather than political justice in the absolute sense.

Objection. Law is a plan of justice. But law concerns the common good of a city or kingdom, not the private good of one person or one family. Therefore, there ought not to be special right, whether master-slave or paternal, since masters and fathers belong to family households.

Reply Obj. Children as such belong to their fathers, and slaves as such likewise belong to their masters. But both children and slaves, considered as particular human beings, are intrinsically subsistent and distinct from other human beings. And so, insofar as they are human beings, there is justice in some respect in relation to them. And it is also for this reason that there are particular laws about the relations of fathers to their children and of masters to their slaves. But insofar as children and slaves belong to others, the relations lack the perfect character of justice or right.

Justice in Itself

Justice is the constant and enduring will to render to others what is due each. It is always in relation to others, a virtue (i.e., a habitual disposition), and inherent in the will rather than the intellect. Justice in general is virtue in general; that is, the goodness of justice is the goodness of every virtue as other virtues are directed to the common good. Particular justice directs human beings in their relations with other human beings regarding particular goods. External actions and external things, not internal emotions, constitute the subject matter of particular justice. The mean of justice is a real mean, not only a mean conceived by reason, such as the mean in fortitude and temperance. Justice is the most important moral virtue, both because of the subject in which it inheres (the will) and because of its object (the good of other human beings). (See Glossary, s.v. Justice.*)*

1. Do we properly define justice as the constant and perpetual will to render to others what is due each?[5]

The aforementioned definition is proper if we rightly understand it. For inasmuch as every virtue is a habit that is the source of good acts, we need to define a virtue by the good act that regards the proper matter of the virtue. But justice concerns things in relation to other things as its proper matter. And so the definition, when speaking of rendering to others what is their due, touches on the acts of justice in relation to the proper matter and object of justice. But for any act regarding any matter to be virtuous, the act needs to be voluntary, steadfast, and enduring. And so we first posit the will in the aforementioned definition of justice in order to show that acts of justice should be voluntary, and we add constancy and perpetuity to the definition in order to designate the steadfastness of the acts. And so the aforementioned definition is the complete definition of justice, except that the act is substituted for the habit specified by the act, since we speak of habits in relation to acts. And if one were to wish to put this into the proper form of a definition, one could say that justice is the habit whereby one with steadfast and enduring will renders to others what is due them.

2. Is justice always in relation to other things?[6]

Justice by its nature consists of our relations to others, since its name signifies equality. For things are equal to other things, not to themselves, and since it belongs to justice to direct human acts rightly, the otherness that justice requires needs to belong to different things capable of acting. And actions belong to subsistent and whole entities and not, properly speaking, to parts and forms, or powers. For example, we do not properly say that hands strike things, but that human beings strike things with their hands. Nor, properly speaking, do we say that heat warms things, but that fire warms things with its heat. Nevertheless, we say metaphorically that hands strike things, and that heat warms things.

---

[5]ST II-II, Q. 58, A. 1.   [6]Ibid., A. 2.

Therefore, properly speaking, justice requires distinct, individual, subsistent substances and so consists only of the relations of one human being to another. But we metaphorically understand different sources of actions in the same human being (e.g., reason and the irascible and concupiscible powers) as if they were different active things. And so we say metaphorically that justice belongs to the same human being insofar as one's reason commands one's irascible and concupiscible powers; and insofar as those powers obey one's reason; and generally insofar as we attribute to each part of a human being what belongs to it.

3. Is justice a virtue?[7]

Human virtues make human acts and human beings themselves good, and this belongs to justice. For human acts are good because they attain the rule of reason, which rightly orders human acts. And so, since justice rightly orders human actions, it clearly renders human acts good.

Objection. What one does out of necessity is not meritorious. But to render to others what is theirs, which belongs to justice, is necessary. Therefore, it is not meritorious. But we merit by virtuous acts. Therefore, justice is not a virtue.

Reply Obj. There are two kinds of necessity. One kind is that of coercion, and this takes away the character of merit, since it is contrary to the will. The other kind is the necessity deriving from the obligation of precepts, or the necessity deriving from a virtuous end; namely, when one can achieve a virtuous end only by doing a particular deed. And such necessity does not exclude the character of merit, since one does willingly what is necessary in this way. But it does exclude the glory of doing more than one's duty.

4. Does justice inhere in the will as its subject?[8]

The power whose acts a virtue aims to direct rightly is the subject of the virtue. But justice does not aim to direct a cognitive act, since we are not called just because we know something rightly. And so the intellect, or reason, which is a cognitive power, is not the subject of justice.

But since we are called just in that we do things rightly, and the proximate source of action is an appetitive power, justice needs to inhere in an appetitive power as its subject. And there are two kinds of appetitive power: namely, the will, which belongs to reason, and sense appetites resulting from sense perceptions; and sense appetites are divided into the irascible and concupiscible powers. But rendering to others what is theirs

---

[7]Ibid., A. 3.   [8]Ibid., A. 4.

cannot issue from a sense appetite, since sense perception does not reach so far as to be able to consider the relation of one thing to another. Rather, such consideration belongs to reason. And so justice cannot inhere in the irascible or concupiscible powers as its subject, but only in the will.

Objection. Justice is not an intellectual virtue, since it is not directed to reason. And so we conclude that it is a moral virtue. But the subject of a moral virtue is a power rational by participation, such as the irascible and concupiscible powers. Therefore, justice resides in the irascible and concupiscible powers as its subject, rather than in the will.

Reply Obj. All appetitive powers and not only the irascible and concupiscible powers are rational by participation, since every appetitive power obeys reason. But the will is one of the appetitive powers. And so the will can be the subject of a moral virtue.

5. Is justice virtue in general?[9]

Justice directs human beings in relation to others, and this can happen in two ways. It can happen in one way in relation to others considered individually. It can happen in a second way in relation to others considered in general; namely, as those serving a community serve all the human beings in the community. Therefore, there can be justice in the strict sense in both ways. But all in a community are clearly related to the community as parts to a whole, and the parts belong to the whole. And so also any good of the part can be ordered to the good of the whole. Therefore, we can accordingly relate the good of any virtue—whether a virtue ordering individual human beings in relation to themselves or a virtue ordering individual human beings in relation to other individual persons—to the common good, regarding which justice disposes the will. And the acts of all the virtues can, in this respect, belong to justice as it directs human beings to the common good. And we call justice virtue in general in this regard. And since it belongs to law to order human beings to the common good, we call justice in general, in the aforementioned way, legal justice. We do so because human beings, by observing justice, are in accord with the law, which orders the acts of all the virtues to the common good.

Objection. As we designate justice a cardinal virtue, so also do we designate temperance and fortitude cardinal virtues. But we do not designate temperance or fortitude virtue in general. Therefore, neither ought we in any respect designate justice virtue in general.

Reply Obj. Temperance and fortitude belong to sense appetites; namely, the concupiscible and irascible powers. And the objects of such appetitive powers are particular goods, just as the objects of the powers of

---

[9]Ibid., A. 5.

sense perception are particular knowable things. But justice inheres in the intellectual appetite as its subject, and the object of the will can be good in general, which the intellect apprehends. And so justice, unlike temperance and fortitude, can be virtue in general.

6. Is justice in general essentially the same as all virtue?[10]

We speak of things being general in two ways. We speak of things being general in one way by predication. For example, animal is something generic to human beings and horses and the like. And something general in this sense needs to be essentially the same as the things in relation to which it is generic, since genera belong to the essence of species and are part of the species' definition.

We call something general in a second way by its power. For example, a universal cause is general in relation to all its effects, as the sun is in relation to all material substances, which its power illumines or affects. And something general in this sense does not need to be essentially the same as the things in relation to which it is general, since the essences of such a cause and its effects differ. And it is in the latter sense that we call legal justice virtue in general; namely, insofar as legal justice directs the acts of other virtues to its end, which is to cause all other virtues by commanding them. For as we can call charity virtue in general, insofar as charity directs the acts of all virtues to the divine good, so also we can call legal justice virtue in general, insofar as legal justice directs the acts of all virtues to the common good. Therefore, as charity, which regards the divine good as its proper object, is a special virtue by its essence, so also legal justice is a special virtue by its essence insofar as it regards the common good as its proper object. And legal justice in this sense resides chiefly and architectonically, as it were, in rulers, and secondarily and ministerially, as it were, in subjects.

But we can call any virtue legal justice insofar as justice, which is essentially particular but general regarding its power, directs the virtue to the common good. And legal justice in this sense is essentially the same as all virtue, although conceptually different.

7. Is there a particular justice besides justice in general?[11]

Legal justice is not essentially all virtue. Rather, there need to be, besides legal justice, which directs human beings immediately to the common good, other virtues that direct human beings immediately regarding particular goods. And these can be either in relation to oneself or in rela-

---

[10]Ibid., A. 6.   [11]Ibid., A. 7.

tion to another individual person. Therefore, as there need to be, besides legal justice, particular virtues that direct human beings in relation to themselves (e.g., temperance and fortitude), so also there needs to be, besides legal justice, a particular justice, which directs human beings regarding things in relation to other individual persons.

Objection. We do not distinguish species of a virtue by whether the virtue regards one or many things. But legal justice directs human beings in relation to others regarding things that belong to many people. Therefore, there is no other species of justice that directs human beings in relation to others regarding things that belong to individual persons.

Reply Obj. The common good of a political community and the individual good of an individual person differ both by the number of persons affected and by a formal difference. For the nature of the common good and the nature of the individual good are different, just as the nature of the whole and the nature of its parts are different.

8. Does particular justice have special subject matter?[12]

All the things that reason can rightly direct are the subject matter of moral virtue, which right reason defines. And reason can rightly direct internal emotions of the soul, and external actions and things that human beings come to use. But we consider the right order of human beings to one another by external actions and external things, by which human beings can share life with one another; and we consider the right order of human beings regarding themselves by their internal emotions. And so particular justice, since it is directed to others, does not concern the whole subject matter of moral virtue, but only external actions and things by a special formal aspect of the object; namely, as the actions and things relate one human being to another.

9. Does justice concern emotions?[13]

Two things make clear the answer to this question. The first is the very subject in which justice inheres; that is, the will, whose movements or acts are not emotions. Rather, we call only movements of sense appetites emotions; and so justice does not concern emotions, as do temperance and fortitude, which belong to the irascible and concupiscible powers.

The second thing making clear the answer is the subject matter, since justice concerns things that are in relation to other things. But internal emotions do not immediately direct us in relation to other things. Therefore, justice does not concern emotions.

---

[12]Ibid., A. 8.   [13]Ibid., A. 9.

Objection. Justice rightly directs actions in relation to others. But we can direct such actions rightly only if we rightly direct our emotions, since disordered actions in relation to others result from disordered emotions. For example, adultery results from sexual lust, and theft from excessive love of money. Therefore, justice needs to concern emotions.

Reply Obj. External actions are in some way in between external things, which are the subject matter of external actions, and internal emotions, which are the sources of external actions. But there may sometimes be a defect in one of these two things without there being a defect in the other. For example, one may steal the property of another out of a desire to harm the other rather than a desire to possess the thing. Or conversely, one may desire the property of another without wanting to steal it. Therefore, it belongs to justice to direct actions rightly insofar as external things are the objects of the actions; but it belongs to other moral virtues, which concern emotions, to direct actions rightly insofar as the actions result from emotions. And so justice prohibits stealing the property of another insofar as this is contrary to the equality that should be established regarding external things, while generosity prohibits stealing out of excessive desire of riches. But internal emotions do not specify external actions; rather, the external things that are the objects of the actions do. Therefore, properly speaking, external actions are the subject matter of justice rather than the subject matter of other moral virtues.

10. Is the mean of justice a real mean?[14]

Other moral virtues chiefly concern emotions, whose right directing we note only in relation to the very human being to whom the emotions belong; namely, as one recoils or desires as one should in different circumstances. And so we understand the mean of such virtues only in relation to the virtuous persons, not by the relation of one thing to another. And so there is, in those virtues, only a mean determined by reason in relation to ourselves. But the matter of justice consists of external actions insofar as they or the things used have the proper relation to other persons. And so the mean of justice consists of a proportional equality of the external thing to an external person. But equality is a real mean between greater and lesser. And so justice has a real mean.

Objection 1. All the species of a genus contain the nature of the genus. But moral virtues are habits of choosing the mean determined by reason in relation to ourselves. Therefore, the mean in justice is likewise one of reason, not a real mean.

---

[14]Ibid., A. 10.

Reply Obj. 1. A real mean is also the mean of reason. And so justice retains the nature of moral virtue.

Obj. 2. We do not understand too much or too little in things absolutely good; and so there is no mean, as there evidently is in the case of virtues. But justice concerns absolutely good things. Therefore, there is no real mean in justice.

Reply Obj. 2. We call something absolutely good in two ways. In one way, we call something absolutely good if it is good in every respect, as virtues are, and then we do not understand means and extremes in such absolutely good things.

We call something absolutely good in a second way because it is such by its nature, although it could become evil by misuse, as is evidently the case with riches and honors. And we can understand too much, too little, and the mean in such things in relation to human beings, who can use them either well or ill; and we say in this sense that justice concerns absolutely good things.

11. Do acts of justice consist of rendering to others what is due them?[15]

The subject matter of justice consists of external actions insofar as they or the things we use through them are related to other persons, and justice directs us in relation to them. But we say that what is, in equal proportion, due other persons belongs to them. And so the proper act of justice consists only of rendering to others what is due them.

12. Is justice the most important moral virtue?[16]

If we should be speaking of legal justice, justice is clearly the most important moral virtue, since the common good surpasses the individual good of a single person.

But even if we should be speaking of particular justice, justice is the most important moral virtue for two reasons. We can understand the first reason regarding the subject—namely, that justice inheres in the more excellent part of the soul (i.e., the rational appetite; namely, the will)—but the other moral virtues inhere in the sense appetites, to which emotions belong. We understand the second reason regarding the object. For we praise other virtues only by reason of the good of the virtuous persons themselves, but we praise justice insofar as virtuous persons are rightly related to others. And so justice is, in one respect, the good of others.

---

[15]Ibid., A. 11.   [16]Ibid., A. 12.

Objection. Only something more worthy adorns something else. But magnanimity is an adornment of justice and all virtues. Therefore, magnanimity is more worthy than justice.

Reply Obj. Magnanimity, insofar as it adds to justice, increases the goodness of justice. But magnanimity without justice would not have the character of virtue.

Injustice

Injustice is a special sin in two ways: as contempt of the common good and as an inequality in relation to others. Someone who does something unjust may not be an unjust person if the unjust result is accidental and unintended, or if the unjust action is unrelated to habitual injustice (namely, the product of emotion). Formally speaking, no one can suffer injustice willingly, although one can do so in a material sense (e.g., if one willingly gives another more than one owes the other). Injustice in substantial matters is contrary to charity and so always a mortal sin.

1. Is injustice a special sin?[17]

There are two kinds of injustice. One kind is contrary to legal justice, and this injustice is essentially a special sin insofar as it concerns a special object: namely, the common good, which it contemns. But regarding its extension, it is a general sin, since contempt of the common good can lead human beings to all kinds of sins. So also do all sins, insofar as they are contrary to the common good, have the character of injustice, derived, as it were, from it.

We speak of injustice in a second way by an inequality in relation to others; namely, as human beings wish to have more goods (e.g., riches and honors) and less evils (e.g., hardships and losses). And then injustice has special matter and is a particular sin contrary to particular justice.

Objection. No special sin is contrary to all the virtues. But injustice is contrary to all the virtues. For example, regarding adultery, it is contrary to chastity; regarding homicide, it is contrary to meekness; and so forth. Therefore, injustice is not a special sin.

Reply Obj. Even particular justice is indirectly contrary to all the virtues; namely, insofar as even external acts belong both to justice and to other moral virtues, albeit in different ways.

---

[17]ST II-II, Q. 59, A. 1.

2. Do we call a person unjust because the person does something unjust?[18]

As the object of justice is an equality in external things, so also the object of injustice is an inequality in those things; namely, as more or less is allotted to someone than belongs to the person. But the habit of injustice is disposed toward this object by the habit's characteristic act, which we call unjust action. Therefore, it may happen in two ways that one who does something unjust may not be an unjust person. It may happen in one way because an action lacks relation to its proper object; and the intrinsic, not an accidental, object specifies and designates an action. And in the case of things done to achieve an end, we call intrinsic the things that one does intentionally, and accidental the things that one does not intend. And so, if one should do something unjust without intending to do anything unjust (e.g., when one does something in ignorance, not thinking that one is doing anything unjust), then one does something unjust only accidentally and materially, as it were, but nothing unjust intrinsically and formally. And we do not call such action unjust.

In a second way, one who does something unjust may not be unjust because the action lacks relation to the habit. For unjust action can sometimes arise from an emotion (e.g., anger or desire). But it sometimes arises by choice—namely, when the unjust action itself as such is agreeable; and then it arises strictly from the habit, since what belongs to a habit is agreeable to one who has the habit.

Therefore, it belongs to an unjust person to do something unjust intentionally and by choice, since we call a person who has the habit of injustice unjust. But a person without the habit of injustice can do something unjust unintentionally or through emotion.

3. Can one suffer something unjust willingly?[19]

Action as such comes from the efficient cause of the action, and undergoing action as such comes from something else. And so the thing causing action and the thing undergoing action cannot be the same thing in the same respect. But the proper source of acting in human beings is the will. And so human beings do, in the proper sense and intrinsically, what they do willingly; and conversely, human beings, in the proper sense, undergo what they undergo unwillingly. This is so because the source of action is from oneself insofar as one wills the action, and so one is active rather than passive insofar as one acts willingly.

Therefore, as such and formally speaking, one can do something unjust only willingly, and one can suffer something unjust only unwillingly. But

---

[18]Ibid., A. 2. [19]Ibid., A. 3.

accidentally and materially speaking, as it were, one can either do something of itself unjust unwillingly, as when does something unintentionally, or suffer something of itself unjust willingly, as when one willingly gives to another more than one owes the other.

Objection. One does something unjust only to one who suffers the injustice. But one may do something unjust to one who is willing (e.g., if one should sell something to a willing person for more than it is worth). Therefore, one may willingly suffer something unjust.

Reply Obj. Undergoing something is the effect of an external action. But in doing and suffering something unjust, we note the matter by what is done externally, considered in itself. And we note what is formal and intrinsic in the matter by the will of the efficient cause and the recipient. Therefore, we should say that the one doing something unjust, and the other suffering something unjust, materially speaking, always accompany each other. But if we should be speaking formally, one can intentionally do something unjust without the other suffering something unjust, since the other will undergo it willingly. And conversely, one can suffer something unjust if one should suffer the injustice unwillingly. But one who unknowingly does something unjust will do something materially, but not formally, unjust.

4. Does one who does something unjust sin mortally?[20]

Anything contrary to charity, which gives life to the soul, is a mortal sin. But every harm one causes to another is of itself contrary to charity, which moves us to will the good of others. And so, since injustice always consists of harm to another, it is clear that doing anything unjust is generically a mortal sin.

Objection 1. Venial sin is contrary to mortal sin. But doing something unjust is sometimes a venial sin, since the unjust things one does in and because of ignorance are venial sins. Therefore, not everyone who does something unjust sins mortally.

Reply Obj. 1. Ignorance of fact (i.e., of particular circumstances) deserves pardon, but ignorance of the law does not excuse. And one who unknowingly does something unjust does it only accidentally.

Obj. 2. One who commits injustice in a small matter deviates little from the mean. But this seems to be tolerable and ought to be counted among the least evils. Therefore, not everyone who does something unjust sins mortally.

Reply Obj. 2. One who commits injustice in small matters lacks the full character of doing something unjust, since we can consider such injustice not to be completely contrary to the will of the one who suffers it. For

---

[20]Ibid., A. 4.

example, such is the case if one should take an apple or the like from another, and the other is probably neither hurt thereby nor displeased about it.

Judicial Judgment

*Judicial judgment is lawful insofar as it is just. (*Lawful *in this context refers primarily to the natural law.) For judicial judgment to be just, the judge should strive for justice, be vested with public authority to judge, and judge prudently. A judge should condemn only on the basis of solid evidence. One should interpret doubtful things in a light favorable to others. The judge should render judgment according to the written law but should interpret the written law by the principle of equity.*

1. Is judicial judgment an act of justice?[21]

Judgment in the proper sense designates the act of a judge as such. But we call a judge one who declares right, as it were, and right is the object of justice. And so the word *judgment* in its primary meaning signifies the definition or determination of justice or right. But to define something rightly regarding virtuous actions results, properly speaking, from habitual virtue. For example, a chaste person rightly determines the things belonging to chastity. And so judgment, which signifies the right determination of what is just, belongs in the proper sense to justice.

Objection. Right judgment regarding the proper subject matter of each virtue belongs to that virtue, since the virtuous person is the rule and measure in particular things. Therefore, right judgment does not belong more to justice than to other moral virtues.

Reply Obj. Other moral virtues direct human beings in relation to themselves, but justice orders them in relation to one another. However, human beings are the masters of things that belong to them but not of things that belong to others. And so, in things regarding other virtues, only the judgment of the virtuous person is required, understanding judgment in a broad sense. But regarding things that belong to justice, the further judgment of a superior, who can reprove and has authority over both parties, is required. And so a more particular kind of judgment belongs to justice than to any other virtue.

2. Is it lawful to judge?[22]

Judicial judgment is lawful insofar as it is an act of justice. But three things are required for judicial judgment to be just. First, the judgment

---

[21]ST II–II, Q. 60, A. 1.   [22]Ibid., A. 2.

should issue from the desire for justice. Second, the judgment should issue from one vested with public authority to judge. Third, right prudential reason should produce the judgment. And the judgment is sinful and unlawful if any of these prerequisites should be lacking. This happens in one way when the judgment is contrary to the rectitude of justice, and then we call the judgment perverse or unjust. It happens in a second way when a judge judges about things over which the judge has no authority. And then we call the judgment usurped. It happens in a third way when a judge lacks reasonable certitude, as, for example, when a judge judges about doubtful and hidden things without any solid evidence; and then we call the judgment suspect or rash.

3. Is judgment based on suspicion unlawful?[23]

Suspicion signifies an opinion of evil based on slight evidence, and this happens in three ways. It happens in one way because someone is himself evil and, for that very reason, being conscious of his own wickedness, as it were, easily thinks evil of others. It happens in a second way because one is biased toward another. For one who contemns or hates, or is angry or envious of, another thinks evil about the other on the basis of slight evidence, since one readily believes what one wishes to believe. It happens in a third way from long experience of the defects of others.

The first two causes of suspicion clearly belong to wicked desires, but the third cause lessens the character of suspicion, since experience helps to produce certainty, and certainty is contrary to the character of suspicion. And so suspicion signifies a sin, and the further one's suspicion extends, the more sinful it is.

There are three grades of suspicion. The first grade is that a human being begins to doubt the goodness of another on the basis of slight evidence, and this is a venial and slight sin. The second grade is that in which one, on the basis of slight evidence, thinks that the wickedness of another is certain; and this, if it should concern something serious, is a mortal sin, since there is no such suspicion without contempt of one's neighbor. The third grade is that in which a judge, on the basis of suspicion proceeds to condemn someone, and this belongs directly to injustice and so is a mortal sin.

Objection. If a judgment should be unlawful, we need to trace it to injustice, since judgment is an act of justice. But injustice is generically always a mortal sin. Therefore, a judgment based on suspicion would always be a mortal sin if it were to be unlawful. But this conclusion is

---

[23]Ibid., A. 3.

false, since we cannot avoid suspicion. Therefore, a judgment based on suspicion does not seem to be unlawful.

Reply Obj. Since justice and injustice concern external actions, a judgment based on suspicion directly belongs to injustice when it proceeds to an external act, and then it is a mortal sin. The internal judgment belongs to justice insofar as it is related to the external judgment, as internal act to external act—as, for example, lustful desire is to fornication, and anger to homicide.

4. Should one interpret doubtful things in a favorable light?[24]

By having a bad opinion of another without sufficient cause, one harms and contemns the other. But no one should contemn or harm another without a compelling reason. And so, where there is no clear evidence of the wickedness of another, we ought to consider the other as good by interpreting in a favorable light what is doubtful.

5. Should one always judge according to the written law?[25]

A judgment is simply a definition or determination of what is just. But something is just in two ways. It is just in one way by the very nature of the thing, and we call this natural right. It is just in a second way by an agreement among human beings, and we call this positive right. But laws are written to declare both kinds of right, one in one way and the other in another way. For written law contains but does not establish natural right, since natural right gets its force from nature, not from the law. And written law both contains and establishes positive right in giving the force of authority to such law. And so judgment needs to be rendered according to the written law. Otherwise, judgment would lack either natural right or positive right.

Objection 1. Unjust judgment should always be avoided. But written laws sometimes contain injustice. Therefore, one should not always judge according to written laws.

Reply Obj. 1. As written law does not give force to natural right, so neither can it lessen or take away the force of natural right, since the will of human beings cannot change nature. And so a written law, if it should contain anything contrary to natural right, is unjust and has no obligatory force, since there is room for positive right only over things in which it does not matter, regarding natural right, whether something is done in this way or that. And so we call unjust laws corruptions of law rather than written laws. And so one should not judge according to them.

---

[24]Ibid., A. 4.   [25]Ibid., A. 5.

Obj. 2. Judgment should concern individual events. But no written law can comprehend all individual situations. Therefore, it seems that one should not always judge according to written laws.

Reply Obj. 2. As unjust laws as such are either always or for the most part contrary to natural right, so also laws rightly laid down are defective in some cases in which it would be contrary to natural right if they were observed. And so one should not judge in such cases by the letter of the law, but have recourse to equity, which is the intention of the lawmaker. And even the lawmaker would judge otherwise than the letter of the law in such cases and would have so determined the matter by law, if the lawmaker were to have considered it.

6. Does usurpation render a judicial judgment unjust?[26]

Since judges should render judgment according to written laws, they in a way interpret the words of the law by applying the words to particular cases. And since it belongs to the same authority to interpret law and to establish law, as only public authority can establish law, so also only public authority, which extends to those subject to the community, can render judicial judgments. And so, as it would be unjust for someone to force another to observe laws not sanctioned by public authority, so also it is unjust for someone to force another to submit to judicial judgments not sanctioned by public authority.

Objection. We distinguish the spiritual power from the earthly power. But religious superiors, who have spiritual power, sometimes interpose themselves regarding matters that belong to the secular power. Therefore, usurped power is not unlawful.

Reply Obj. The secular power is subject to the spiritual power as the body is subject to the soul. And so judicial judgment is not usurped if a spiritual superior interposes himself about earthly affairs regarding matters in which the secular power is subject to him, or which the secular power relinquishes to him.

Subjective Parts

There are two species of particular justice: commutative justice and distributive justice. Commutative justice, which consists of mutual exchanges, directs the relation of private persons to one another. Distributive justice directs the distribution of common goods to private persons. The mean in commutative jus-

---

[26]Ibid., A. 6.

tice is the arithmetic—that is, the quantitatively exact—quid pro quo. For example, the wages paid to a laborer should be quantitatively equal to the value of the service received. The mean in distributive justice is the geometric—that is, proportional—quid pro quo whereby each receives common goods in proportion to the services rendered to the community. For example, the person who contributes twice as much to the community than another person should receive twice as much of the common goods as the other.

Exchanges are involuntary when one uses the property or person or deeds of another against the other's will (the other's property in theft, the other's person in homicide, and the other's deeds in defamation), and then one violates commutative justice. Exchanges are voluntary when one transfers property to another in various ways (e.g., when one leases or sells property to another).

Retaliation, as Thomas defines it, is the equal recompense of suffering loss imposed on a person because of the person's previous action inflicting loss on another. Thomas applies the concept not only to equal recompense for harm caused to the person or property of another, but also to the equal recompense in voluntary exchanges, in which both parties suffer loss.

1. Do we appropriately posit two species of justice; namely, distributive and commutative justice?[27]

Particular justice is directed to private persons, who are related to the community as parts to a whole, and we can consider two relationships regarding parts. There is one relationship of parts to other parts. The relationship of one private person to another is similar, and commutative justice, which consists of mutual exchanges between two persons, directs this relationship.

We consider a second relationship of the whole to its parts. The relationship of community goods to individual persons is similar, and distributive justice, which distributes common goods to individual persons proportionally, directs this relationship. And so there are two species of justice: namely, commutative and distributive justice.

Objection. Distributive justice concerns common goods. But common goods pertain to legal justice. Therefore, distributive justice is a species of legal justice, not of particular justice.

Reply Obj. Movements take their species from their goals. And so directing things that belong to private persons to the common good belongs to legal justice. But conversely, distributing common goods to particular persons belongs to particular justice.

---

[27]ST II-II, Q. 61, A. 1.

2. Do we understand the mean in distributive and commutative justice in the same way?[28]

Distributive justice allots things to private persons insofar as what belongs to the whole is due the parts. And the more important the parts are, the greater the distribution is to the parts. And so, in distributive justice, the more important the persons in a political community are, the more common goods are allotted to them. And we gauge the importance of persons in aristocratic regimes by the standard of virtue; of persons in oligarchic regimes by the standard of wealth; of persons in democratic regimes by the standard of freedom; and of persons in other regimes in other ways.

And so we do not understand the mean in distributive justice by the equality of one thing to another. Rather, we understand the mean by the proportion of things to persons; namely, that as one person surpasses another, so also the things allotted to the one surpass the things allotted to the other. And so such a mean is by geometric proportionality, wherein we consider equality proportionally, not quantitatively. This is as if we should say that three is to two as six is to four, since the proportion in both cases is one and a half to one, and the greater number in each couplet is one-and-a-half times the lesser number. But the difference between the greater and lesser numbers in the two couplets is not quantitatively the same, since six exceeds four by two, and three exceeds two by one.

But in exchanges, things are rendered to individual persons because of things received from them, and this is most apparent in buying and selling, in which we first note the character of commutation. And so the things exchanged need to be equal, so that one should restore to another as much as one is enriched by what belongs to the other. And then there is an equality by an arithmetic mean, which we note by equal quantitative differences from the mean. For example, five is the mean between six and four, since six exceeds the mean by one, and the mean exceeds four by one. Therefore, if each party to an exchange started off with five, and one of the parties received one from of the other party's five, the one receiving will have six, and the other will be left with four. Therefore, there will be justice if both are brought back to the mean, so that the one with four receives one from the other with six, and the one with six gives one to the other with four, since both parties will then have five, which is the mean.

Objection. Both distributive justice and commutative justice are included in particular justice. But we understand the mean in every part of temperance or fortitude in the same way. Therefore, we should understand the mean in distributive and commutative justice in the same way.

---

[28]Ibid., A. 2.

Reply Obj. In other moral virtues, we understand the mean as one of reason, not a real mean. But we understand the mean in justice as a real mean. And so we understand the mean of justice in different ways by real differences.

3. Do commutative justice and distributive justice have different subject matters?[29]

Justice concerns certain external actions—namely, distributions and exchanges—and these actions consist of the treatment of particular external things or persons or deeds. Actions concern the treatment of things when one takes away from or restores to another the other's property. And actions concern the treatment of persons when one does an injustice to the very person of a human being (e.g., by striking or insulting a person), or when one shows respect to another. And actions concern the treatment of deeds when one justly requires a deed of or renders a service to another. Therefore, if we should understand as the subject matter of commutative and distributive justice the things of which external actions treat, distributive and commutative justice have the same subject matter. For things can be both distributed from common goods to individuals and exchanged from one person to another. And laborious tasks can be distributed and recompensed.

But if we should understand as the subject matter of commutative and distributive justice the chief actions themselves whereby we treat of persons, things, and deeds, then there is different subject matter in each. For distributive justice directs distributions, and commutative justice directs the exchanges that we may consider between two persons.

Some exchanges are involuntary, and others voluntary. Exchanges are involuntary when one deals with the property or person or deeds of another against the other's will. And this happens sometimes secretly, by fraud, and sometimes openly, by coercion. In either case, the offense can be against the property or against the proper or closely associated person of another. In the case of offenses against the property of another, we call it theft if one should take the property secretly, and robbery if one should take the property openly.

In the case of offenses against the proper person of another, the offense may regard the very substance or the reputation of the other. If the offense regards the substance of another, then one harms the other secretly by killing, striking, or poisoning the other covertly; and one harms the other openly by killing or imprisoning or maiming the other publicly. If the offense regards the reputation of another, one harms the other secretly by

---

[29]Ibid., A. 3.

false witness or detraction (in both of which one takes away the other's reputation) or the like; and one harms the other openly by bringing charges in courts of law against, or by shouting insults at, the other.

And if the offense regards the closely associated person of another, one harms the other in the other's wife by adultery, usually in secret, and in the other's slaves when one induces them to leave their master. And one can also do these things openly. The same argument applies to other closely associated persons, and one can commit offenses against them in all the ways that one can against the chief person. But adultery and inducing slaves to leave their masters are, strictly speaking, offenses against the persons; although inducing slaves to leave their masters is related to theft, since slaves are a form of property.

We call exchanges voluntary when one voluntarily transfers one's property to another, and if one should alienate property to another without the other incurring debt, as in the case of gifts, this is an act of generosity, not of justice. But voluntary transfers of property belong to justice insofar as they partake of the nature of debt.

This happens in three ways. It happens in one way when one alienates one's property to another in exchange for other property, as in buying and selling.

Voluntary transfers of property partake of the nature of debt in a second way when one grants the use of one's property to another, and the other is obliged to return it. If one grants the use of one's property without compensation, we call such transfers usufruct regarding productive property, or simply borrowing and lending in the case of nonproductive property (e.g., money, dining utensils, and the like). If one grants the use of one's property in return for compensation, we call such transfers leasing or renting.

In a third way, one transfers property to another, placing the other under obligation to return it, not for the other's use but in order to safeguard the property, as in the case of entrusted goods, or in connection with an obligation, as when one pledges one's property as security for oneself or another.

And all such actions, whether voluntary or involuntary, have the same nature of understanding the mean by equal recompense. And so all these actions belong to the same species of justice; namely, commutative justice.

4. Is justice absolutely the same as retaliation?[30]

The word *retaliation* signifies the equal recompense of suffering imposed on someone for that one's previous action, and we speak of

---

[30]Ibid., A. 4.

retaliation in the strictest sense with respect to the wrongful sufferings by which someone harms the person of one's neighbor (e.g., that if one strikes another, the other strikes back). And because taking the property of another also does something harmful, so also we secondarily speak of retaliation in the case of such things; namely, as the person who inflicted loss on another should also suffer loss of the person's property. Third, the word *retaliation* is broadened to cover voluntary exchanges, in which both parties inflict harm and suffer harm, although the voluntariness of such exchanges subtracts from the aspect of suffering harm.

There should be equal recompense in all these things according to the nature of commutative justice; namely, that the suffering repaid be equal to the action inflicting harm. But the suffering repaid would not always be equal if one were to suffer specifically the same thing that one caused. First, this is so because when one injuriously harms another who is a greater person, the action inflicting harm is greater than specifically the same suffering that the offender would undergo. And so one who strikes a ruler is not only struck back, but is much more severely punished.

Second, when one inflicts property loss on another against the other's will, the action inflicting harm on the victim is greater than the suffering of the offender would be if only the victim's property were taken away from the offender, since the offender would suffer no loss of the offender's own property. And so the offender is punished by being obliged to make restitution several times over, since the offender has inflicted loss on the commonwealth by infringing the security of its protection, as well as the loss on the private person.

Third, the suffering repaid would also not always be equal in voluntary exchanges if the person receiving the property of another were to give the person's own property in exchange, since the property of the other may be worth more than the person's own property. And so it is necessary in exchanges to equate the suffering of one party with the action of the other party by a proportionate common measure, and money was invented for this purpose.

But retaliation has no place in distributive justice, since we consider the equality in distributive justice by the proportion of things to persons, not of one thing to another or of loss suffered to action inflicting loss. And we speak of retaliation regarding the latter proportion.

Objection 1. In both kinds of justice, something is given to someone according to some kind of equality. In distributive justice, something is given to someone in relation to the worthiness of the person, which we seem most to note by the services that the person has rendered to the community. And in commutative justice, something is given to someone in relation to the thing in which one has suffered loss. But in each kind of equality, one is repaid according to one's deeds. Therefore, it seems that justice is absolutely the same as retaliation.

Reply Obj. 1. If something were paid to someone for services that the person had rendered to the community, this would belong to commutative, not distributive, justice. For in distributive justice, we consider the equality of what one person receives to what another person receives in relation to each person, not the equality of what one person receives to what that person expends.

Obj. 2. Because of the difference between the voluntary and the involuntary, it especially seems that one need not receive as much retribution as the harm one caused, since one who has involuntarily caused a wrong is punished less severely than one who has done so willfully. But we do not distinguish the mean of justice, which is a real mean and not one in relation to ourselves, by the voluntary and the involuntary, which we understand in relation to ourselves. Therefore, justice seems to be absolutely the same as retaliation.

Reply Obj. 2. The wrong is greater when the wrongful action is voluntary, and so we understand the wrong as something greater. And so a greater punishment needs to be repaid to the offender because of a real difference, not because of a difference in relation to ourselves.

Restitution

One is obliged in commutative justice to restore another's property to the other, whether the property was unjustly taken or is held in trust. One is obliged to recompense any harm caused to the body or reputation of another. One is obliged to pay punitive damages if and only if a court imposes them. One is obliged to make partial, but only partial, restitution if one prevented another from using the other's property to gain profit. One is not obliged to make restitution if it is impossible or imprudent in particular circumstances to do so. But one is obliged to make restitution when one becomes capable of doing so, and to safeguard the property to be returned, if it exists, until it is prudent to return it. One who loses entrusted property is obliged to make restitution only if one's custody of the property has been grossly negligent. One who has unjustly taken the property of another is obliged to make restitution even if one no longer has the property. The chief perpetrators of theft or robbery are most obliged to make restitution, but accomplices before and after the fact are also, though secondarily, obliged. One is obliged to make immediate restitution insofar as this is possible.

1. Is restitution an act of commutative justice?[31]

It seems that to make restitution is simply to reestablish a person in possession of, or mastery over, the person's property. And so we note the equality of justice in restitution by the recompense of one thing for another, and this belongs to commutative justice. And so restitution is an act of commutative justice: namely, when one person holds the property of another, whether by the other's consent, as in the case of something lent or entrusted, or contrary to the other's will, as in robbery or theft.

Objection 1. One cannot restore what has passed away and no longer exists. But justice and injustice regard particular actions and being acted upon, which pass away and do not abide. Therefore, restitution does not seem to be an act of any part of justice.

Reply Obj. 1. The word *restitution,* insofar as it signifies a restoration, supposes something identical. And so, in its primary meaning, it would seem to apply chiefly to external things, which remain the same both substantially and regarding the right of ownership, and can pass from one person to another. But as the word *commutation* has been extended from such things to cover the acting and being acted upon that belong to the respect or injury, or the harm or benefit, of a person, so also the word *restitution* has been extended to cover things that abide in their effects, although not in themselves. Such things abide either in a material effect (e.g., when a person's body is wounded by another's blow) or in reputation (e.g., when a person remains defamed by scurrilous words or dishonored).

Obj. 2. Restitution is a recompense, as it were, of something taken away. But something can be taken away from a human being in distributions as well as commutations (e.g., when one distributing things gives less to another than the other should have). Therefore, restitution is as much an act of distributive justice as of commutative justice.

Reply Obj. 2. We calculate, by the relation of one thing to another, the recompense that the distributor makes to the other to whom the distributor gave less than what was owed. For example, the less the other received than was owed, the more the distributor should give the other. And so this then belongs to commutative justice.

2. Is it necessary for salvation that one make restitution of what one has taken?[32]

Restitution is an act of commutative justice, which consists of an equality. And so making restitution signifies returning the very thing unjustly taken, since returning the thing restores equality. (But if the

---

[31]ST II-II, Q. 62, A. 1.   [32]Ibid., A. 2.

thing is justly taken, there will be inequality if there is restitution for it, since justice consists of equality.) Therefore, since observance of justice is necessary for salvation, it is necessary for salvation to return what one has unjustly taken.

Obj. 1. Nothing impossible is necessary for salvation. But it is sometimes impossible to restore what one has taken (e.g., a limb or life). Therefore, it does not seem to be necessary for salvation to return what one has taken from another.

Reply Obj. 1. Regarding things for which one cannot repay anything equivalent (e.g., the honor due God or one's parents), it suffices to repay what one can. And so when one cannot recompense something taken with something equivalent, one should make restitution as far as one can. For example, a person who has severed another's limb should recompense the victim either in money or some honor, with due consideration of both parties according to the judgment of a good person.

Obj. 2. One cannot undo what has been done. But one sometimes takes away the personal honor of another by unjustly insulting the other. Therefore, one cannot restore to the other what one has taken away, and it is not necessary, for salvation, to restore what one has taken away.

Reply Obj. 2. Insults cannot be undone. But showing respect can undo the action's effect; namely, the lowering of the other's personal honor in public opinion.

3. Is it sufficient to restore only the thing unjustly taken?[33]

There are two things involved when one unjustly takes another's property. The first is the inequality regarding the thing, and this is sometimes without injustice, as in the case of lending. The other is the wrongdoing of injustice, which can also happen without real inequality, as, for example, when one intends to do violence but fails. Therefore, regarding the first, restitution applies the remedy, since restitution restores equality, for which it suffices that one restores as much as one has of something belonging to another. But regarding wrongdoing, punishment applies the remedy, and inflicting punishment belongs to a judge. And so, before the court has imposed sentence, one is not bound to restore more than one took; but after the court has imposed sentence, one is bound to pay the penalty.

4. Should one recompense what one did not take?[34]

Whoever inflicts loss on another seems to take away from the other that in which one inflicts the loss, since loss means that the other has less than

---

[33]Ibid., A. 3.   [34]Ibid., A. 4.

the other should have. And so human beings are bound to restitution of that in which they inflicted loss on the other. But loss is inflicted on another in two ways. Loss is inflicted in one way because what the other actually had is taken away. And one should always make restitution to the other for such loss by the recompense of something equivalent. For example, if one inflicts loss on another by destroying the other's house, one is bound to make restitution for as much as the house is worth.

One inflicts loss on another in a second way by preventing the other from obtaining what the other was in the process of obtaining, and one need not recompense such loss with something equivalent. For having something potentially is less than having it actually, and the other who is in the process of obtaining something has it only virtually or potentially. And so if one were to make restitution to the other as if the other were actually to possess it, one would restore to the other more than the thing taken away, and restitution does not require this. Nevertheless, one is bound to make some recompense according to the circumstances of persons and occupations.

Objection. One who holds a creditor's money beyond the contract's terminal date seems to inflict loss on the creditor regarding any profit the creditor could gain with the money. But the debtor himself does not take away this profit. Therefore, it seems that one is bound to make restitution for what one did not take.

Reply Obj. One in possession of money has profit only virtually, not yet actually, and profit can be prevented in many ways.

5. Is it always necessary to make restitution to the person from whom one has taken something?[35]

Restitution reestablishes the equality of commutative justice, which consists of equating one thing to another. And one could not equate one thing with another unless whatever is lacking is restored to the person who has less than what is owed the person. And to supply this, one needs to make restitution to the person from whom one has taken something.

Objection. 1. We should harm no one. But it would sometimes be to the harm of the person from whom one had taken something, or of others, if one were to return the thing taken to its owner. Such would be the case if one were to return a sword held in trust to a madman. Therefore, one should not always return something to the person from whom one has taken it.

---

[35]Ibid., A. 5.

Reply Obj. 1. One should not return something to its owner when the thing to be returned is likely to be seriously harmful to the owner or another, since restitution is directed to the benefit of the person to whom something is returned. For all possessions fall within the category of the useful. But one who holds the property of another should not appropriate it. Rather, such a person should either keep it in order to return it at a suitable time, or deposit it elsewhere in order for it to be more safely preserved.

Obj. 2. A person who unlawfully gave something does not deserve to recover it. But a person sometimes unlawfully gives what another also unlawfully receives (e.g., the seller and buyer in the practice of simony). Therefore, one should not always make restitution to the person from whom one has received something.

Reply Obj. 2. A person gives something unlawfully in two ways. A person gives something unlawfully in one way because the very giving is unlawful and contrary to the law, as is evident in the case of the practice of simony. Such a person deserves to lose what the person gave, and so no restitution should be made to that person in regard to these things. A person gives something unlawfully in a second way for the sake of something illicit, although the giving itself is lawful (e.g., when one pays a prostitute for fornication). And so also the woman can keep the money for herself, but she would be bound to make restitution to the customer if she were to have extorted any payment by fraud or guile.

Obj. 3. No one is bound to do the impossible. But it is sometimes impossible to make restitution to the person from whom one has taken something, whether because the person is dead, or because the person is too far away, or because the person is unknown. Therefore, one should not always make restitution to the person from whom one has taken something.

Reply Obj. 3. If the person to whom one should make restitution should be completely unknown, one should give back insofar as one can; namely, by giving alms for the salvation of the person, whether the person be living or dead—but only after a diligent search for the person.

If the person should be dead, one ought to make restitution to the person's heir, who is reckoned as if the same person.

And if the person should be very far away, one ought to transmit to the person what is owed the person, and especially if the property should be of great value and could be easily sent. Otherwise, one should deposit it in a safe place to keep it for the person, and notify the owner.

Obj. 4. One should more recompense a person from whom one received a greater favor. But human beings received more benefit from others (e.g., their parents) than from those who lend things to them or entrust things with them. Therefore, human beings should sometimes assist another person rather than make restitution to a person from whom they have received something.

Reply Obj. 4. One should, out of one's own possessions, recompense one's parents or those from whom one received greater favors. But one should not recompense a benefactor out of another's property, which would be the case if one were to compensate someone with what one owes another. There is perhaps an exception in the case of extreme necessity, in which one could and should even take away the property of another in order to assist one's father.

6. Is the person who took the property bound to restitution?[36]

We should consider two things regarding the person who took the property of another: namely, the property taken and the taking itself. By reason of the property, one is bound to return it as long as one has it in one's possession, since the essence of commutative justice is that one should subtract what one has beyond what is one's own and give it to the one who lacks it.

And we can consider the taking of the property in three ways. For the taking is sometimes wrongful: namely, being against the will of the one who is the owner of the property, as is clearly the case in theft and robbery. And then one is bound to make restitution both by reason of the property and by reason of the wrongful action, even if the property does not remain in the taker's possession. For one who strikes another is bound to recompense the wrong to the one who suffered it, even though nothing stays in the attacker's possession. Just so, a thief or robber is bound to recompense the loss inflicted, even if the thief or robber should have none of the stolen goods; and the thief or robber should be further punished for the wrong inflicted.

In a second way, one takes the property of another for one's own benefit without wrong: namely, with the consent of the owner of the property, as is clearly the case with loans. And then the person who took the property is bound to restitution of what the person took, both by reason of the property and by reason of the taking. This is so even if the person should have lost the property, since the person is bound to recompense the other who did the favor, which the other will not do if the other would incur loss by lending the property.

In a third way, one takes the property of another without wrong but not for one's own benefit, as is clearly the case with entrusted goods. And so

---

[36]Ibid., A. 6.

the one who took the property in this way is in no way bound by reason of the taking. (Rather, the one taking the property does a favor.) But one who took the property is bound by reason of the property. And so a person is not bound to restitution if the property should be taken away through no fault of the person. But the person would be bound to restitution if the person were to lose the entrusted property through gross negligence.

Objection 1. Restitution restores the equality of justice, which consists of taking away from the person who has more than the person should have and giving to the person who has less than the person should have. But sometimes the person who has taken property from another does not have it, and it comes into the possession of still another. Therefore, the other who has the property, not the one who took it, is bound to make restitution.

Reply Obj. 1. The chief aim of restitution is that the person who has less than the person ought to have should be compensated, not that the person who has more than the person ought to have should cease to possess the property taken. And so, in things that one can take from another without loss to the other, there is no room for restitution, as, for example, when one takes light from the candle of another. And so, although the person who took the property has transferred it to another and does not have it, the victim is nonetheless deprived of the property. And so both the one who took the property, by reason of wrongfully taking the property, and the one who has the property, by reason of the property itself, are bound to make restitution to the victim.

Obj. 2. One is not obliged to reveal one's crime. But in making restitution, one sometimes reveals one's crime, as is clearly so in the case of theft. Therefore, the one who took property is not always obliged to make restitution.

Reply Obj. 2. Although one is not obliged to reveal one's crime to human beings, one is obliged to reveal one's crime to God in confession. And so the thief can make restitution of another's property through a confessor.

Obj. 3. Restitution of the same property should not be made many times over. But many in concert sometimes steal property, and one of them makes entire restitution of it. Therefore, the one who took the property is not always bound to make restitution.

Reply Obj. 3. The chief aim of restitution is to remove the loss of the one from whom something has been unjustly taken. Therefore, after one thief has made adequate restitution to the victim, the other thieves are not bound to make further restitution to the victim. Rather, they are bound to reimburse the thief who made the restitution, although the latter thief may forgive the debt of the others.

7. Are those who did not take property bound to make restitution?[37]

One is bound to make restitution both by reason of the property of another that one took and by reason of wrongfully taking it. And so whoever causes the unjust taking is held to make restitution, and this happens in two ways: namely, directly and indirectly. It happens directly when one induces another to take property, and one does so in three ways. The first way is by inducing the other to the very taking, which one does by commanding it, expressly counseling it, consenting to it, and praising the other for the other's skill, as it were, in taking the property of another. The second way regards the thief or robber himself; namely, in that one shelters or in any way assists him. The third way regards the property taken; namely, in that one participates in the theft or robbery as an accomplice, as it were, in the crime. It happens indirectly when one does not prevent the theft or robbery when one can and should, whether because one withholds a command or counsel to prevent the theft or robbery, or because one withholds help to resist the thief or robber, or because one hides the thief or robber after the deed.

All these things are summed up in the saying that one causes unjust taking by commanding it, counseling it, consenting to it, encouraging it, providing shelter, participating in it, not speaking against it, not resisting it, or hiding the criminal.

But we should note that five of the foregoing things always oblige one to make restitution. First, commanding the theft or robbery obliges one to do so because the person who commands the theft or robbery is its chief cause and so chiefly bound to make restitution. Second, consenting—namely, in the case of one without whose consent a robbery is impossible—obliges one to make restitution. Third, giving shelter—namely, when one gives shelter to robbers and offers them protection—obliges one to make restitution. Fourth, participating—namely, when one participates in the crime of robbery and shares in the booty—obliges one to make restitution. Fifth, one who does not resist, although bound to do so, is obliged to make restitution. For example, rulers, who have the duty to secure justice on earth, are obliged to make restitution if robbers flourish because of the rulers' dereliction of duty, since the remuneration that rulers receive is payment, as it were, established in order that they preserve justice on earth.

In the other enumerated cases, one is not always obliged to make restitution. For example, counseling or flattery, or any such thing, is not always the efficacious cause of robbery. And so one who counsels or encourages

---

[37] Ibid., A. 7.

(i.e., flatters) is bound to make restitution only when that person can, with probability, calculate that the unjust taking resulted from such a cause.

Objection. Justice does not oblige one to increase the property of another. But if both the one who took property and those who in any way cooperated were bound to make restitution, the property of the one from whom something has been taken would thereby be increased. This is so both because restitution would be made to the latter many times over, and because people sometimes try their best to take property from someone but do not succeed. Therefore, persons other than the thief or robber are not bound to make restitution.

Reply Obj. The chief person in the deed is the one chiefly bound to make restitution: primarily, the person who commands the theft or robbery; secondarily, the one who executes it; and then the others sequentially. But if one of these persons makes restitution to the person who suffered the loss, the others are not bound to make restitution to that person. Rather, the chief perpetrators of the deed and those who acquired the property are bound to reimburse the others if those others have made restitution.

Nevertheless, when one commands an unjust taking that does not result, there is no need to make restitution, since restitution is chiefly directed to making whole the property of the one who has unjustly suffered loss.

8. Is one bound to make immediate restitution, or can one lawfully defer it?[38]

As taking the property of another is a sin against justice, so also is it a sin against justice to retain the property, since, by retaining the property of another against that other's will, one prevents the owner from using the property and so causes injury to the owner. But it is clear that everyone is bound to abandon sin immediately and not permitted to remain in sin, even for a little while. And so everyone is bound to make immediate restitution or to seek delay from the one who can grant use of the property.

Objection. No one is bound to do the impossible. But one sometimes cannot make immediate restitution. Therefore, no one is bound to make immediate restitution.

Reply Obj. When one cannot make immediate restitution, the impossibility itself absolves one from making immediate restitution, just as one is completely absolved from making restitution if one is completely unable to do so. But one, either by oneself or through another, should seek remission or delay from the person to whom one owes restitution.

---

[38]Ibid., A. 8.

Preferential Treatment of Persons

Distributive justice requires that common goods be distributed according to the recipient's deserts. But giving preferential treatment to persons because of who they are rather than what they are is not proportional to the persons' worthiness, and so such treatment is a violation of distributive justice. One may, however, favor one's relatives in certain things (e.g., willing one's property to one's relatives), and worldly considerations may make less holy persons more worthy of spiritual preferment than holier persons. One may and should show honor and respect to temporal and spiritual officeholders in spite of their moral defects. Preferential treatment of persons should have no place in judicial proceedings.

1. Is preferential treatment of persons a sin?[39]

Favorable treatment of persons is contrary to distributive justice. For the equality of distributive justice consists of different things being distributed to different persons in proportion to the persons' worthiness. Therefore, if one should consider the attribute of a person the reason why the thing conferred is due the person, there will be favorable estimation of the reason, not favorable treatment of the person. For example, if one should promote a person to a professorship because of the person's adequate knowledge, one considers the proper reason, not the person. But if one should consider only the fact that the person on whom one confers something is a particular person (e.g., Peter or Martin), and not the reason why the thing given would be proportionate to or due the person, one gives preferential treatment to the person. This is because one distributes something to the person absolutely and not for a reason that would make the person worthy to receive it.

And any condition not indicating a reason why a person is worthy of a particular gift regards the person. For example, if one should promote a person to a prelature or professorship because the person is rich or a blood relative, this gives preferential treatment to the person. But the condition of a person may make the person worthy regarding one thing but not another. For example, consanguinity makes a person worthy to be constituted the heir of a patrimony, but not worthy that an ecclesiastical prelate should be conferred on the person. And so the same condition of the person amounts to preferential treatment of the person if we consider the condition in relation to one occupation, but not if we consider the condition in relation to another occupation.

---

[39]ST II–II, Q. 63, A. 1.

Therefore, preferential treatment of persons is clearly contrary to distributive justice, since it is disproportionate. But only sin is contrary to virtue. Therefore, preferential treatment of persons is a sin.

2. Is the preferential treatment of persons in the distribution of spiritual things a sin?[40]

Preferential treatment of persons is a sin because it is contrary to justice. But the greater the things in which one transgresses justice are, the more serious the sin is. And so, since spiritual things are more important than temporal things, the preferential treatment of persons in the distribution of spiritual things is a more serious sin than such treatment in the distribution of temporal things.

And since there is preferential treatment of persons when one distributes something to a person beyond the person's proportional worth, we need to consider that we can note the worth of a person in two ways. We can do so in one way absolutely and as such, and then one who abounds more in the spiritual gifts of grace is of greater worth. We can do so in a second way in relation to the common good. For it sometimes happens that one who is less holy and less knowledgeable can contribute more to the common good because of the person's worldly power, diligence, or the like. And since distributions of spiritual things are directed to the common benefit, persons less good absolutely are sometimes thus preferred to persons better absolutely, without preferential treatment of the former. Just so, even God sometimes grants freely bestowed graces to persons who are less good.

3. Is the preferential treatment of persons in showing honor and respect a sin?[41]

Honor is a witness to the virtue of the one who is honored, and so only virtue is the proper reason of honor. But we should note that a person can be honored both because of the person's virtue and because of the virtue of another. For example, we honor rulers and prelates even if they should be evil, since they represent the person of God and the community of which they are in charge. We should honor parents and masters for the same reason, since they share in the dignity of God, who is the father and master of all. We should honor the elderly because they have a sign of virtue: that is, old age. And we should honor the rich because they hold a higher position in communities, but if the rich are honored only with an eye on their riches, there will be the sin of preferential treatment of persons.

---

[40]Ibid., A. 2.   [41]Ibid., A. 3.

4. Is the preferential treatment of
persons in judicial judgments a sin?[42]

Judicial judgment is an act of justice, since a judge brings back to the equality of justice things that can cause a contrary inequality. But preferential treatment of persons has an inequality, since one distributes something to a person beyond the person's proportional worth, and the equality of justice consists of such a proportion. And so preferential treatment of persons corrupts judicial judgment.

Homicide

Thomas now turns his attention to violations of commutative justice, beginning with homicide and then other injuries against the person. He considers culpable homicide without regard to technical legal categories (e.g., murder in the first or second degree, voluntary or involuntary manslaughter). Plants and irrational animals are for the benefit of other things, and so human beings may destroy plants and kill animals for human benefit. Killing law-abiding human beings is sinful. Those vested with public authority may execute convicted criminals for the good of the community, but private persons may not. Suicide is a sin, not only because it is contrary to the love one ought to have for oneself, but also because it is contrary to justice in relation to the community and God. Since just persons promote the common good, no one is permitted to kill an innocent person. But one may forcibly resist an aggressor in moderate self-defense, even if the force results in aggressor's death. Accidental deaths are not homicides unless they, although not actually and as such intended, result from criminal activity or negligence.

1. Is it lawful to kill any living thing?[43]

No one sins by using something for the purpose for which it exists. But in the order of things, the less perfect are for the sake of the more perfect. Just so, nature in the process of generation goes from the less perfect to the more perfect. And so, as in begetting human beings, there is first something alive, then something animal, and lastly a human being; so also all things that have the lowest form of life, such as plants, are universally for the sake of all animals, and all animals for the sake of human beings. And so it is lawful for a human being to use plants for the benefit of animals, and animals for the benefit of human beings. But the most necessary of all uses seems to be that animals use plants for food, and human beings animals, and this cannot be done without killing plants and animals. And

---

[42]Ibid., A. 4.   [43]ST II-II, Q. 64, A. 1.

so it is lawful, by God's order of things, both to kill plants for the use of animals and to kill animals for the use of human beings.

Objection. Homicide is a sin because it deprives a human being of life. But life is common to all animals and plants. Therefore, it seems, by the same argument, that it is a sin to kill irrational animals and plants.

Reply Obj. Irrational animals and plants do not have rational life, by means of which they would act on themselves. Rather, something else—a natural impulse, as it were—always acts on them. And this is a sign that they are by nature at the service of, and suitable for use by, other things.

2. Is it lawful to kill sinful human beings?[44]

It is lawful to kill irrational animals insofar as they are by nature ordered to the use of human beings, as the imperfect is ordered to the perfect. But every part is by nature ordered to the whole of which it is a part, as the imperfect is to the perfect. And so every part is for the sake of the whole of which it is a part. And on that account, we perceive that if the amputation of a limb should be expedient for the health of the whole human body (e.g., when a limb is gangrenous and infecting other parts of the body), the amputation is praiseworthy and beneficial to health. But any individual person is related to the whole community as a part to the whole. And so, if any human being should be dangerous to the community and corrupting it because of some sin, it is praiseworthy and beneficial to kill that human being in order to safeguard the common good.

Objection. It is unlawful that one do anything intrinsically evil for any good end. But killing a human being is intrinsically evil, since we ought to have charity toward all human beings. Therefore, it is never lawful to kill a sinner.

Reply Obj. Human beings by sinning withdraw from the order of reason and so fall from human dignity: namely, as human beings, who are by nature free and exist for their own sakes, fall somehow into the slave status of irrational animals. And so such human beings are subordinate to other things insofar as they are useful to those things. And so, although killing a human being who maintains human dignity is intrinsically evil, it can nonetheless be good to kill a sinner, just as it can be good to kill an irrational animal, since an evil human being is worse than an irrational animal and causes more harm.

3. Is it lawful for a private person to kill a sinful human being?[45]

It is lawful to kill an evildoer insofar as the killing is directed to the well-being of the whole community. Thus, killing an evildoer belongs only to

---

[44]Ibid., A. 2.   [45]Ibid., A. 3.

the one to whom the care of preserving the community is committed, as it belongs to a doctor to amputate a gangrenous limb when care of the health of the whole body has been committed to the doctor. But the care of the common good has been committed to rulers having public authority. And so it is lawful only for them, and not for private persons, to kill evildoers.

Objection. We compare sinful human beings to irrational animals. But it is lawful for a private person to kill wild animals, especially dangerous ones. Therefore, by like argument, it is lawful for a private person to kill a sinner.

Reply Obj. Irrational animals are by nature different from human beings, and so no judicial judgment is necessary to decide whether a wild animal should be killed. If the animal should be domestic, judicial judgment will be necessary because of loss to the owner, not because of the animal itself. But a sinful human being is not by nature different from the just. And so there needs to be a public judicial judgment to decide whether the sinful human being should be killed for the sake of the common well-being.

4. Is it lawful to kill oneself?[46]

It is altogether unlawful to kill oneself, for three reasons. First, suicide is unlawful because each thing by nature loves itself, and it belongs to this self-love that each thing should naturally preserve itself in existing and resist destructive things as much as it can. And so suicide is contrary to the inclination of nature and to charity, which requires that each one love oneself. And so suicide, being contrary to the natural law and charity, is always a mortal sin.

Second, suicide is unlawful because any part belongs to the whole of which it is a part. But each human being is part of the community. And so each human being belongs to the community, and in killing oneself, one causes injury to the community.

Third, suicide is unlawful because life is a gift from God to human beings and is subject to the power of the one who causes life and takes it away. And so those who deprive themselves of life sin against God, as one who kills another's slave sins against the slave's master, and as a person who presumes to pass judicial judgment on something not committed to the person sins. For judgment over life and death belongs only to God.

Objection 1. Homicide is a sin inasmuch as it is contrary to justice. But no one can commit injustice against oneself. Therefore, no one sins by killing oneself.

---

[46]Ibid., A. 5.

Reply Obj. 1. Homicide is a sin both because it is contrary to justice and because it is contrary to the charity one should have toward oneself. And in the latter regard, suicide is a sin in relation to oneself. But it is also sinful by being contrary to justice in relation to the community and God.

Obj. 2. It is lawful for one voluntarily to undergo a lesser danger in order to avoid a greater one. For example, it is lawful for a person to amputate a gangrenous limb in order to save the whole body. But by killing oneself, one sometimes avoids a greater evil, whether it is an unhappy life or the disgrace of some sin. Therefore, it is lawful for one to kill oneself.

Reply Obj. 2. Free choice makes human beings masters of themselves, and so human beings can lawfully make dispositions about themselves regarding things that belong to this life, which the free choice of human beings governs. But the passage from this life to another, happier one is subject to the power of God, not to the free choice of human beings. And so it is not lawful for human beings to kill themselves in order to pass to a happier life.

Second, it is not lawful for human beings to kill themselves to escape any miseries of the present life, since death is the ultimate and most terrible evil of this life. Thus, bringing death on oneself in order to escape other miseries of this life is to take on the greater evil in order to avoid the lesser one.

Third, it is not lawful to kill oneself because of a sin one has committed. This is so both because one most harms oneself by taking away the time needed for repentance, and because it is not lawful to kill an evildoer except by the judicial judgment of the public power.

Fourth, it is not lawful for a woman to kill herself in order to avoid being raped. This is so because she should not commit the greatest crime against herself—that is, suicide—in order to avoid the lesser crime of another. (For the woman commits no crime by rape if there is no consent.) And it is evident that fornication and adultery are lesser sins than homicide, and especially suicide, which is the most serious homicide, since one thereby harms oneself, to whom one owes the greatest love. Suicide is also the most dangerous, since it leaves no time to expiate the sin by repentance.

Fifth, it is not lawful to kill oneself in order not to consent to sin. This is so because one should not do evil things in order that good things result, or in order to avoid evil things, especially lesser and less certain evils. For it is uncertain whether one would in the future consent to sin, since God can deliver human beings from sin, no matter what the temptation.

5. Is it ever lawful to kill an innocent human being?[47]

We can consider a human being in two ways: in one way, as such; in the second way, in relation to something else. In considering a human being as such, it is unlawful to kill anyone, since we should love in all human beings, even sinners, their nature, which God made, and which killing them destroys. But killing a sinner is lawful in relation to the common good, which sin corrupts, while the lives of the just preserve and promote the common good, since the just constitute the more important part of the community. And so it is never lawful to kill an innocent person.

6. Is it lawful to kill another in self-defense?[48]

Nothing prevents one action from having two effects, only one of which is intended, and the other of which is unintended. But what one intends specifies moral acts, not what one does not intend, since the latter result is incidental. Therefore, one's action in self-defense can result in two effects: one, saving one's own life; the other, slaying the aggressor. Therefore such an action, since one intends to preserve one's life, does not have the character of being unlawful, since it is natural to preserve oneself in existence as much as one can. But an act proceeding out of a good intention can be rendered unlawful if the act is not proportionate to the end. And so, if one should use more force to defend one's own life than necessary, this will be unlawful; but if one should resist force moderately, this will be lawful self-defense. Nor is it necessary for salvation that one omit acts of moderate self-defense in order to avoid killing another, since one is more bound to safeguard one's own life than the life of another.

But since it is only lawful for the public authority to kill a human being for the sake of the common good, it is unlawful that human beings other than those vested with public authority intend to kill another in self-defense. And those vested with public authority who intentionally kill a human being in self-defense relate such killing to the public good. This is evident, for example, in the case of soldiers warring against enemies, and in the case of a judge's marshal resisting robbers, although even these would sin if they should be motivated by private animosity.

7. Does one who by chance kills another incur the guilt of homicide?[49]

Chance causes an unintended effect, and so things happening by chance, absolutely speaking, are neither intended nor voluntary. And

---

[47]Ibid., A. 6.   [48]Ibid., A. 7.   [49]Ibid., A. 8.

since every sin is voluntary, things happening by chance, as such, are not sins. But what one does not, actually and as such, will or intend may be accidentally willed and intended, as we call removing something that prevents an effect an accidental cause of the effect. And so one who does not, when one should, remove things that result in homicide will be in some way guilty of voluntary homicide.

The latter happens in two ways. It happens in one way when a person engaged in unlawful things, which the person should have avoided, incurs the guilt of homicide. It happens in a second way when a person does not use due care. And so, if a person should engage in lawful things and use due care, in the course of which homicide results, the person will not incur the guilt of homicide. But if a person should engage in unlawful activity or not use due care in the course of lawful activity, the person will not escape the guilt of homicide if the activity results in the death of a human being.

War

There are three conditions for a just decision to wage war: (1) legitimate authority should declare or initiate the war; (2) the cause should be just (i.e., because of wrongdoing by the enemy); (3) the intention should be to promote good or prevent evil. (The rules in connection with homicide make clear regarding war conduct that just warriors should not kill innocent persons [i.e., ordinary civilians] intentionally or through negligence.) A nation's rulers should never lie and always keep their treaty obligations, but they may deceive the enemy about their intentions and plans.

1. Is it always sinful to wage war?[50]

Three things are required for a war to be just. First, the war needs to have the authority of the ruler, at whose command the war should be waged. This is because it belongs to no private person to initiate war, since private persons can vindicate their rights in the courts of the superior, and since it belongs to no private person to convoke the people to wage war, which is necessary in war. Rather, since the care of the commonwealth has been committed to rulers, it belongs to them to safeguard the commonweal of the city or kingdom or region subject to them. And as they lawfully use the sword to defend the commonwealth against domestic disturbers of the peace when they punish criminals, so also it belongs to them to safeguard the commonwealth from foreign enemies by the sword of war.

---

[50]ST II–II, Q. 40, A. 1.

Second, a just cause is required; namely, that the enemy attacked deserve to have war waged against them because of some wrong.

Third, a right intention in waging war is required; namely, that one intend that good be promoted, or that evil be avoided. Even if there should be lawful authority to declare war, and just cause, the war may be rendered unlawful because of an evil intention.

2. Is it lawful to lay ambushes in wars?[51]

Ambushes aim to deceive enemies, and the deeds or words of another may deceive a person in two ways. A person can be deceived in one way because another tells the person something false, or another does not keep his promise. This is always unlawful, and no one should deceive enemies in this way, since one should observe laws of war and treaties, even with enemies.

Our words or deeds can deceive a person in a second way because we do not reveal to the person what we intend or understand. But we are not always obliged to do this, since even many things in sacred teachings should not be revealed, particularly to unbelievers, lest they ridicule these things. And so, much more should one conceal plans of attack against enemies from those enemies; and among other advice on military affairs, it is especially important that one should conceal such plans, lest they fall into the enemy's hands. And such secrecy belongs to the nature of ambushes that one may lawfully lay in just wars. Strictly speaking, we do not call such ambushes deceptions. Nor are they contrary to justice. Nor are they contrary to a rightly ordered will, since a person's will would be wrongly ordered if the person were to want that others conceal nothing from him.

Insurrection[52]

Insurrection is armed conflict between factions of the same people or a conspiracy to initiate such a conflict. This is contrary to the unity and peace of the people, and so a special and mortal sin. The leaders of an insurrection are the most guilty of the sin, but supporters are also guilty. Disruption of (i.e., rebellion against) tyrannical regimes is not insurrection, since the tyrant seeks his own good, not the common good.

1. Is insurrection always a mortal sin?[53]

Insurrection is a special sin that is like war and private strife in one respect and differs from them in another respect. It is like them in signi-

---

[51]Ibid., A. 3.　　　[52]See also ST II-II, Q. 104, A. 6, on obedience to secular powers.　　[53]ST II-II, Q. 42, A. 1.

fying opposition, but differs from them in two ways. It differs from them in one way in that war and private strife signify actual fighting between two parties, while we can say of insurrection either that there is such actual fighting, or that there is preparation for such fighting.

Insurrection differs from war and strife in a second way. War, strictly speaking, is against foreigners and enemies—between one people and another people, as it were—and private strife is between two persons or between two groups of few persons. But insurrection, strictly speaking, is between hostile factions of the same political community (e.g., when one faction of the political community is incited to war against another faction). And so insurrection, because it is contrary to a special good—namely, the unity and peace of the people—is a special sin.

2. Is insurrection always a mortal sin?[54]

Insurrection is contrary to the unity of the multitude (i.e., the people) of a city or kingdom. But the people are a community bound together by legal consent and common benefits. And so the unity of which insurrection is the contrary is clearly a unity of law and common benefit. Therefore, it is clear that insurrection is contrary to both justice and the common good. And so insurrection is by its nature a mortal sin; and the more the common good, which insurrection subverts, surpasses the private good, which private strife subverts, the more serious the sin is.

The sin of insurrection first and chiefly belongs to the leaders of the insurrection, who sin most seriously. Second, the sin belongs to the supporters of the insurrection, who disrupt the common good. But we should not call those who resist the insurrectionists and defend the common good insurrectionists, just as we do not call those who defend themselves brawlers.

Objection. We praise those who deliver the people from the power of a tyrant. But this cannot be easily done without a popular insurrection in which one faction of the people strives to maintain the tyrant, and another faction strives to remove him. Therefore, there can be insurrection without sin.

Reply Obj. A tyrannical regime is unjust, since it is directed to the private good of the ruler, not to the common good. And so disruption of this regime does not have the character of insurrection, except, perhaps, in cases where the tyrant's regime is so inordinately disrupted that the subject people suffer greater harm from the resulting disruption than from the tyrant's regime. Rather, the tyrant, who supports discontent and fac-

---

[54]Ibid., A. 2.

tionalism in the subject people in order to be able more securely to dominate them, is the insurrectionist, since it is tyranny when governance is directed to the ruler's own good to the harm of the people.

Other Injuries against the Person

Individuals may have a bodily member amputated for the health of the whole body, and doctors may amputate a patient's limb with the patient's consent. Just so, public authority may inflict punishment on convicted criminals by maiming them for the sake of the body politic. Parents may strike their children in moderation as a means of discipline. Imprisonment is only lawful (i.e., in accord with the natural law) by public authority to punish criminals and by private persons to prevent an imminent evil. There is a double sin in imprisoning a person closely associated with another person (e.g., someone's wife, child, or servant).

1. Is it ever lawful to maim the bodily member of another?[55]

Bodily members, since they are parts of the whole human body, exist for the sake of the whole body, as the imperfect for the sake of the perfect. And so one should make dispositions regarding members of the human body insofar as such dispositions are expedient for the whole body. And members of the human body are intrinsically useful for the good of the whole body, but they may by accident be harmful to the whole body (e.g., when a gangrenous limb is infecting the whole body). Therefore, if a bodily member should have been hitherto healthy and remain in its natural condition, it cannot be amputated without detriment to the whole human being.

But the whole human being is directed to the end of the whole community of which the human being is a part. Therefore, it can happen that the amputation of a bodily member, although tending to the detriment of the whole body, is nonetheless directed to the good of the community, since the amputation is inflicted on a person as punishment in order to restrain sin. And so, as it is lawful for the public power totally to deprive individuals of life because of greater sins, so also it is lawful for the public power to deprive individuals of a bodily member because of lesser sins. But this is not lawful for any private person, even with the consent of the person to whom the bodily member belongs, since this injures the community, to which the very individual and all the individual's parts belong.

---

[55]ST II–II, Q. 65, A. 1.

But if a bodily member, because of its gangrene, should be infecting the whole body, then it is lawful, at the direction of the one to whom the member belongs, to amputate the gangrenous member for the health of the whole body, since the care of one's health is committed to each individual. And there is the same argument if this should be done at the direction of the person to whom caring for the health of the person with the gangrenous member belongs. But it is otherwise altogether unlawful for anyone to amputate a bodily member.

2. Is it lawful for parents to strike their children or for masters to strike their slaves?[56]

Striking someone inflicts a harm on the body of the one struck, but in another way than in maiming, since maiming takes away integrity of the body, but striking only inflicts pain on the senses. And so there is much less harm in striking someone than maiming someone's bodily member. But it is lawful to inflict harm on someone only by way of punishment because of justice. And no person justly punishes another unless the other should be subject to the authority of that person. And so it is lawful only for a person who has authority over the one who is struck. And since children are subject to the authority of their parents, and slaves to the authority of their masters, parents may lawfully strike their children, and masters their slaves, for the sake of correction and discipline.

Objection. Parents should not provoke their children to anger, nor masters their slaves. But some children or slaves are provoked to anger on account of being struck. Therefore, parents should not strike their children, nor masters their slaves.

Reply Obj. Anger, since it is the desire for retribution, is chiefly incited when one thinks oneself unjustly hurt. And so parents are not prohibited from striking their children for the sake of discipline, but from inflicting blows on them immoderately.

3. Is it lawful to imprison a human being?[57]

We consider three things in order regarding bodily goods. First, we consider the integrity of the body's substance, and killing and maiming inflict detriment on this good. Second, we consider the pleasure or quiet of the senses, and striking or anything inflicting pain on the senses is contrary to this good. Third, we consider the movement and use of bodily members, which bondage or imprisonment or any detention prevents. And so imprisoning or in any way restraining someone is unlawful unless

---

[56]Ibid., A. 2.   [57]Ibid., A. 3.

it should be according to the order of justice, either as punishment or as a precaution to avoid some evil.

Objection. A person should be restrained only from an evil deed, and anyone can lawfully prevent another from such. Therefore, if imprisoning a person in order to restrain the person from an evil deed were lawful, it would be lawful for anyone to imprison someone. But that conclusion is clearly false. Therefore, it is unlawful to imprison someone.

Reply Obj. It is lawful for anyone to restrain a person for a brief time from an unlawful deed the person is imminently about to commit, as, for example, when one restrains a person from jumping off a cliff or from killing another. But holding another absolutely in custody or bondage belongs only to one who has the right to dispose universally about the acts and life of the other, since custody or bondage prevents a person from doing good things as well as evil things.

4. Is sin more serious if the aforementioned injuries are inflicted on persons closely associated with other persons?[58]

The more people an injury affects, other things being equal, the more serious the sin is. And so a sin is more serious if one should strike the ruler rather than a private person, since the former sin redounds to the injury of the whole community. But when one inflicts injury on a person who is in some way closely associated with another person, the injury belongs to two persons. And so, other things being equal, a sin is more serious by that very fact. But it can happen that a sin against a person not closely associated with any other is in some circumstances more serious because of the dignity of the person or the magnitude of the harm.

Objection. Injuries inflicted on people closely associated with other people have the character of sin insofar as one inflicts harm on another against the other's will. But the evil inflicted on someone's own person is more contrary to the other's will than the evil inflicted on the other's close associate. Therefore, the injury inflicted on the closely associated person is lesser.

Reply Obj. An injury inflicted on a closely associated person harms the chief person less than if the injury were directly inflicted on the chief person, and the injury inflicted on the closely associated person is, in this regard, a lesser sin. But all of what belongs to the injury against the chief person is added to the sin that one incurs because one wounds another person as such.

---

[58]Ibid., A. 4.

Theft and Robbery

Thomas here considers sins inflicting harm on others in their property and against their will. Human beings have a natural dominion over external things, and they may use these things for human benefit. Private ownership of property is preferable to common ownership for several reasons (better care of property, greater precision about duties, and less potential for conflict). But regarding the use of property, owners should possess property as common (i.e., share it with those in need).

Both theft and robbery are contrary to justice. Theft takes another's property secretly, and robbery takes it forcibly. Both theft and robbery are contrary to the will of the victim, theft because of the victim's ignorance of the taking, and robbery because of force. Finders should return found property to its owner if the property belongs to another. Taking property of slight value may not be a serious sin or even any sin. Those in immediate need who take the property of another are not guilty of theft. No private person may forcibly take the property of another, which is robbery, but public authority may do so in the course of administering justice (e.g., to punish criminals or collect taxes). Robbery is a more serious sin than theft because robbery inflicts insult and injury on the victim in addition to taking property.

1. Is the possession of external things natural to human beings?[59]

We can consider external things in two ways. We can consider them in one way regarding their nature, which is subject only to divine, not human, power. We can consider them in a second way regarding their use, and then human beings have a natural dominion over external things, since human beings, by their reason and will, can use external things for human benefit, as things made for their sake, as it were. This is because less perfect things are always for the sake of more perfect things. The possession of external things is for that reason natural to human beings; and the very creation of human beings manifests their natural dominion over other creatures, since the dominion belongs to human beings on account of their reason, and the image of God consists of reason.

Objection. No one should assign to oneself what belongs to God. But dominion over all creatures belongs strictly to God. Therefore, possession of things is not natural to human beings.

Reply Obj. God has the chief dominion over all things. He has, by his providence, ordained certain things for the material sustenance of human beings. And human beings for that reason have a natural dominion over things regarding the power to use them.

---

[59]ST II–II, Q. 66, A. 1.

2. Is it lawful for human beings to possess things as their own, as it were?[60]

Regarding external things, two things are proper to human beings. One of these is the power to manage and dispense things, and it is lawful in this regard that human beings should possess things as their own. And this is also necessary for human life for three reasons.

First, the power of individuals to manage and dispense things is necessary for human life because each individual is more careful to manage things that belong only to the individual than to manage things that are common to all or many persons. For each individual, avoiding work, leaves to others what belongs to the care of common goods, as happens when there are many servants.

Second, the power of individuals to manage and dispense things as their own is necessary for human life because human affairs are conducted in a more orderly manner if the requisite care of managing things should be entrusted to individuals. On the other hand, there would be confusion if unspecified individuals were to manage everything.

Third, the power of individuals to manage and dispense things as their own is necessary for human life because the condition of peace among human beings is better preserved when each individual is content with the individual's own possessions. And so we perceive that quarrels more frequently arise among those who possess things in common, not individually.

The other thing proper to human beings regarding external things is use of the things, and human beings in this regard should possess external things as common, not as their own; namely, they should be ready to share them when others are in need.

Objection. Everything contrary to natural right is unlawful. But all things are common by natural right, and individual ownership is contrary to common possession. Therefore, it is unlawful for individual human beings to appropriate external things for themselves.

Reply Obj. We attribute common possession of things to natural right because natural right does not determine who owns what, not because natural right dictates that all things should be possessed in common, and nothing as one's own, as it were. Rather, human agreement, which belongs to positive law, determines who owns what. And so individual ownership of property is not contrary to natural right, but supplements it through the inventiveness of human reason.

---

[60]Ibid., A. 2.

3. Does secret taking of another's property belong to the nature of theft?[61]

The nature of theft consists of a combination of three things. The first characteristic belongs to theft as contrary to justice, which renders to each what belongs to each. And so it is characteristic of theft that one takes something that belongs to someone else. And the second characteristic belongs to theft as distinguished from sins against the person (e.g., homicide and adultery). And so it belongs to theft to concern property. For if one should take what belongs to another as part of the other, as it were (e.g., amputating the limb of another), or what belongs to another as a closely associated person (e.g., abducting the daughter or wife of another), this does not have the nature of theft in the strict sense. The third difference—namely, that one takes another's property secretly—completes the nature of theft. And so the proper nature of theft is the secret taking of the property of another.

4. Are theft and robbery specifically different sins?[62]

Theft and robbery are sins contrary to justice, since one does something unjust to another. But no one suffers injustice willingly. And so theft and robbery have the nature of sin because the taking of property is involuntary regarding the one from whom it is taken. And we call something involuntary in two ways: namely, through ignorance or the use of force. Therefore, robbery has one aspect of sin, and theft another aspect, and they differ specifically.

5. Is theft always a sin?[63]

If one should consider the nature of theft, one will find two aspects of sin in it. First, theft is sinful because it is contrary to justice, which renders to each what belongs to each. And so theft is contrary to justice, since theft is the taking of the property of another. Second, theft is sinful by reason of the deception or fraud that the thief commits by taking the property of another secretly and deceitfully, as it were. And so every theft is clearly a sin.

Objection. Those who find and keep things that are not their own seem to commit theft. But this seems to be lawful according to natural justice. Therefore, it seems that theft is not always a sin.

Reply Obj. We should make distinctions about found things, since some found things were never in the possession of anyone (e.g., precious stones and jewels found on the seashore), and finders are allowed to keep

---

[61]Ibid., A. 3.   [62]Ibid., A. 4.   [63]Ibid., A. 5.

such things. The argument is the same regarding long-buried treasures, which belong to no one, except that civil laws require finders to give half to the owner of the field if the treasures should have been found in someone else's field. Some found things have been found close to the goods of another, and then one does not commit theft if one should take these things, not intending to keep them but intending to return them to their owner, who does not consider them abandoned. Likewise, finders do not commit theft in keeping things for themselves if the found things should be considered abandoned, and the finders should so believe. In all other cases, finders who keep things commit the sin of theft.

6. Is theft a mortal sin?[64]

Mortal sin is contrary to charity, which gives spiritual life to the soul. And charity consists chiefly of love of God and secondarily of love of neighbor, to which our willing and doing good to our neighbor belong. But human beings by theft inflict harm on their neighbor in the neighbor's property, and human society would perish if human beings were to steal from one another at will. And so theft, being contrary to charity, is a mortal sin.

Objection. One can commit theft in small as well as large matters. But it seems inappropriate that one be punished by eternal death for the theft of a small thing (e.g., a needle or a pen). Therefore, theft is not a mortal sin.

Reply Obj. Reason understands something slight as if nothing. And so, regarding very little things, human beings do not think that they suffer harm, and those who take such things can presume that this is not contrary to the will of the owner. And persons can be excused from mortal sin insofar as they should take such very little things secretly. But if they should intend to steal and inflict harm on their neighbor, there can be mortal sin even regarding such very little things, just as there can be mortal sin in only a thought by reason of consent.

7. Is it lawful for one to steal because of need?[65]

Things of human right cannot derogate from natural or divine right. But the natural order instituted by divine providence has ordained inferior things for alleviation of human beings' need. And so the division and appropriation of things, which derive from human law, do not preclude that property should be used to alleviate human beings' need. And so natural right requires that the excess possessions of particular persons be used for sustenance of the poor. But since many suffer need, and the same things cannot assist everyone, dispensing one's goods to help those in

---

[64]Ibid., A. 6.   [65]Ibid., A. 7.

need is left to the discretion of each individual. But if one's need is so pressing and evident that there is an immediate need to be met out of things at hand (e.g., when personal danger threatens, and there is no other way to alleviate it), then one can lawfully alleviate one's need with the goods of another, whether taken openly or secretly. Strictly speaking, this does not have the nature of theft or robbery.

Objection. Human beings should love their neighbor as they love themselves. But it is not lawful for one to steal in order to assist one's neighbor by alms. Therefore, it is also unlawful to steal to alleviate one's own need.

Reply Obj. One can also, in case of like necessity, secretly take the property of another in order to assist one's neighbor in need.

8. Can one commit robbery without sin?[66]

Robbery signifies a force or coercion whereby, contrary to justice, one takes something belonging to another from the other. But no one can exercise coercion in society except by the public authority. And so those who forcibly take things from others, if the former be private persons not exercising public power, act unlawfully and commit robbery, as robbers evidently do. But public power is committed to rulers in order that they safeguard justice. And so it is lawful for them to use force and coercion only in the course of justice, whether in wars against enemies or in punishing civilian criminals. And property taken by such force does not have the nature of robbery, since the taking is not contrary to justice. On the other hand, if, contrary to justice, some in the exercise of public authority forcibly take the property of others, they act unlawfully and commit robbery and are held to restitution.

Objection 1. Warriors take spoils by force of arms, and this seems to belong to the nature of robbery. But it is lawful in wars to take spoils from enemies. Therefore, robbery is in some cases lawful.

Reply Obj. 1. We should distinguish about the spoils of war. For if those who despoil the enemy wage just war, property forcibly acquired in the war becomes theirs, and this does not have the nature of robbery. And so they are not obliged to make restitution. Nonetheless, those engaged in just war, in taking spoils, could sin by covetousness or wicked intention: namely, if they chiefly wage war for the sake of spoils and not for the sake of justice. And if those who take spoils should engage in an unjust war, they commit robbery and are obliged to make restitution.

Obj. 2. Earthly rulers forcibly extort many things from their subjects, and this seems to belong to robbery. But it seems grievous to say that they

---

[66]Ibid., A. 8.

sin in this, since then almost all rulers would be condemned. Therefore, robbery is lawful in some cases.

Reply Obj. 2. If rulers exact from their subjects what is proper according to justice in order to preserve the common good, this is not robbery. But if rulers unduly extort things by force, this is robbery. And so they are also obliged to make restitution. And the more dangerously and generally they act against public justice, of which they are constituted the guardians, the more grievously they sin than robbers do.

9. Is theft a more serious sin than robbery?[67]

Robbery and theft have the nature of sin because they are contrary to the will of the victim—contrary to the victim's will through the victim's ignorance in the case of theft, and contrary to the victim's will through force in the case of robbery. But something is more involuntary through force than through ignorance, since force is more directly contrary to the will than ignorance is. And so robbery is a more serious sin than theft is. And there is a second reason, since robbery both inflicts loss on a person in the person's property and tends to insult and injure the person; and the latter outweighs the fraud and deception that belong to theft.

Injustice by Judges

In this and the next four sections, Thomas considers the criminal judicial process. Those vested with public authority can judge other persons if they have jurisdiction over the persons. Judges should judge only according to the evidence submitted, not their knowledge as private persons, and only on charges brought by others. Judges should not remit punishment, both in justice to the accuser and in deference to higher authority.

1. Can a person justly judge someone who is not subject to the person?[68]

A judge's decision is, as it were, a particular law regarding a particular deed. And so, as law in general should have coercive force, so also should a judge's decision have coercive force, which constrains each party to observe the judge's decision. Otherwise, the decision would not be effective. But only one who wields public authority lawfully has coercive power in human affairs, and we consider those who wield public authority superiors in relation to those over whom, as their subjects, they hold power, whether ordinary or delegated power. And so it is clear that one person

---

[67]Ibid., A. 9.   [68]ST II-II, Q. 67, A. 1.

can judge another person only if the latter is in some way a subject of the former, whether by delegation or ordinary power.

2. Is it lawful for a judge, on the basis of the evidence submitted, to rule contrary to what the judge knows to be true?[69]

Judging belongs to a judge insofar as the judge exercises public authority. And so, in judging, the judge should be informed by what the judge knows as a public person, not by what the judge knows as a private person. As a public person, the judge knows certain things in general and other things in particular. The judge knows things in general through public laws, whether divine or human, and the judge should not admit any arguments against them. And the judge knows other things in a particular case through written evidence and oral witnesses and other such legal proofs; and the judge, in judging, should follow these things rather than what the judge knows as a private person. But what the judge knows as a private person can help the judge to discern more precisely the evidence introduced, so as to be able to find its weakness. And if the judge cannot legally reject the evidence, the judge, in rendering judgment, should follow it.

3. Can a judge judge someone even if there should be no accuser?[70]

The judge interprets justice. But justice is in relation to another, not in relation to oneself. And so a judge needs to adjudicate between two parties, and the judge does this when one party is the plaintiff and the other party the defendant. And so, in criminal cases, a judge cannot judicially convict any person unless another brings a charge against the person.

4. Can a judge lawfully remit punishment?[71]

We should consider two things regarding what pertains to this question. First, we should consider that the judge has the power to judge between the accuser and the accused. Second, we should consider that the judge passes judicial sentence by public authority and not by the judge's own power, as it were. Therefore, there are two reasons why a judge cannot absolve a criminal from punishment. The first reason concerns the accuser, to whose right it sometimes belongs that the criminal be punished (e.g., because of a wrong committed against the accuser). And then remitting punishment is not at the discretion of the judge, since every judge is bound to render to each person that person's right.

The second reason concerns the commonwealth, whose power the judge wields, and it belongs to the good of the commonwealth that crimi-

---

[69]Ibid., A. 2.   [70]Ibid., A. 3.   [71]Ibid., A. 4.

nals be punished. But regarding the latter, there is a difference between lower judges and the supreme judge—namely, the ruler—to whom the public power has been fully committed. For a lower judge has no power to absolve a criminal of punishment, which would be contrary to the laws imposed on the lower judge by the superior judge. Nevertheless, if the one who suffered injury should wish to remit it, the ruler, who has full power in the commonwealth, could lawfully absolve the criminal if this should seem not to be harmful to the public benefit.

Unjust Criminal Charges

In medieval continental Europe, private citizens were the ordinary prosecutors of crime. According to Thomas, a private person is obliged to bring a criminal charge if the crime involves material or spiritual detriment to the community, and if the person can adduce sufficient proof. The charge and the judicial proceedings should be in writing. There is injustice if the charge is false, if the accuser colludes with the defendant to undermine the case, or if the accuser withdraws the charge. Those who deliberately bring false charges should be punished as much as the punishment they sought to inflict on the accused.

1. Is a person obliged to bring a criminal charge?[72]

There is a difference between giving a warning and bringing a criminal charge. We look to the emendation of a brother in the case of a warning, but punishment of the crime in the case of a criminal charge. But one does not seek the punishments of the present life as such, since this is not the final time of retribution. Rather, one seeks such punishments insofar as they are medicinal, leading either to the emendation of the sinner or to the good of the commonwealth, whose peace the punishment of sinners procures. But one intends the emendation of the sinner in the case of a warning, and the good of the commonwealth belongs strictly to bringing a criminal charge. And so, if the crime should have been such as to lead to the detriment of the commonwealth, a person is obliged to bring a criminal charge (e.g., when someone's sin tends to the material and spiritual corruption of the community), provided that the person can sufficiently prove it, which is the duty of the accuser. But if the sin should have been such as not to affect the community, or if one should be unable to adduce sufficient evidence of it, one is not obliged to press the criminal charge, since no one is obliged to seek what one cannot appropriately accomplish.

---

[72]ST II-II, Q. 68, A. 1.

Objection. No one is obliged to act against the trust that one owes to a friend, since one should not do to another what one does not wish to be done to oneself. But bringing a criminal charge against someone is sometimes contrary to the trust that one owes to a friend. Therefore, a human being is not obliged to bring a criminal charge.

Reply Obj. Revealing secrets to a person's detriment is contrary to the trust one owes the person, but not if one reveals the secrets for the sake of the common good, which one should always prefer to the private good. And so it is not lawful to keep any secret contrary to the common good. (Nor is anything that enough witnesses can substantiate altogether secret.)

2. Does the criminal charge need to be in writing?[73]

When it is a matter regarding the charge in a criminal case, the accuser is a party, and so the judge is an intermediary between the accuser and the accused in the judicial trial. In the trial, the judge should proceed with regard for as much certitude as possible. And since the exact words spoken easily slip from memory, the judge would be unable to be certain what was said and how it was said, when the judge has to pass sentence, unless the words were put in writing. And so it has for good reason been established that charges, as well as other things transacted in court, be put in writing.

3. Do false representations, collusion, and withdrawal render a criminal charge unjust?[74]

A criminal charge is directed to the common good, which one aims to promote by making a crime known. But no one should harm a person unjustly in order to promote the common good. And so there may be sin in an accusation in two ways. There may be sin in one way by acting unjustly against the accused, by falsely imputing crimes to the accused. There may be sin in a second way regarding the commonwealth, whose good one chiefly intends to promote by bringing a criminal charge, when one wickedly prevents the punishment of sin. And this likewise happens in two ways. It happens in one way by using deception in presenting the charge, and this belongs to collusion with the accused, since the accuser thereby helps the accused and betrays the accuser's cause.[75] It happens in a second way by withdrawing completely from the criminal charge.

---

[73]Ibid., A. 2.　　[74]Ibid., A. 3.　　[75]Thomas is perhaps thinking of cases in which the accused has bribed or coerced the accuser into collusion.

4. Is the accuser who has failed to prove a criminal charge held to retaliatory punishment?[76]

The accuser in a criminal case is a party seeking punishment of the accused, and it belongs to the judge to determine the equality of justice between the two parties. But the equality of justice requires that one suffer the harm that one seeks for the other. And so the person who puts another in danger of grave punishment suffers a like punishment justly.

Objection. One may sometimes bring a criminal charge because of an honest mistake, and the judge in such a case absolves the accuser. Therefore, the accuser who has failed to prove the charge is not held to retaliatory punishment.

Reply Obj. Retaliation does not belong to justice absolutely, since it differs greatly whether one harms another voluntarily or involuntarily. Something voluntary deserves punishment, but something involuntary deserves pardon. And so a judge does not impose the punishment of retaliation if the judge knows that someone has falsely accused another involuntarily, out of ignorance, by an honest mistake and with no intention to harm the other.

Injustice by Defendants

The defendant is obliged to answer the judge's questions that are in accord with legal process about matters over which the judge has jurisdiction, but may avoid answering other questions. (Note that Thomas does not allow the defendant a right not to incriminate himself.) The defendant may not defend himself by making false accusations against others. The defendant, if and only if the defendant is innocent, may appeal the judge's adverse decision. Only those condemned to death unjustly may resist the ruler, and then only when resistance would not risk serious public disturbance. Those condemned to death may take flight.

1. Can a defendant without mortal sin deny the truth that would convict the defendant?[77]

Anyone who acts contrary to the obligation of justice sins mortally, and it belongs to the obligation of justice that one should obey one's superior in matters that the superior's jurisdiction reaches. But a judge is the superior in relation to the one judged. And so the defendant is duty bound to explain the truth that the judge demands from the defendant in accord with legal process. And so, if the defendant has refused to tell the truth

---

[76]Ibid., A. 4.   [77]ST II-II, Q. 69, A. 1.

that the defendant is obliged to tell, or if the defendant has falsely denied the truth, the defendant commits mortal sin. But if the judge should demand anything incompatible with legal process, the defendant is not obliged to answer the judge. Rather, the defendant can lawfully avoid answering, either by an appeal or by legal evasion in other ways. Nevertheless, it is unlawful for the defendant to lie.

Objection. One is not obliged to reveal oneself in public or incriminate oneself before others. But if the defendant were to confess the truth in court, the defendant would reveal and incriminate himself. Therefore, the defendant is not obliged to tell the truth, and the defendant does not commit mortal sin if the defendant lies in court.

Reply Obj. When a judge interrogates a person in accord with legal process, the person does not reveal himself. Rather, the judge reveals the person, since the judge, whom the person is obliged to obey, imposes the necessity to answer.

2. Is it lawful for the accused to defend himself by false representation?[78]

It is one thing to say nothing about the truth, and another thing to propose falsehood. And it is lawful in a particular case to say nothing about the truth, since a person is obliged to admit only the truth that the judge can and should require of the person in accord with legal process, not every truth. For example, the defendant is not obliged to tell the judge whether there was a prior accusation of crime against the defendant, whether there was some clear evidence against the defendant in the case, or whether the evidence against the defendant was almost conclusive. But it is never lawful for one to propose falsehood.

And regarding what is lawful, one can proceed in ways lawful and suitable for an intended end, and this belongs to prudence. Or one can proceed in ways unlawful and incompatible with the proposed end, and this belongs to cleverness, which one uses in fraud and guile. The first procedure is praiseworthy, but the second is wicked. Therefore, it is lawful for those accused of crime to defend themselves by suitable means, by hiding truth that they are not obliged to admit (e.g., by refusing to answer questions that they are not obliged to answer). And this is to be prudently evasive, not to defend themselves by misrepresenting the truth. But it is not lawful for the accused to tell lies or hide the truth that the accused is obliged to admit, nor to use any fraud or guile, since fraud and guile are the same as lying, and that is to defend oneself by misrepresenting the truth.

---

[78]Ibid., A. 2.

3. Is it lawful for the defendant to put off judgment by appealing?[79]

A defendant may appeal a decision on two bases. A defendant may appeal in one way because of confidence in the justice of the defendant's cause; namely, because the judge unjustly sentences the person. And then it is lawful to appeal, since this is prudent evasion. A defendant may appeal in a second way for the sake of causing delay in order that a just sentence not be carried out, and this is to defend oneself by misrepresentation, which is unlawful. For the defendant causes injury both to the judge, the execution of whose duty the defendant prevents, and to the defendant's adversary, whose vindication the defendant disrupts as much as possible.

4. Is it lawful for one condemned to death to defend oneself, if possible?[80]

One is condemned to death in two situations. One is condemned to death in one situation justly, and then it is unlawful for the one condemned to defend himself, since it is lawful for the judge to attack the condemned man if the latter resists. And so we conclude that the one condemned to death unjustly resorts to force, and such a one undoubtedly sins. One is condemned to death in a second situation unjustly, and such judgment is like the use of force by robbers. And so, as it is lawful to resist robbers, so it is lawful in such a case to resist wicked rulers, except, perhaps, in order to avoid scandal, when resistance might risk a serious public disturbance.

Objection 1. That to which nature always inclines is always lawful, being of natural right, as it were. But human beings, animals, and insensate things have a natural inclination to resist things that destroy. Therefore, it is lawful for the condemned criminal to resist, if possible, in order not to be handed over to death.

Reply Obj. 1. Reason is given to human beings so that things to which nature inclines be followed according to the order of reason, not indiscriminately. And so a defense with due moderation, not any defense, is lawful.

Obj. 2. As a person avoids a death sentence by resistance, so also does the person by flight. But it seems to be lawful that one free oneself from death by flight. Therefore, it is also lawful to resist.

Reply Obj. 2. One is condemned to suffer death, not to inflict death on oneself; and so one is not obliged to do anything that results in one's own

---

[79]Ibid., A. 3.   [80]Ibid., A. 4.

death, that is, such as remaining in the place from which one is brought to death. Nevertheless, a person is obliged not to resist the executioner in order not to suffer what is just for the person to suffer. So also, if a person is condemned to die of hunger, the person does not sin by eating food secretly provided, since not to eat the food would be to kill oneself.

Injustice by Witnesses

Individuals are obliged to testify when a superior with authority over them demands it regarding public matters and reports of past crime. They are obliged to testify in order to deliver those accused from unjust punishment, false accusation, or unjust loss, even if a superior with no authority over the individuals demands it. Individuals are obliged to testify about matters incriminating someone only if a superior requires it according to legal form.

The testimony of two or three witnesses is sufficient to convict the defendant. Fault on the part of witnesses sometimes makes their testimony unreliable (e.g., the testimony of public criminals). Lack of reason (e.g., in the case of the insane), emotional predispositions (e.g., in the case of enemies or members of the family), and external factors (e.g., those subject to the command of the accuser or accused) sometimes make testimony unreliable with no fault on the part of the witness. False testimony is always a serious sin because it is perjury and contrary to justice.

1. Is a person obliged to testify?[81]

We should distinguish about testifying, since one is sometimes required to testify and sometimes not. If a superior with authority over a person in matters belonging to justice requires the person's testimony, the person is undoubtedly obliged to testify about matters regarding which the testimony is demanded according to legal form. For example, a person is obliged to testify regarding public matters and matters about which there has been a prior report of crime. If testimony is required of the person about other things (e.g., secret matters and matters about which there have been no prior reports of crime), the person is not obliged to testify.

And if a superior without authority to command a person to testify should require the person's testimony, we need to distinguish. If such testimony should be required in order to deliver someone from unjust death or any punishment, false report of crime, or unjust loss, then the person is obliged to testify. And if the person's testimony should not be required,

---

[81]ST II-II, Q. 70, A. 1.

the person is obliged to do what the person can to declare the truth to someone who could help to deliver the accused.

And in matters pertinent to incriminating someone, a person is obliged to testify only if a superior requires the testimony according to legal form. For if the person should conceal the truth about the matter by not coming forward to testify, no particular harm thereby results to anyone. Or if danger should threaten the accuser, the person should not be concerned, since the accuser willingly put himself into the danger. But it is a different matter regarding the accused, who is unwillingly threatened with danger.

Objection. No one is obliged to act deceitfully. But a person who does not keep the secrets a friend commits to the person acts deceitfully. Therefore, a person is not always obliged to testify, especially about matters a friend commits to the person under secrecy.

Reply Obj. A priest should never testify about matters committed to him under secrecy in confession, since he knows such things as God's minister, not as a human being, and the sacramental bond is greater than any human precept.

But we should distinguish about things otherwise committed to a person under secrecy. For these things are sometimes such that a person is obliged to manifest them as soon as the person knows them. For example, a person is obliged to make public things regarding spiritual or material harm of the community, the grave injury of a person, or any other such thing by testifying in court or giving a warning. And the commitment of a secret to a person cannot oblige the person contrary to this duty, since the person would thereby break the fidelity the person owes to another. But things committed to a person under secrecy are sometimes such that the person is not obliged to divulge them. And so a person can be obliged not to divulge these things because they are committed to the person under secrecy. And then one is never obliged to divulge them, even at the command of a superior, since keeping faith belongs to natural right, and human beings cannot be commanded to do anything contrary to what concerns natural right.

2. Is the testimony of two or three witnesses sufficient?[82]

We should not seek the same certitude in every kind of subject matter. For example, we cannot have demonstrative certitude in the case of human acts, about which we make judgments and testimonies are required, since human acts are contingent and variable. And so probable certitude, which attains truth for the most part, although it falls short of

---

[82]Ibid., A. 2.

truth in rather few cases, suffices regarding human acts. But the testimony of many witnesses is more likely to be true than the testimony of one person. And so, when the defendant denies a crime, and many witnesses affirm what the accuser says, divine law and human law reasonably establish that the testimony of the witnesses should prevail. And so two witnesses in agreement are required, or, for greater certitude, three.

3. Should the testimony of a witness be rejected apart from fault on the witness's part?[83]

Testimony has probable, not absolute, certitude. And so any probability to the contrary renders testimony unreliable. And sometimes fault on the part of the witness (e.g., of unbelievers, the notorious, and those guilty of a public crime, who cannot even bring a criminal charge) makes it probable that the testimony of the witness is unreliable. And the witness's testimony is sometimes unreliable without fault on the part of the witness. Some faultless witnesses are unreliable because they lack reason (e.g., children, the insane, and women). Some faultless witnesses are unreliable because of their emotional dispositions (e.g., enemies, closely associated persons, and household members). And some faultless witnesses are unreliable because of an external condition (e.g., paupers, slaves, and those subject to another's command, who can in all probability be easily induced to testify falsely). And so it is clear that the testimony of a witness is rejected both because of, and apart from, fault on the part of a witness.

4. Is false testimony always a mortal sin?[84]

False testimony is deformed in three ways. It is deformed in one way because it is perjury, since witnesses are permitted to testify only under oath, and false testimony is always a mortal sin in this respect. It is deformed in a second way because it violates justice, and so, just like any injustice, it is by its nature a mortal sin in this respect. It is deformed in a third way because of the falsehood itself, since every lie is a sin; but it is not for this reason that false testimony is always a mortal sin.

Injustice by Lawyers

Lawyers cannot and need not offer counsel to all the poor, but they should do so when relatively necessary and give the highest consideration to those poor who are most closely connected to them. Some persons are barred from the legal profession because they lack the requisite ability (the deaf and the dumb). Others

---

[83]Ibid., A. 3.   [84]Ibid., A. 4.

are barred because they are unsuitable (e.g., the blind, persons of ill repute, and those convicted of a serious crime). Lawyers should not defend unjust causes, since they would then be cooperating with evil. Lawyers may receive just compensation for their counsel.

1. Are lawyers obliged to offer counsel to the poor?[85]

Since offering counsel to the poor belongs to works of mercy, we should say the same thing about the former as about the latter. For no one person can take on works of mercy for all the needy. And so we should give the highest consideration to those who are more closely united to us by the suitability of time, place, or other things. When the combination of these circumstances is suitable, it remains for us to consider whether the person suffers such need that it is not readily apparent how the person can be otherwise helped. And in such a case, one is obliged to take on the work of mercy to help the person. But if it should be readily apparent how the person can be otherwise helped, whether by himself or another person who is more closely associated or has greater means, one is not absolutely so obliged to help the person in need that one sins if one does not do so. But if one should help the person in the absence of such necessity, one would act in a praiseworthy manner.

And so lawyers are not always obliged to offer counsel to the poor, but only under the combination of the aforementioned suitable circumstances. Otherwise, lawyers would need to put aside all other business and attend only to the suits of the poor. And we should say the same thing about doctors in regard to taking care of the poor.

2. Do the laws fittingly exclude some persons from legal practice?[86]

A person is prevented from performing an act in two ways: in one way, by incapacity; in a second way, by unsuitability. But incapacity absolutely excludes a person from performing an act, while unsuitability does not altogether exclude a person, since necessity may take away the unsuitability. Therefore, some persons are barred from legal practice on account of their incapacity because they lack sense, whether internal (e.g., the insane and children) or external (e.g., the deaf and the dumb). For lawyers need both internal skill, with which they would be able suitably to demonstrate the justice of the case they have undertaken to represent, and speech and hearing, with which they would be able to communicate to others and to hear what others say to them. And so those who are deficient in these things are altogether forbidden to practice law, whether in their own behalf or in behalf of others,

---

[85]ST II-II, Q. 71, A. 1.   [86]Ibid., A. 2.

And the suitability of practicing law is taken away in two ways. It is taken away in one way because a person is obligated to do greater things. And so it is unfitting that monks or priests be lawyers in any case, or that clerics be lawyers in secular courts, since such persons are restricted to divine things. The suitability of practicing law is taken away in a second way because of a personal defect. The defect may be material, as in the case of the blind, who could not suitably attend the judge; or spiritual, since it is unfitting that a person who contemned justice in regard to himself should plead the cause of justice for another. And so persons of ill repute, unbelievers, and those convicted of serious crimes are not fit to be lawyers.

But necessity outweighs unsuitability, and so unsuitable persons can exercise the office of lawyer for themselves or persons closely associated with them. And so also clerics can be lawyers for their churches, and monks for their monasteries, if their abbot has commanded them to do so.

3. Does a lawyer sin if the lawyer should defend an unjust cause?[87]

It is unlawful for anyone to cooperate in doing evil, whether by counseling or assisting or in any way approving the evil, since those who counsel or assist are in some respect participants. And so also all such are obliged to make restitution. But it is clear that lawyers offer counsel and assistance to their clients. And so, if a lawyer knowingly defends an unjust cause, the lawyer undoubtedly sins seriously and is obliged to make restitution of the loss that, contrary to justice, the other party incurs because the lawyer helps the unjust cause. But if the lawyer, thinking a cause just, unknowingly defends an unjust cause, the lawyer is excused from sin in the way in which ignorance can excuse.

Objection. It is lawful to desist from any sin. But lawyers are punished if they have abandoned their case. Therefore, a lawyer does not sin by defending an unjust cause if the lawyer has undertaken its defense.

Reply Obj. If a lawyer initially believed a cause just, and it should become evident later in the process that the cause is unjust, the lawyer is not obliged to give it up so as to help the other party or reveal secrets of the case to the other party. But the lawyer can and should abandon the case or induce his client to yield or compromise without loss to the other party.

4. Is it lawful for lawyers to receive compensation for their counsel?[88]

A person can justly receive payment for services that one is not obliged to provide for another. But it is clear that lawyers are not always obliged to

---

[87]Ibid., A. 3.   [88]Ibid., A. 4.

offer or give counsel in behalf of others. And so, if lawyers should sell
their services or counsel, they do not act contrary to justice. And the argument is the same about doctors giving help to cure patients and about all
other such persons, provided that they are moderately compensated, taking into account the circumstances of persons and occupations, the work
involved, and the country's customs. But if a lawyer, out of wickedness,
should exact anything excessive, the lawyer sins against justice.[89]

Fraud in Buying and Selling

Exchanged goods should be of the same value, and money measures their value.
And so selling goods more dearly or buying them more cheaply is unjust. But
the seller may raise the price to compensate for a particular disadvantage that
the seller would suffer by the sale, and buyers whom the sale greatly benefits
may freely pay the seller something extra.

The seller who knowingly sells goods that are essentially, quantitatively, or
qualitatively different from what the buyer contracts to buy (e.g., copper sold
as gold) commits fraud and is bound to make restitution. The seller who
unknowingly sells goods with such defects does not commit fraud but is bound to
make restitution when notified of the defects. Likewise, the buyer who know-
ingly buys goods that are essentially, quantitatively, or qualitatively different
from what the seller contracts to sell (e.g., gold bought as copper) commits
fraud and is bound to make restitution. The seller is also bound to disclose hid-
den defects that would cause the buyer loss or danger.

Families make exchanges to provide for their needs of life, and such
exchanges are praiseworthy. People in the business of trading make exchanges
for the sake of profit, and such exchanges are ignoble but not sinful. And so peo-
ple in the business of trading may seek moderate profit to earn a livelihood or
benefit the public.

1. Can one lawfully sell something for more than it is worth?[90]

It is altogether sinful to use fraud in order to sell something for more
than its just price, since one deceives one's neighbor to the neighbor's
loss. But absent fraud, we can speak about buying and selling in two ways.
We can speak about buying and selling in one way as such. And in this
way, buying and selling seem to have been introduced for the common
benefit of both parties; namely, the buyer needs something belonging to
the seller, and vice versa. But things introduced for the common benefit

---

[89]In ST II-II, QQ. 72–76, there follows an exposition, omitted here, of injustice in
speech (insult, detraction, gossip, derision, and cursing).   [90]ST II-II, Q. 77,
A. 1.

of both parties should not burden one party more than the other. And so the equality of the goods exchanged should be the basis of contracts between the parties. But we measure the value of goods useful to human beings by the price paid for them, and money was invented for this purpose. And so, if either the price exceeds the value of the goods or, conversely, the goods exceed the price, the equality of justice is taken away. And so selling something more dearly or buying something more cheaply than the thing is worth is, as such, unjust and unlawful.

We can speak of buying and selling in a second way insofar as the buying and selling incidentally benefits one party and disadvantages the other party (e.g., if one party has a great need of a particular thing, and the other suffers without it). And the just price in such a case will be related both to the goods sold and to the loss the seller incurs because of the sale. And so one could lawfully sell such goods for more than they are worth in themselves, although not for more than they are worth to the owner.

But if the buyer benefits greatly from the goods bought from the seller, and the seller suffers no loss by being without the goods, the seller should not raise the price. The seller should not raise the price because the benefit accruing to the buyer does not come from the seller but from the condition of the buyer, and no one ought to sell to another what is not one's own, although one can charge another for the loss one suffers. But buyers who are greatly benefited by goods received from sellers can, of their own free will, pay the sellers something extra, and this belongs to the buyer's virtue.

2. Is a sale rendered unjust and unlawful because of a defect in the goods sold?[91]

We can consider three defects regarding the goods sold. One defect concerns the type of goods. But if the seller should know of such defect in the goods sold, the seller commits fraud in the sale. And so this renders the sale unlawful. The second defect concerns the quantity of the goods, which we determine by measuring it. And so a seller who knowingly uses a false measure in a sale commits fraud, and the sale is unlawful. The third defect regards the quality of the goods (e.g., if one should sell a sick animal as if it were healthy). And one who does this knowingly commits fraud, and so the sale is unlawful.

And the seller in such cases both sins by making the unjust sale and is obliged to make restitution. But if any of the aforementioned defects were in the goods sold unbeknownst to the seller, the seller does not sin, since the seller does something unjust in a material sense without his action

---

[91]Ibid., A. 2.

being unjust. Nonetheless, the seller is obliged to compensate the loss to the buyer when the defect comes to the attention of the seller.

And we should also understand about the buyer what we said about the seller. For sellers may sometimes believe that their property is less valuable as to its kind. For example, if a seller should sell gold as copper, the buyer who knows this buys it unjustly and is obliged to make restitution. And the argument is the same about defects of quality and quantity.

3. Is the seller obliged to tell the buyer of defects in the goods sold?[92]

It is always unlawful to occasion danger or loss to another, although human beings need not always give help or counsel to another regarding anything to the other's advantage. Rather, human beings need give help or counsel only in particular cases (e.g., when another is subject to one's care, or when no one else can help the other). But the seller, by the very fact of offering something defective for sale to the buyer, occasions loss or danger to the latter if the latter could incur loss or danger because of the thing's defect. The buyer could incur loss if the thing offered for sale were to be less valuable because of such a defect, and the seller were not to reduce the price because of the defect. And the buyer could run into danger if such a defect renders use of the thing troublesome or harmful (e.g., if one should sell the buyer a lame horse for an agile one, or an unstable house for a stable one, or rotten or poisonous food for healthy food). And so, if such defects are hidden and the seller does not disclose them, there will be unlawful and deceitful selling, and the seller is obliged to recompense the loss.

But if the defect is evident (e.g., when a horse has only one eye; or when use of the thing, although unsuitable for the seller, can still be suitable for others), and if the seller, because of the defect, reduces the price as much as the seller should, the seller is not obliged to point out the thing's defect. This is because the buyer would perhaps wish that the price, because of such a defect, be reduced more than it should be. And so sellers may lawfully look to their own security by keeping quiet about such a defect.

4. Is it lawful in trade to sell something for more than one paid for it?[93]

It belongs to businessmen to engage in trading things, and there are two ways of trading things. There is one kind of exchange that is natural and necessary, as it were: namely, an exchange of one thing for another, or

---

[92]Ibid., A. 3.   [93]Ibid., A. 4.

of something for money, to provide for the needs of life. And such exchanges, strictly speaking, do not belong to businessmen. Rather, they belong to household managers and statesmen, who have a duty to provide for a household or a political community regarding the needs of life. And there is another kind of exchange of money for money, or any things for money, for the sake of profit, not to provide for the needs of life; and this business of trading seems, in the strict sense, to belong to businessmen. The first kind of exchange is praiseworthy, since it is in the service of natural need; but the second kind of exchange is rightly censured, since, as such, it is beholden to the desire for profit, which desire knows no bounds and always strives for more and more. And so the business of trading, considered as such, has something base, since it does not essentially signify a worthy or necessary end.

But profit, which is the end of the business of trading, although it does not essentially signify anything worthy or necessary, signifies nothing essentially sinful or contrary to virtue. And so nothing prevents profit from being directed to a necessary or worthy end, and then the business of trading is rendered lawful. For example, one may direct a moderate business profit to maintaining one's household or helping the needy. Or one may engage in the business of trading for the benefit of the public— namely, lest one's country lack things necessary for life—and seek profit as payment for one's labor, not as an end, as it were.

The Sin of Interest-Taking

The ownership of real and much personal property is separable from its use (e.g., one person may own a house, and another person may rent it). But some things are consumed in their very use (e.g., wine), and the ownership and use of such things cannot be separated. Therefore, one cannot seek separate payment for the ownership and the use of such things. According to Thomas, money is such a thing, since its chief use is as a means of exchange; and the value of money as a means of exchange is consumed in its use in exchanges. Therefore, one may not lend money at interest or seek any other advantage measurable by money (e.g., use of the borrower's property). But lenders may seek to be compensated for any actual loss they incur because they lend money, and those who invest money with merchants or craftsmen may share in the profits.

Lenders are obliged to return money taken as interest, but not any profit obtained from the money.

It is never lawful to induce a person to lend at interest, but it is lawful in case of need to borrow at interest from moneylenders who make a regular practice of charging interest.

1. Is it a sin to take interest for money lent?[94]

Taking interest for money lent is intrinsically unjust, since this is to sell something that does not exist, and clearly constitutes inequality, which is contrary to justice. To prove this, we should note that there are some things, the use of which consists of consumption of the things themselves. For example, we consume wine by using it for drink, and we consume wheat by using it for food. And so, regarding such things, we should not reckon the value of their use separately from the value of the things themselves. Rather, we give up the things to whomever we grant their use, and so lending in such cases transfers ownership. Therefore, if one were to want to sell wine and the use of wine separately, one would be selling the same thing twice, that is, something that does not exist. And so one would clearly commit a sin against justice.

By like argument, lenders of wine or wheat who seek double recompense for themselves—namely, the recompense of something equivalent and payment for use of the wine or wheat, which we call interest—commit injustice.

But there are some things, the use of which does not consist of their consumption (e.g., one uses a house by dwelling in it, not by consuming it). And so, regarding such things, one can grant each separately. For example, one may grant ownership of a house to another while keeping for oneself the use of the house for a period of time. Or conversely, one may grant use of the house to another but retain ownership of the house. And human beings can, for that reason, lawfully both receive payment for the use of a house and reclaim the house at the expiration of the lease, as is evident in the leasing and renting of houses.

And human beings invented money chiefly to facilitate exchanges, and so the special and chief use of money consists of its very consumption or alienation as it is spent in exchanges. And on that account, it is intrinsically unlawful to receive payment for the use of money lent, payment that we call interest. And as human beings are obliged to make restitution for other things unjustly acquired, so also are they required to make restitution for the money they received as interest.

2. Can one seek any other advantage for money lent?[95]

We consider as money anything whose value money can measure; and those who, by tacit or explicit contract, accept money for the loan of money, or of anything else consumed in its very use, sin against justice. Just so, those who, by tacit or explicit contract, should receive anything

---

[94]ST II–II, Q. 78, A. 1.   [95]Ibid., A. 2.

else whose value money can measure incur the like sin. But a lender does not sin if the lender should receive something as a free gift, not as if requiring it or by any tacit or explicit obligation, as it were. This is because the lender could have received a free gift even before lending the money, and the lender is made no worse off because the lender lent money. And it is lawful to require, in exchange for a loan, recompense of things that money does not measure (e.g., benevolence and love of the lender, or the like).

Objection 1. Persons can lawfully take into account compensation against loss. But persons sometimes suffer loss because they lend money. Therefore, it is lawful for them to expect or even require something for their loss, over and above the money lent.

Reply Obj. 1. Lenders can without sin contract with borrowers to compensate them for loss of things that they should have, since this is to avoid loss, not to sell the use of money. And borrowers may avoid greater loss than lenders will incur; and so borrowers, out of their gains, recompense the loss of lenders. But lenders may not contract with borrowers to be compensated for loss of profit from the money lent, since lenders should not sell what they do not yet have and can in many ways be prevented from having.

Obj. 2. Those who transfer the ownership of money by lending it alienate it more that those who invest money with merchants or craftsmen. But it is lawful to receive profit from money invested with merchants or craftsmen. Therefore, it is also lawful to receive profit from money lent.

Reply Obj. 2. Lenders transfer ownership of money to borrowers. And so the borrower possesses it at the borrower's risk and is obliged to return all of it, and the lender should not require more. But one who invests money with a merchant or craftsman by forming a partnership does not transfer ownership of the money to the merchant or craftsman. Rather, the money remains the investor's, so that merchants carry on their business and craftsmen their craft, with risk to the investor. And so investors may lawfully expect to share in profits from the business or craft, as something that belongs to them.

Obj. 3. A person can take security for money lent (e.g., borrowers give their farms or homes to lenders as security), and lenders could sell use of the security. Therefore, it is lawful to make a profit from money lent.

Reply Obj. 3. If borrowers should give, as security for money lent them, things whose use money can measure, lenders should calculate use of the things toward the repayment of what they lent. Otherwise, if lenders should want free use, as it were, of the things in addition to repayment, this is the same as if they were to receive money for their loan. And this is interest-taking, unless the thing were perhaps such as friends usually grant the use of without charge, as is evidently the case with borrowed books.

Obj. 4. Because of loans, persons sometimes sell things more dearly, or buy things more cheaply, or increase the price of their goods in return for giving buyers a longer time to repay the loans, or lower the price of the goods in return for buyers repaying the loans earlier. In all of the above cases, recompense seems to be made for lending money, as it were. But this is not clearly unlawful. Therefore, it seems that it is lawful to seek, or even require, an advantage from money lent.

Reply Obj. 4. Persons evidently take interest if they should want to sell their goods on credit for more than the just price, since such credit has the nature of a loan. And so everything required in exchange for such credit beyond the just price is like a charge on the loan, which belongs to the nature of taking interest.

Likewise, if buyers should want to buy goods more cheaply than the goods' just price by paying for the goods before delivery, this is the same as taking interest. For such prepayment has the nature of a loan, the charge for which is the reduction of the just price of the goods purchased.

But if sellers should want to reduce the price to less than the just price in order to get their money sooner, they do not commit the sin of taking interest.

3. Are lenders obliged to return any profit they make from the money they took as interest?[96]

There are things whose use consists of their very consumption, things that have no use separate from consumption. And so, if lenders have extorted such things (e.g., money, wheat, wine, and the like) through the taking of interest, they are obliged to return only what they took, since anything they obtain out of these things is the fruit of their human effort, not that of the things. A possible exception is if the borrower, by losing some goods as interest, should suffer loss through the lender's retention of the goods, since the lender is then obliged to recompense the harm to the borrower.

But there are some things whose use does not consist of their consumption (e.g., houses, farms, and the like), and there is a separate use of such things. And so, if lenders were to have extorted the house or farm of another by taking interest, they would be obliged to return both the house or farm and the fruits derived from them, since the latter are the fruits of property owned by the other and so fruits owed to the other.

---

[96]Ibid., A. 3.

4. Is it lawful to borrow money at interest?[97]

It is never lawful to induce a person to sin, but it is lawful to use the sin of another for good. For God uses all sins for some good, since he draws some good out of any evil. And so it is never lawful to induce a person to lend at interest; but it is lawful to borrow at interest from those who are ready to lend at interest and make a practice of doing so, for the sake of some good; namely, to alleviate the need of oneself or another. Just so, it is lawful for one who falls into the hands of robbers to reveal the goods in one's possession, in the taking of which the robbers sin, in order not to be killed.

Equity

Established laws cannot anticipate all contingencies, and it is sometimes contrary to the equality of justice and the common good to observe the law (e.g., returning a sword to its mad owner). And so one should sometimes not follow the letter of the law, but do what justice and the common good require. One should do so only in clear cases. This is equity and virtuous. Equity is a subjective part—that is, a species—of justice, and a higher rule of human action than legal justice.

1. Is equity a virtue?[98]

There cannot be a rule of established law that could not be deficient in a particular case, since human actions, regarding which laws are laid down, consist of many contingent particulars. Rather, lawmakers, in framing laws, consider what happens for the most part; but to observe laws in some cases is contrary to the equality of justice and to the common good, for which the laws strive. For example, law establishes that entrusted goods should be returned to their owners, since this is just in most cases. But it happens that that would sometimes be harmful (e.g., if a madman who had entrusted his sword to someone should demand its return, or if one should demand the sword back in order to fight against the country). Therefore, in these and like cases, it would be evil to follow the established law, and it would be good to bypass the letter of the law and follow what the nature of justice, and the common benefit, demand. Equity is directed to this, and so equity is evidently a virtue.

Objection. It seems to belong to equity to consider the intention of the lawmaker. But it belongs only to the ruler to interpret the intention of the lawmaker. Therefore, an act of equity is unlawful, and equity is not a virtue.

---

[97]Ibid., A. 4.   [98]ST II-II, Q. 120, A. 1.

Reply Obj. There is room for interpretation in doubtful matters, in which it is not lawful to depart from the letter of the law without the ruler so determining. But in clear maters, there is need to execute the law, not to interpret it.

2. Is equity part of justice?[99]

A virtue has three kinds of parts: namely, subjective, integral, and potential. But a subjective part is something of which the whole virtue is essentially predicated, and is something less than the whole virtue. This happens in two ways. For something is sometimes predicated of several things by the same consideration (e.g., *animal* of horses and cattle). And something is sometimes predicated of several things by what is prior and what is consequent (e.g., *being* of substances and accidents). Therefore, equity, as a certain kind of justice, is a part of justice in the general sense. And so equity is a subjective part of justice. And predicating *justice* of equity has priority over predicating *justice* of legal justice, since equity governs legal justice. And so equity is the higher rule, as it were, of human actions.

Integral Parts

Doing the good one owes to God and the community, and avoiding the contrary evil, are the constitutive parts of justice in general; and doing the good one owes to one's neighbor, and avoiding the contrary evil, are the constitutive parts of particular justice. Conversely, transgression (doing what one should not) and omission (not doing what one should) are the constitutive parts of injustice. Transgression consists of doing something prohibited by a negative precept (e.g., do not commit perjury), and omission consists of not doing something commanded by an affirmative precept (e.g., show respect to one's parents).

Omission is a special sin regarding justice in general insofar as we understand the obligatory good in relation to divine or human law, and regarding particular justice insofar as we understand the obligatory good in relation to our neighbor. One incurs the sin of omission at the time when one is supposed to do something, although the sin may be imputed only because of antecedent fault.

Transgression, absolutely speaking is a more serious sin than omission, since doing evil is absolutely contrary to doing good, but not doing good is not always evil.

---

[99]Ibid., A. 2.

1. Are avoiding evil and doing good parts of justice?[100]

If we should be speaking of good and evil in general, doing good and avoiding evil belong to every virtue. In this respect, they cannot be posited as parts of justice, unless we perhaps understand justice as all virtue. But even justice so understood regards a special aspect of good; namely, good as due in relation to divine or human law.

And justice as a special virtue regards good under the aspect of something owed to our neighbor. In this respect, it belongs to particular justice to do good under the aspect of something due in relation to our neighbor, and to avoid the contrary evil; namely, what harms our neighbor. And it belongs to justice in general to do the good owed in relation to the community or God, and to avoid the contrary evil.

Objection. It belongs to every virtue to do good deeds and avoid evil deeds. But parts do not exceed the whole. Therefore, avoiding evil and doing good should not be parts of justice, which is a special virtue.

Reply Obj. We understand good and evil here under a special aspect by which they are applied to justice. And so we posit good and evil as parts of justice by a special aspect of good and evil, not the aspect of any other moral virtue, since other moral virtues regard emotions. And in the latter, doing good is arriving at the mean, which consists of avoiding the extremes as evils, as it were. And so, regarding the other virtues, doing good and avoiding evil amount to the same thing. But justice regards external actions and things, in which it is one thing to establish equality and another thing to destroy the established equality.

2. Is transgression a special sin?[101]

We derive the word *transgression* from bodily movement and apply it to moral acts. But we say that one transgresses by bodily movement if one crosses a prefixed boundary, and in moral matters, negative precepts establish for human beings the boundary beyond which they should not go. And so we speak of transgression in the strict sense when one does something contrary to a negative precept.

And in a material sense, transgression can be contrary to all kinds of sin, since human beings transgress divine precepts by any kind of mortal sin. But if we should understand transgression in a formal sense—namely, by the special aspect of doing something contrary to a negative precept—then it is a special sin in two ways. As a part of justice, transgression is a special sin in one way insofar as it is contrary to types of sin that are contrary to other virtues. For, as it belongs to the proper nature of

---

[100]ST II-II, Q. 79, A. 1.   [101]Ibid., A. 2.

legal justice to consider the obligation of a precept, so it belongs to the proper nature of transgression to consider the contempt of a precept. Transgression is a special sin in a second way insofar as we distinguish it from omission, which is contrary to an affirmative precept.

Objection. No species includes other species of the same genus to which it belongs. But the sin of transgression extends to all capital sins and sins of thought, word, and deed. Therefore, transgression is not a special sin.

Reply Obj. All the mentioned species of sin can involve transgression because of a special characteristic, not because of their own nature. But a sin of omission is completely different from a transgression.

3. Is omission a special sin?[102]

Omission signifies the omission of an obligatory good, not any good. But good under the aspect of being obligatory belongs strictly to justice: to legal justice if we should understand obligation in relation to divine or human law, and to particular justice insofar as we consider obligation in relation to one's neighbor. And so, in the way in which justice is a special virtue, omission is also a special sin different from sins contrary to other virtues. And in the way in which doing good, of which omission is the contrary, is a special part of justice different from avoiding evil, of which transgression is the contrary, omission is also different from transgression.

Objection. For any special sin, one needs to determine when it begins. But one does not fix a particular time when a sin of omission begins, since one is similarly disposed whenever one does not do something, but one does not always sin in not doing something. Therefore, omission is not a special sin.

Reply Obj. As sins of transgression are contrary to negative precepts, which belong to avoiding evil, so sins of omission are contrary to affirmative precepts, which belong to doing good. Affirmative precepts oblige in relation to a fixed point of time, not at all times, and a sin of omission begins at that time. And one may at that time be unable to do what one ought. And a person does not commit a sin of omission if the inability to do what the person should do is blameless on the part of the person.

But if the inability to do what one ought is due to one's prior sin (e.g., if a monk has gotten drunk late at night and cannot get up for matins as he should), some say that the sin of omission began when the monk committed himself to the unlawful action incompatible with the obligatory action. But this does not seem to be true, since, were someone to rouse the

---

[102]Ibid., A. 3.

monk forcibly, and were the monk to go to matins, the monk would not omit attending matins. And so it is clear that the prior drunkenness caused the absence from matins and was not the omission. And so we should say that an omission begins to be imputed to a person as a sin when it was the time for the person to do something, but the omission is imputed to the person because of the prior cause, which renders the subsequent omission voluntary.

4. Is a sin of omission more serious than a sin of transgression?[103]

The farther a sin is from virtue, the more serious the sin is. But there is the greatest distance between contraries, and so something is farther away from its contrary than a simple negation of the contrary is. For example, black is absolutely more distant from white than nonwhite is from white, since every black thing is nonwhite, but not the converse. But transgression is clearly contrary to virtuous action, and omission signifies the negation of virtuous action. For example, there is a sin of omission if one should fail to show due reverence to one's parents, and there is a sin of transgression if one should insult them or cause any injury to them. And so, simply and absolutely speaking, transgression is clearly a more serious sin than omission, although a particular omission can be more serious than a particular transgression.

Objection. A sin of commission can be venial or mortal. But a sin of omission seems always to be mortal, since such a sin is contrary to an affirmative precept. Therefore, omission seems to be a more serious sin than transgression is.

Reply Obj. As omissions are contrary to affirmative precepts, so transgressions are contrary to negative precepts. And so both, if understood in the strict sense, signify the character of mortal sin. But we can speak of transgression or omission in a broad sense because something disposing a person to the contrary of affirmative or negative precepts is contrary to the precepts. And so both, broadly understood, can be venial sins.

Potential Parts

Certain virtues are potential parts of justice, that is, connected to justice but falling short of its perfect character. Religion, filial devotion, and respect for the virtuous fall short because they lack the characteristic of equality between the parties. Other connected virtues fall short because they lack the characteristic of strict legal obligation to another. Truth, gratitude, and retribution are so

---

[103]Ibid., A. 4.

necessary that one cannot preserve moral rectitude without them. Generosity and friendship are necessary as conducive to greater rectitude. Thomas treats each of these virtues in ST II-II, QQ. 81–119.

1. Do we suitably assign the virtues connected to justice?[104]

We should note two things about the virtues connected to a chief virtue. First, we should note that the connected virtues have something in common with the chief virtue. Second, we should note that they lack something of the perfect character of the chief virtue. And because justice is in relation to another, all virtues in relation to another can be connected to justice by this common aspect. But the nature of justice consists of rendering to another what one owes the other according to equality. Therefore, a particular virtue in relation to another falls short of justice in two ways. A virtue falls short of justice in one way insofar as the virtue lacks the characteristic of equality. A virtue falls short of justice in a second way insofar as the virtue lacks the characteristic of obligation.

Some virtues render to another what one owes the other but cannot render anything equal. First, anything human beings render God is due him but cannot be equal; namely, in that human beings render God as much as they owe him, and **religion** is connected to justice in this way. Second, one cannot equally recompense one's parents what one owes them, and **filial devotion** is connected to justice in this way. Third, one cannot recompense a virtuous person with an equal reward, and **respect** for such a person is connected to justice in this way.

And we can consider falling short of the obligation of justice in regard to two kinds of obligation: namely, moral and legal. Legal obligation is what the law obliges one to render another, and justice, the chief virtue, considers such obligation in the strict sense. Moral obligation is what one owes another out of the uprightness of virtue. And since obligation signifies necessity, such obligation has two grades. For some things are so necessary that one cannot preserve moral rectitude without them, and this has more of the characteristic of obligation. We can consider this obligation regarding the one obliged. And then it belongs to this obligation that human beings show themselves to others in words or deeds just as they are, and **truth** is connected to justice in this way. We can also consider this obligation regarding the other to whom one is obliged; namely, as one recompenses the other according to the other's deeds. And this sometimes consists of good things, and **gratitude** is connected to justice in this way. And this sometimes consists of evil things, and **retribution** is connected to justice in this way.

---

[104]ST II-II, Q. 80, A. 1.

The second kind of moral obligation is necessary as conducing to greater rectitude, but without which one can preserve rectitude; and **generosity, affability** (or **friendship**), and the like consider such obligation.

Objection. Equity is connected to justice. But it seems that none of the aforementioned designations mention equity. Therefore, the virtues connected to justice have been inadequately enumerated.

Reply Obj. Equity is connected to legal, not particular, justice and seems to be the same as higher power of judgment.

The Ten Commandments and Justice

The Ten Commandments direct human beings in relation to others and so necessarily belong to justice. The first three concern religion, the relation to God; the fourth concerns filial devotion, the relation to one's parents; and the others concern relations to one's fellow human beings.

1. Are the Ten Commandments precepts of justice?[105]

The Ten Commandments are the primary precepts of the Law, and natural reason at once assents to them as most evident. And the characteristic of obligation, which is necessary for a precept, is most clearly evident in justice, which is in relation to another. This is because it seems at first glance that human beings are masters of themselves in matters relating to themselves, and that it is lawful for them to do anything in such regard. But in relation to another, it is clearly evident that human beings are obliged to render to another what is due the other. And so the Ten Commandments necessarily belong to justice. The first three Commandments[106] concern acts of religion, which is the most important part of justice. The Fourth Commandment concerns acts of filial devotion, which is the second part of justice. And the other six Commandments are laid down about acts of justice in the general sense, which we consider between equals.

---

[105]ST II-II, Q. 122, A. 1.   [106]The numbering of the Ten Commandments is that of the Vulgate. The Hebrew Bible and the King James Version divide the Vulgate's First Commandment into two (the First and the Second) and combine the Vulgate's Ninth and Tenth Commandments into one (the Tenth).

3

Fortitude

In Itself

Fortitude is the moral virtue by which one resists difficulties that repel the will from acting according to reason. It is a special virtue insofar as it signifies firmness of spirit to endure and resist the greatest difficulties. It concerns fear of the difficulties and boldness in attacking them. It most concerns mortal dangers, including those faced in just war and just self-defense. Endurance in the face of danger is more important than attacking causes of danger. The brave person acts for the sake of the goodness of the virtue of bravery, expressing the likeness of the virtue in brave acts. Despite deriving spiritual pleasure in acting virtuously, the brave person experiences spiritual sorrow because of the risk of death, and also because of physical pain. A brave person should think about threatening dangers beforehand, but the person most manifests bravery without forethought in the face of sudden dangers. The brave person uses only moderate anger to facilitate prompt action. Since standing fast in the good of reason is a common condition of virtue, and fortitude stands fast against the greatest difficulties (physical pain and threat of death), fortitude is a cardinal virtue. But prudence and justice are more important capital virtues than fortitude, which acts only to preserve virtue by controlling fear and moderating boldness.

1. Is fortitude a virtue?[1]

The virtue of human beings makes them good and their actions good. But the good of human beings consists of being in accord with reason. And so it belongs to human virtue to make human beings and their actions to be in accord with reason. This happens in three ways. It happens in one way insofar as one causes right reason itself, and intellectual virtues do this. It happens in a second way insofar as one establishes right reason in human affairs, and this belongs to justice. And it happens in a third way insofar as one removes impediments to the rectitude to be established in human affairs.

And the human will is prevented from following right reason in two ways. The human will is prevented in one way by something pleasurable drawing the will to something other than what right reason requires, and the virtue of temperance takes away this impediment. The human will is prevented in a second way by something repelling the will from something

---

[1]ST II-II, Q. 123, A. 1.

in accord with reason, because of some difficulty that presses hard on the will. And fortitude of mind—namely, the fortitude by which the will resists such difficulties—is required to take away these impediments, just as human beings overcome and repel bodily impediments by bodily strength.

Objection. Human virtue, since it is good quality of mind, most belongs to the soul. But fortitude seems to belong to the body, or at least to result from one's bodily constitution. Therefore, it seems that fortitude is not a virtue.

Reply Obj. We speak of fortitude of the soul, which we posit as a virtue, by analogy to bodily strength. But it is not contrary to the nature of virtue that one have a natural inclination to virtue by reason of one's natural constitution.

2. Is fortitude a special virtue?[2]

We can understand the word *fortitude* in two ways. We can understand it in one way insofar as it signifies a firmness of spirit absolutely. And in this respect, it is virtue in general, or rather the condition of any virtue, since virtue requires that one act firmly and unwaveringly. We can understand fortitude in a second way insofar as it signifies firmness of spirit in enduring and resisting things in which it is most difficult to have firmness; namely, in the face of grave dangers. And so we posit fortitude as a special virtue, one that has fixed subject matter.

3. Does fortitude concern fear and boldness?[3]

It belongs to the virtue of fortitude to remove impediments that draw the will away from following reason. But that one should be drawn away from something difficult belongs to the aspect of fear, which signifies a retreat in the face of an evil involving difficulty. And so fortitude chiefly concerns fear of difficult things, which can draw the will away from following reason,

And one needs not only to endure firmly the onslaught of such difficult things by restraining fear, but also to attack them moderately; namely, when one needs to root them out in order to be secure in the future. And this seems to belong to the aspect of boldness. And so fortitude regards fear and boldness: restraining fear and moderating boldness, as it were.

4. Does fortitude concern only mortal dangers?[4]

It belongs to the virtue of fortitude to guard a person's will against withdrawing from the good of reason because of fear of bodily evil. But

---

[2]Ibid., A. 2.   [3]Ibid., A. 3.   [4]Ibid., A. 4.

one needs to hold firmly to the good of reason against any such evil, since no bodily evil is equivalent to the good of reason. And so we need to call fortitude of spirit the virtue that firmly keeps a person's will in the good of reason against the greatest evils, since one who stands firm against greater evils stands firm against lesser evils, but the converse is not true. And it also belongs to the nature of virtue to concern the most extreme thing. But death, which takes away all bodily goods, is the most terrible of all bodily evils. And so the virtue of fortitude concerns fear of mortal dangers.

Objection 1. Fortitude is love that readily endures all things for the sake of what is loved, and fears neither death nor any other adversity. Therefore, fortitude concerns both mortal dangers and all other adversities.

Reply Obj. 1. Fortitude well disposes one to bear all adversities. But we consider humans brave only because they bear the greatest evils well, not because they bear any kind of adversity well. And we call persons brave in one respect because they bear adversities other than death well.

Obj. 2. No virtue consists of extremes. But fear of death consists of an extreme, since such fear is the greatest fear. Therefore, the virtue of fortitude does not concern fear of death.

Reply Obj. 2. We consider extremes in relation to virtues by what exceeds right reason. And so it is not contrary to virtue if one should undergo the greatest dangers in accord with reason.

5. Does fortitude in the strict sense concern the danger of death in combat?[5]

Fortitude strengthens the spirit of a human being against the greatest danger, that is, the danger of death. But since fortitude is a virtue, and it always belongs to the nature of virtue to tend to some good, it is in order to seek some good that human beings do not flee from the danger of death. And the danger of death from sickness, storms at sea, attacks by robbers, or other such things do not seem directly to threaten one because one is seeking some good. But the danger of death in combat directly threatens human beings because of a good; namely, insofar as one is defending the common good in just combat.

And there can be a just combat in two ways. In one way, there can be just conflict in general, as when soldiers fight in a battle. In a second way, there can be just combat in particular, as, for instance, when a judge or even a private person does not retreat from a just judgment out of fear of a threatening sword or any danger, even if it should be life-threatening. Therefore, it belongs to fortitude to show firmness of spirit against mortal

---

[5]Ibid., A. 5.

dangers, whether they threaten in general combat or in a particular conflict, which we can call combat by the general term. And we should accordingly grant that fortitude in the strict sense concerns the danger of death in war.

But a brave person is also rightly disposed regarding the danger of any other death, especially since human beings can undergo the danger of any death for the sake of virtue. For example, a brave person does not flee from attending a sick friend because one fears a mortal infection, or from traveling to carry out a virtuous task because one fears shipwreck or robbers.

6. Is endurance the chief act of fortitude?[6]

Fortitude concerns suppressing fear more than moderating boldness. For it is more difficult to suppress fear than to moderate boldness, since the very danger, the object of boldness and fear, of itself contributes something to suppress boldness, but acts to increase fear. But it belongs to fortitude to attack as it moderates boldness, while endurance results from suppressing fear. And so endurance—that is, standing fast in the face of danger—is a more important act of fortitude than attacking.

7. Does a brave person act for the sake of the goodness of the habit of fortitude?[7]

There are two kinds of ends: namely, the proximate and the final. And the proximate end of any efficient cause is to bring the likeness of its form in something else. For example, the end of fire heating something is to produce the likeness of the fire's heat in what is being heated, and the end of a builder is to produce the likeness of the builder's skill in the material. And we can call whatever good results from this, if it be striven for, the remote end of the efficient cause. And as skill disposes external matter in making things, so also prudence disposes human acts in doing things. Therefore, we should say that brave persons intend as their proximate end to express in brave acts the likeness of their habit of fortitude, since they intend to act in suitable accord with the habit. And their remote end is happiness, that is, God.

8. Do brave persons take pleasure in their brave acts?[8]

When it is a question of emotions, there are two kinds of pleasure. The first belongs to the body and results from physical contact, and the second belongs to the soul and results from the soul's understanding.

---

[6]Ibid., A. 6.   [7]Ibid., A. 7.   [8]Ibid., A. 8.

And the latter in the strict sense results from virtuous acts, since we consider the good of reason in them. But the chief act of fortitude consists of bearing sorrows in the way that the soul understands them. For example, a human being is sad to lose physical life, which the virtuous person loves both as a natural good and as something necessary for virtuous deeds, and sad to lose the things proper to physical life. And the chief act of fortitude also consists of enduring some painful things regarding physical contact: for example, wounds and blows. And so a brave person in one respect has something that causes pleasure; namely, spiritual pleasure—that is, pleasure in the very act of virtue and its end. And a brave person in another respect has something that causes sorrow, both spiritual sorrow when contemplating loss of one's life, and physical pain.

And perceptible physical pain renders the spiritual pleasure of virtue imperceptible (except, perhaps, when God's superabundant grace raises the soul to divine things, in which the soul delights, with greater force than physical pain afflicts it). But the virtue of fortitude causes reason to overcome physical pain. And the pleasure in virtue overcomes spiritual sorrow, since a virtuous person prefers the goodness of virtue to physical life and the properties of life. And so a brave person need not feel pleasure, but it is enough that the person should not feel sad.

Objection. Something stronger conquers something weaker. But brave persons love virtuous good more than their own body, which they expose to mortal dangers. Therefore, pleasure regarding the virtuous good overcomes physical pain. Therefore, the brave person acts completely with pleasure.

Reply Obj. The pleasure in virtue conquers spiritual sorrow in a brave person. But since physical pain is more sensibly perceptible, and sense perception more apparent to human beings, great physical pain causes spiritual pleasure, which concerns the end of virtue, to disappear, as it were.

9. Does fortitude most consist of sudden things?[9]

We should consider two things about acts of bravery. One regards choosing to be brave, and then fortitude does not concern sudden things. For a brave person chooses to think about threatening dangers beforehand in order to be able to resist them or bear them more readily. And the second thing we should consider about acts of fortitude regards manifesting the virtuous habit; and then fortitude most concerns sudden things, since one most manifests the habit of bravery in sudden dangers. For habits operate like nature. And so the fact that one should, without forethought, do things proper to the virtue when, because of sudden danger, there is imminent need to do so, most manifests that fortitude is firmly present in

---

[9]Ibid., A. 9.

the soul as a habit. One without the habit of fortitude can also prepare the soul against dangers by daily forethought, and the brave person uses this preparation at the opportune moment.

10. Does a person use anger in acts of bravery?[10]

Aristotelians and Stoics have spoken about anger and other emotions in different ways. For Stoics excluded both anger and all other emotions of the soul from the spirit of a wise—that is, virtuous—person. Aristotelians, following Aristotle, attributed anger and other emotions of the soul, as moderated by reason, to the virtuous. And the two schools perhaps differed only in mode of expression and not in substance. For Aristotelians called all movements of sense appetites, howsoever disposed, emotions of the soul. And since commands of reason cause sense appetites to help one to act more promptly, they held that the virtuous should use anger and other emotions of the soul, as moderated by the commands of reason, to do so. And Stoics called emotions of the soul immoderate affections of sense appetites, and so sicknesses or diseases. Therefore, the brave person uses moderate, but only moderate, anger in acts of bravery.

Objection. As some persons carry out brave acts more forcibly because of anger, so also some persons do so because of sorrow or desire. But fortitude does not use sorrow or desire to assist brave acts. Therefore, neither should fortitude use anger.

Reply Obj. Fortitude involves two activities: namely, enduring and attacking. But fortitude uses anger to assist the activity of attacking, not the activity of enduring, since only reason causes endurance. And fortitude uses anger rather than other emotions for attacking because it belongs to anger to attack what causes sorrow, and so anger directly assists fortitude in attacking. But sorrow by its nature yields to harmful things, although sorrow incidentally helps one to attack, either because sorrow causes anger, or because one exposes oneself to danger in order to escape sorrow. Likewise, desire by its nature tends to pleasurable good, and attacking in the face of danger is intrinsically contrary to that good, although desire sometimes incidentally helps attacking; namely, because one prefers to risk danger than to lack something pleasurable.

11. Is fortitude a cardinal virtue?[11]

Cardinal, or chief, virtues are those that especially claim for themselves what commonly belongs to all virtues. But we posit standing fast as one of the common conditions of virtue, and fortitude most claims for itself praise for steadfastness. And the more one is impelled to lose cour-

[10]Ibid., A. 10.   [11]Ibid., A. 11.

age and retreat, the more we praise one who endures. And both a pleasing good and an afflicting evil impel a human being to retreat from what is in accord with reason, but physical pain impels a human being more than pleasure. And of spiritual sorrow and dangers, a human being most fears those that lead to death, against which the brave person stands fast. And so fortitude is a cardinal virtue.

12. Does fortitude surpass all other virtues?[12]

In qualitatively great things, being greater is the same as being better. And so the better a virtue is, the greater it is. But the good of reason is the good of human beings, and prudence, which is the perfection of reason, has this good essentially. And justice produces this good, inasmuch as it belongs to justice to put the order of reason in all human affairs. And other virtues preserve this good; namely, inasmuch as they control emotions, lest the latter lead human beings away from the good of reason. And fortitude holds the first place in the rank of such virtues, since fear of mortal danger most causes human beings to retreat from the good of reason. And temperance ranks after fortitude, since the pleasures of touch also prevent the good of reason more than other things do.

And what something is essentially is more important than what it causes, and the latter is more important than what it preserves by removing obstacles. And so prudence is the most important cardinal virtue, justice the second most important, fortitude the third most important, and temperance the fourth most important. And other virtues rank after the cardinal virtues.

Fear

One sins against fortitude in several ways. One does so in one way if one fears mortal dangers too much and avoids them when, according to reason, one should not. This is a mortal sin if the will consents to such fear. A person should avoid some evils (e.g., loss of one's life) more than other evils (e.g., loss of one's property), and so one may yield property to robbers in order to save one's life but may not commit sin in order to avoid physical harm or death. Fear of imminent danger lessens but does not excuse sin committed out of fear.

1. Is fear a sin?[13]

We call something a sin regarding human actions because of a disorder, since the goodness of a human act consists of a certain order. But it is due

---

[12]Ibid., A. 12.   [13]ST II-II, Q. 125, A. 1.

order that one's will be subject to the rule of reason, and reason dictates that some things should be avoided, and other things sought. And some things are to be avoided more than other things, and some things are likewise to be sought more than other things; and the more a good should be sought, the more the contrary evil should be avoided. And so reason dictates that some goods are more to be sought than some evils are to be avoided. Therefore, when one's will avoids things that reason dictates should be endured lest one desist from other things that one should seek, the fear is inordinate and has the nature of sin. But when one's will, out of fear, avoids what according to reason one should avoid, the will is neither inordinate nor sinful.

2. Is the sin of fear contrary to fortitude?[14]

Every fear derives from love, since one fears only the contrary of what one loves. And love is not limited to any genus of virtue or vice. Rather, ordered love is included in any virtue, since all virtuous persons love the goodness of their virtue; and inordinate love is included in any sin, since inordinate desire derives from inordinate love. And so inordinate fear is likewise included in any sin, as, for example, a miser fears the loss of money, the intemperate person the loss of pleasure, and so forth. But the chief fear concerns mortal dangers. And so the disorder of such fear is contrary to fortitude, which concerns mortal dangers. And we accordingly say by synecdoche that timidity is contrary to fortitude.

Objection. All despair derives from a fear. But despair is contrary to hope, not fear. Therefore, the sin of fear is not contrary to despair.

Reply Obj. As hope is the source of boldness, so fear is the source of despair. And so, as hope is a prerequisite for the brave person, who uses boldness moderately, so, conversely, despair derives from some fear. But it is not necessary that any despair result from any kind of fear. Rather, it is necessary that any despair result from fear of the same type of thing. And the despair contrary to hope is related to a different type of thing—namely, divine things—than the fear contrary to fortitude, which belongs to mortal dangers. And so the argument fails.

3. Is fear a mortal sin?[15]

Fear is a sin insofar as it is inordinate; namely, insofar as it avoids what according to reason one should not avoid. This disordered fear sometimes consists only of the sense appetite, without the added consent of the will, and so can be only a venial, not a mortal, sin.

---

[14]Ibid., A. 2.   [15]Ibid., A. 3.

But such disordered fear sometimes extends to the rational appetite, which we call the will; and the will by free choice, contrary to reason, avoids something. And such disordered fear is sometimes a mortal sin and sometimes a venial sin. For if a person, on account of the fear whereby the person avoids mortal danger or any other temporal evil, is thereby disposed to do something prohibited or omit something commanded by divine law, such fear is a mortal sin. Otherwise, it will be a venial sin.

4. Does fear excuse a person from sin?[16]

Fear has the nature of sin insofar as it is contrary to the order of reason. But reason judges that a person should avoid some evils more than other evils. And so it is no sin if a person, in order to avoid evils that according to reason should be more avoided, does not avoid evils that should be less avoided. For example, a person should avoid physical death more than loss of property. And so, if one were to promise or give something to robbers out of fear for one's life, one would be excused from the sin one would incur if one were, without a legitimate reason, to give something to sinners in preference to giving it to the virtuous, whom one should prefer.

And if a person who, out of fear, avoids evils that according to reason should be less avoided, should incur evils that according to reason should be more avoided, the person could not be completely excused from sin. This is because such fear would be inordinate. But one should fear evils of the soul more than evils of the body, and evils of the body more than evils regarding external things. And so, if a person should incur evils of the soul (i.e., sins) in order to avoid evils of the body (e.g., blows or death) or evils regarding external things (e.g., loss of money), or if a person should endure evils of the body in order to avoid loss of money, the person is not completely excused from sin. But the person's sin is nonetheless somewhat lessened, since what one does out of fear is less voluntary. For an imminent danger imposes on a person a certain necessity to do something, and so such things that one does out of fear are not absolutely voluntary, but partially voluntary and partially involuntary.

Objection. Every fear is either of a temporal evil or of a spiritual evil. But fear of a spiritual evil cannot excuse one from sin, since such fear does not induce one to sin but draws one away from it. Nor does fear of a temporal evil excuse one from sin, since one need not fear poverty, sickness, or anything other than what comes from one's own wickedness. Therefore, it seems that fear never excuses one from sin.

---

[16]Ibid., A. 4.

Reply Obj. The Stoics held that temporal goods are not human goods, and so temporal evils are not human evils and should never be feared. But Augustine and Aristotelians held that such temporal things are the lowest goods, and so one should fear contrary things but not so much that one retreats in the face of them from what is good regarding virtue.

Lack of Fear

One also sins if one should have too little fear of losing one's life, which one should love in a proper way. Spiritual pride and stupidity cause one to lack the fear of losing one's life that one should have. Fortitude consists of the mean between too little and too much fear.

1. Is lack of fear a sin?[17]

Since fear derives from love, there seems to be the same judgment about love and fear, and we are now treating of the fear of temporal evils, which derives from the love of temporal goods. But nature endows each one to love one's own life and the things ordered to one's life, though to do so in the proper way; namely, that one love such things insofar as one uses them for the sake of one's final end, not as if they constitute one's end. And so not loving them in the way one should is contrary to the inclination of nature and consequently a sin. But one never completely falls away from love of one's life, since one cannot completely lose what belongs to nature. And so those who kill themselves do this out of love of their flesh, which they wish to free from present distresses.

And so it can happen that one fears death and other temporal evils less than one should because one loves their contraries less than one should. But not fearing death and other temporal evils at all cannot arise out of complete lack of love. Rather, this lack of fear happens because one thinks that the evils contrary to the goods one loves cannot happen to oneself. And this sometimes happens out of pride of spirit presumptuous about self and contemptuous of others. And it sometimes happens out of lack of reason. And so, being without fear is clearly sinful, whether caused by spiritual pride or by stupidity, which nonetheless excuses one from sin if the stupidity should be invincible.

2. Is lack of fear contrary to fortitude?[18]

Fortitude concerns fear and boldness. But all moral virtue posits the mean of reason in the matter the virtue concerns. And so the fear tem-

---

[17]ST II–II, Q. 126, A. 1.   [18]Ibid., A. 2.

pered by reason belongs to fortitude: namely, that human beings fear what they should fear, and when they should fear, and so forth. But excess and defect can destroy this measure of reason. And so, as timidity is contrary to fortitude by too much fear—namely, inasmuch as one fears what one should not, or as one should not—so also temerity is contrary to fortitude by too little fear; namely, inasmuch as one does not fear what one should fear.

Boldness

Boldness, like fear, is an emotion, and emotions should be subject to reason. And so excessive boldness in attacking the cause of a mortal danger is a sin and contrary to fortitude.

1. Is boldness a sin?[19]

Boldness is an emotion. But emotion sometimes is moderated by reason and sometimes lacks the measure of reason, whether by excess or deficiency, and emotion is sinful in this respect. And we sometimes understand the names of emotions by their excess. For example, we speak of anger as excessive anger; namely, as sinful anger, not any anger. And we also in this way hold that boldness, meaning excessive boldness, is a sin.

2. Is boldness contrary to fortitude?[20]

It belongs to moral virtue to observe the measure of reason in the matter that the virtue concerns. And so every sin signifying lack of moderation about the matter of a moral virtue is contrary to the virtue as the immoderate is to the moderate. But boldness, insofar as the word denotes a sin, signifies the excessive emotion we call boldness. And boldness in this sense is clearly contrary to the virtue of fortitude, which concerns fear and boldness.

Parts

There are no subjective parts (i.e., species) of fortitude, since fortitude itself has a very specific subject matter.

There are four integral (i.e., constitutive) parts of fortitude: confidence, magnificence (nobility of character), patience, and perseverance. Acts attacking the causes of mortal dangers require confidence and magnificence. Acts of endurance require patience and perseverance.

---

[19]ST II–II, Q. 127, A. 1.   [20]Ibid., A. 2.

These integral parts, if related to other, less difficult subject matter, are potential parts of fortitude (i.e., connected virtues). For example, the connected virtue of magnificence concerns great expenses for public benefactions, and the connected virtue of magnanimity (high-mindedness), which Thomas regards as equivalent to confidence, concerns great public honors. Thomas particularly considers these connected virtues and the sins contrary to them in ST II-II, QQ. 129–38.

1. Do we suitably designate the parts of fortitude?[21]

There can be three kinds of parts of any virtue: namely, subjective, integral, and potential. And we cannot assign subjective parts to fortitude, in that it is a special virtue, since it concerns very special subject matter and so cannot be divided into many, specifically different virtues. But we assign integral parts, as it were, and potential parts. We assign **integral parts** regarding things that necessarily accompany acts of fortitude. And we assign **potential parts** insofar as things that fortitude observes regarding the most difficult things—namely, mortal dangers—other virtues observe regarding other, less difficult subject matters. And the latter virtues are connected to fortitude as secondary virtues to the chief virtue.

And there are two kinds of brave acts: namely, acts of attack and acts of endurance. And two things are required for acts of attack. One of these belongs to preparing the soul; namely, that one have a spirit ready to attack. And we posit **confidence** regarding this. The second belongs to executing the attack; namely, that one not fail to execute the things one has begun confidently. And we posit **magnificence** regarding this. And so these two things, if restricted to the proper subject matter of fortitude—namely, mortal dangers—will be its integral parts, as it were, without which there can be no fortitude. But if they are related to certain other subject matters in which there is less difficulty, they will be virtues specifically different from fortitude but connected to it as something secondary to something primary. For example, there is magnificence regarding great expenses for public benefactions, and magnanimity, which seems to be the same as confidence, regarding great public honors.

And two things are required for the other kind of brave acts, that is, acts of endurance. The first of these is in order that the difficulty of the threatening evils does not break the spirit through sorrow and cause it to fall away from its greatness. And we posit **patience** regarding this. And the second thing is in order that the lengthy suffering of difficulties does not weary human beings to the point that they give up trying. And we

---

[21]ST II-II, Q. 128, A. 1.

posit **perseverance** regarding this. These two things also, if restricted to the proper subject matter of fortitude, will be its integral parts, as it were. But if they are related to any difficult subject matters, they will be virtues different from fortitude and yet connected to it as secondary virtues to the chief virtue.

4

Temperance

In Itself

The virtue of temperance concerns moderation. Temperance is virtue in general insofar as reason moderates all human actions and emotions, but temperance is a special virtue insofar as reason restrains desires and pleasures of the senses. As a special virtue, temperance chiefly concerns the emotions tending toward sensibly pleasurable goods and the sorrows resulting from the absence of such pleasures. It concerns the chief sense pleasures: those of food and drink, which nature requires for the preservation of the life of the individual human being; and that of sex, which nature requires for the preservation of the human species. Since such pleasures result from touch, temperance concerns the pleasures of touch but secondarily concerns the pleasures in tasting and smelling foods and drink, and in seeing beautiful women. Temperance takes the needs of this life as the norm governing the use of pleasurable things. Temperance is a cardinal virtue because moderation is chiefly praiseworthy in connection with the pleasures of touch, which are more natural, more necessary, and more difficult to resist. Since temperance concerns only the sense desires and pleasures of individual human beings, it is less excellent than justice and fortitude, which concern the good of the community.

1. Is temperance a virtue?[1]

It belongs to the nature of virtue to incline human beings to good. But the good of human beings is to be in accord with reason. And so human virtue inclines human beings to what is in accord with reason. But temperance clearly inclines human beings to this, since the name signifies a moderating or tempering, which reason does. And so temperance is a virtue.

Objection 1. No virtue is contrary to an inclination of nature. But temperance draws a person away from pleasures of the senses, to which nature inclines the person. Therefore, temperance is not a virtue.

Reply Obj. 1. Nature inclines things to what befits each thing. And so human beings by nature seek pleasure befitting them. But since human beings as such are rational, pleasures that are in accord with reason befit them; and temperance draws human beings away from pleasures that are contrary to reason, not those that are in accord with reason. And so tem-

[1]ST II-II, Q. 141, A. 1.

perance is evidently in accord with, not contrary to, the inclination of human nature, although temperance is contrary to the inclination of an animal nature not subject to reason.

Obj. 2. Virtues are interrelated. But some persons have temperance without having other virtues. For example, many persons are temperate but greedy or cowardly. Therefore, temperance is not a virtue.

Reply Obj. 2. Temperance, insofar as it fully possesses the character of virtue, does not exist without prudence, which sinners lack. And so those who lack other virtues, being subject to contrary sins, do not have the temperance that is a virtue. Rather, they perform temperate acts from a natural disposition, as some imperfect virtues are natural to human beings, or by acquired habituation, which does not have the perfection of reason apart from prudence.

2. Is temperance a special virtue?[2]

In ordinary human speech, some general terms are restricted to the things that are the chief ones in the group. For example, we understand the word *city* to mean Rome by synecdoche. Therefore, we can understand the word *temperance* in two ways. We can understand it in one way by its general meaning. And then temperance is virtue in general, not a special virtue, since the word signifies a tempering—that is, a moderating—that reason imposes on human actions and emotions, and this is common to all moral virtues. Nonetheless, temperance differs conceptually from fortitude even as we understand each as virtue in general. For temperance draws human beings away from things that entice desires contrary to reason, while fortitude impels human beings to withstand or attack things on account of which human beings avoid the good of reason.

But if we should consider temperance by synecdoche, insofar as temperance bridles desire from things that most entice human beings, then temperance is a special virtue with special subject matter, just as fortitude is.

3. Does temperance concern only desires and pleasures of the senses?[3]

It belongs to moral virtue to preserve the good of reason against emotions contrary to reason. But there are two kinds of movements of the soul's emotions. There is one insofar as sense appetites seek after sensibly perceptible and bodily goods, and the second insofar as the sense appetites avoid sensibly perceptible and bodily evils. The first kind of move-

---

[2]Ibid., A. 2. [3]Ibid., A. 3.

ment of sense appetite is chiefly contrary to reason by lack of moderation. For sensibly perceptible and bodily goods, specifically considered, are not contrary to reason but rather serve reason as means that reason uses to attain its own end. But they are chiefly contrary to reason insofar as a sense appetite does not tend toward them according to the measure of reason. And so it especially belongs to moral virtue to moderate emotions that signify seeking some good.

And movements of a sense appetite avoiding sensibly perceptible evils are chiefly contrary to reason by their effect, not by their lack of moderation; namely, as a person, by avoiding sensibly perceptible and bodily evils, which sometimes accompany the good of reason, departs from that good of reason. And so it belongs to moral virtue in such things to show firmness in the good of reason.

Therefore, the virtue of fortitude, to the nature of which showing firmness belongs, chiefly concerns the emotion that belongs to avoiding bodily evils—namely, the emotion of fear—and so concerns boldness, which attacks fearful things in hope of some good. Just so, temperance, which signifies a moderation, chiefly concerns emotions tending toward sensibly perceptible goods—namely, the emotions regarding desires and pleasures of the senses—and so concerns sorrows that result from the absence of such pleasures. For just as boldness presupposes fearful things, so also such sorrow comes from the absence of the aforementioned pleasures.

Objection. Temperance is the firm and moderate mastery of reason over sexual lust and other evil impulses of the spirit. But we call all emotions of the soul impulses of the spirit. Therefore, it seems that temperance does not concern only sense desires and pleasures.

Reply Obj. Emotions that belong to avoiding evil presuppose emotions that belong to seeking good, and emotions of the irascible power presuppose emotions of the concupiscible power. And so, while temperance directly moderates emotions of the concupiscible power tending toward good, temperance as a result moderates all other emotions, since moderating prior emotions results in moderation of subsequent emotions. For one who desires moderately then hopes moderately, and is moderately saddened about the absence of sensibly desirable things.

4. Does temperance concern only desires and pleasures of touch?[4]

Temperance concerns sense desires and pleasures of the senses as fortitude concerns fears and boldness. But fortitude concerns fears and boldness regarding the greatest evils, which destroy nature itself: that is,

---

[4]Ibid., A. 4.

mortal dangers. And so temperance likewise needs to concern desires of the greatest sense pleasures. And since sense pleasure results from connatural action, the more natural the actions that result in certain sense pleasures, the more vehement the pleasures are. But most natural to animals are the actions that preserve the nature of the individual through food and drink and preserve the nature of the species by the sexual union of man and woman. And so temperance in the strict sense concerns the pleasures of food and drink and the pleasure of sex. But such pleasures result from the sense of touch. And so we conclude that temperance concerns the pleasures of touch.

Objection 1. Things that belong to the same genus seem equally to belong to the subject matter of a virtue. But all pleasures of the senses seem to belong to the same genus. Therefore, they equally belong to the subject matter of temperance.

Reply Obj. 1. The pleasures of senses other than touch are differently disposed in human beings and other animals. For in other animals, pleasures from the other senses are caused only in relation to sensibly perceptible objects of touch. For example, a lion takes pleasure in seeing a stag or hearing its voice because of the food it will provide. But human beings take pleasure by the other senses both because of the relationship of things to the objects of touch and because of the harmony of sensibly perceptible objects. And so temperance concerns pleasures of the other senses, insofar as they are related to pleasures of touch, but only secondarily, not chiefly. And insofar as sensibly perceptible objects of the other senses are pleasurable because of the objects' harmony, as when a human being takes pleasure in harmonious sound, the pleasure does not belong to the preservation of nature. And so emotions connected with the pleasures of other senses do not have the chief place. And so we do not use the word *temperance* regarding them by synecdoche.

Obj. 2. Spiritual pleasures are greater than pleasures of the body. But some persons at times depart from the laws of God and the condition of virtue because of desires for spiritual pleasures (e.g., excessive inquisitiveness for knowledge). Therefore, temperance does not concern only the pleasures of touch.

Reply Obj. 2. Although spiritual pleasures are by their nature greater than pleasures of the body, the senses do not perceive spiritual pleasures in the way of pleasures of the body. And so spiritual pleasures do not so forcefully affect sense appetites, against the impulses of which moral virtue preserves the good of reason. Or we should say that spiritual pleasures, absolutely speaking, are in accord with reason, and so we should restrain them only incidentally; namely, inasmuch as a spiritual pleasure draws one away from a better and more requisite pleasure.

Obj. 3. If the pleasures of touch were the proper subject matter of temperance, temperance would need to concern all pleasures of touch. But temperance does not concern all such pleasures (e.g., the ones involved in games). Therefore, the pleasures of touch are not the proper subject matter of temperance.

Reply Obj. 3. Some pleasures of touch do not belong to the preservation of nature. And so it is not necessary that temperance concern all pleasures of touch.

5. Does temperance concern pleasures proper to taste?[5]

Temperance concerns the chief pleasures, which most belong to the preservation of human life, whether of the species or the individual. And we consider some things as primary and some things as secondary. We indeed consider as primary the very use of something necessary (e.g., a woman, who is necessary for the preservation of the species, or food and drink, which are necessary for the preservation of the individual). And the very use of these necessary things has an essential pleasure attached. And we consider as secondary regarding each kind of use something that contributes to the use being more pleasurable (e.g., the beauty and adornment of women, and the pleasurable taste and smell of food). And so temperance chiefly regards the pleasure of touch, which intrinsically results from the very use of necessary things, the entire use of which consists of touching them. And there is temperance, or its lack, as secondary regarding pleasures of taste or smell or sight, since the sensibly perceptible objects of these senses contribute to the pleasurable use of necessary things. But since the sense of taste is closer to the sense of touch than the other senses are, temperance more concerns taste than the other senses.

6. Should we understand the rule of temperance by the needs of the present life?[6]

The goodness of moral virtue consists chiefly of the order of reason, since the good of human beings is to be in accord with reason. And the chief order of reason consists of directing particular things to their ends; and the good of reason most consists of this order, since good has the nature of an end, and the end itself is the rule governing means to the end. But all pleasurable things that human beings use are directed to some need of this life as their end. And so temperance takes the needs of this life as the rule governing the pleasurable things one uses; namely, that one should use them insofar as the needs of this life require their use.

---

[5]Ibid., A. 5.   [6]Ibid., A. 6.

Objection 1. One who exceeds a rule sins. Therefore, if bodily needs were to be the rule of temperance, one who uses any pleasure beyond the needs of nature, which are satisfied with little things, would sin against temperance. But this seems to be improper.

Reply Obj. 1. We can consider the needs of human life in two ways. We consider such needs in one way as we say that that without which something cannot exist at all is necessary, as, for example, food is necessary for animals. We consider the needs of human life in a second way as we say that that without which something cannot exist in a suitable way is necessary. But temperance considers the needs of human life in both senses. And so the temperate person seeks pleasurable things for the sake of health or a good constitution. And we can consider other things, things unnecessary for human life, in two ways. For some things are impediments to health or a good constitution, and in no way does a temperate person use such things, since this would be a sin against temperance. But some things are not impediments to health or a good constitution, and a temperate person uses these things moderately, according to the right place and the right time and the thing's compatibility with those with whom the person lives. And so the temperate person also seeks other pleasurable things; namely, those unnecessary for health or a good constitution, if the things are not impediments to them.

Obj. 2. No one who observes a rule sins. Therefore, if bodily needs were the rule of temperance, anyone who uses a pleasure because of a bodily need (e.g., for the sake of health) would be free of sin. But this seems to be false. Therefore, bodily needs are not the rule of temperance.

Reply Obj. 2. Temperance concerns needs regarding the fitness of one's life. But we consider such needs regarding both the fitness of body and the fitness of external things—namely, riches and responsibilities—and, much more, the fitness of honorable character. And so, in the pleasurable things that the temperate person uses, the person considers not only that the things should not impede the person's health or good bodily disposition, but also that the things should not be contrary to goodness—that is, honorable character—and that they should not be beyond the person's financial means. And so the temperate person regards both the needs of this life and the person's responsibilities.

7. Is temperance a cardinal virtue?[7]

We call a virtue chief or cardinal that we most highly praise because it has one of the things universally required for the character of virtue. But moderation, which is required in every virtue, is most praiseworthy

---

[7]Ibid., A. 7.

regarding pleasures of touch, which temperance concerns. This is so both because such pleasures are more natural to us, and so more difficult to abstain from and to restrain desires for, and because their objects are more necessary for the present life. And so we posit temperance as a chief or cardinal virtue.

8. Is temperance the greatest virtue?[8]

The good of the people is more excellent than the good of the individual. And so the more a virtue belongs to the good of the people, the better it is. But justice and fortitude belong to the good of the people more than temperance does. This is because justice consists of exchanges, which are in relation to others; and fortitude consists of the dangers in wars, which are sustained for the common welfare; while temperance moderates only the sense desires and pleasures of things that belong to the individual person. And so justice and fortitude are clearly more excellent virtues than temperance, and prudence and the theological virtues are better than justice and fortitude.

Objection. The more general something is, the more necessary and the better it seems to be. But fortitude concerns mortal dangers, which happen more rarely than pleasures of touch that happen every day; and so the practice of temperance is more general than the practice of fortitude. Therefore, temperance is more excellent than fortitude.

Reply Obj. The generality whereby something belongs to many human beings contributes more to the excellence of goodness than the generality that we consider insofar as something happens frequently. But fortitude excels in the former, and temperance in the latter. And so fortitude is absolutely better, although we can say that temperance is in one respect better than both fortitude and justice.

Contrary Sins

The natural order requires that human beings use pleasures necessary for preserving the individual human being and the human species, and one would sin if one should act contrary to the natural order. But it is sometimes praiseworthy to abstain from the pleasures of food, drink, or sex for the sake of a greater good (e.g., abstaining for the sake of bodily health or in preparation for athletic contests).

An intemperate person is like a child in seeking base things, in becoming increasingly self-indulgent, and in the need for correction. Intemperance is a

---

[8]Ibid., A. 8.

more serious sin than cowardice, with respect to their respective subject matters, because the desire for pleasure is not so great as the desire to avoid mortal dangers. It is also a more serious sin than cowardice regarding the sinner, because the desire for pleasure, unlike the fear of mortal danger, does not paralyze the mind; because intemperance is more voluntary than cowardice; and because intemperance is easier to remedy than cowardice. Intemperance is most worthy of reproach because it is most contrary to human excellence regarding pleasures common to human beings and irrational animals, and because it is the most contrary to the beauty of human beings produced by the light of reason.

1. Is it a sin to avoid pleasures of touch?[9]

Everything contrary to the natural order is sinful. But nature appointed pleasure for actions necessary for the life of human beings. And so the natural order requires that human beings use such pleasures as much as they are necessary for human welfare, whether regarding preservation of the individual or preservation of the species. Therefore, if one were to avoid pleasure to the degree of omitting things necessary for natural preservation, one would sin, acting contrary to the natural order, as it were. And this belongs to the sin of avoiding pleasures of touch.

But we should note that, for the sake of an end, it is sometimes praiseworthy or even necessary to abstain from the pleasures resulting from such actions. For example, for the sake of bodily health, some persons abstain from certain pleasures in food, drink, and sex. And some persons also abstain from such pleasures for the sake of executing a function. For example, athletes and soldiers need to abstain from many pleasures in order to perform their functions. And likewise penitents, in order to restore the health of their souls, practice abstinence from pleasures as if on a diet. And human beings wishing to be free for contemplation and divine things need to withdraw themselves more from things of the flesh. But none of the foregoing belongs to the sin of avoiding pleasures of touch, since they are in accord with right reason.

Objection. The good of human beings is to be in accord with reason. But abstaining from all pleasures of touch most advances human beings in the good of reason. Therefore, avoidance of pleasures of touch, which totally rejects such pleasures, is not sinful.

Reply Obj. Since human beings cannot use reason apart from sense powers, which need bodily organs, human beings need to sustain their bodies in order to use their reason. But pleasurable actions cause sustenance of

---

[9]ST II-II, Q. 142, A. 1.

the body. And so the good of reason cannot be in human beings if they should abstain from all pleasurable things. But insofar as human beings need more or less bodily power to engage in acts of reason, they have more or less need to use pleasurable material things. And so human beings who have assumed the responsibility to be free for contemplation and to transmit spiritual good to others by a spiritual generation, as it were, laudably abstain from many pleasurable things. But those who are duty bound to be available for manual labor and carnal generation do not laudably abstain from those pleasurable things.

2. Is intemperance a childish sin?[10]

We say that something is childish in two ways. We say that something is childish in one way because it is suitable for children, and the sin of intemperance is not childish in this sense. We say that something is childish in a second way analogously, and we call sins of intemperance childish in this sense. For the sin of intemperance is a sin of excessive sense desire, and the sin is childlike in three respects.

First, the sin of intemperance is childlike regarding what both a person desiring excessively and a child seek. For both a person desiring excessively and a child seek base things, since we consider things beautiful in human affairs insofar as they are directed by reason. But a child does not consider the order of reason, and excessive sense desire likewise does not listen to reason.

Second, the sin of intemperance is childlike regarding the result. For a child, if left to its own will, grows in self-will. So also desire, if indulged, grows stronger.

Third, the sin of intemperance is childlike regarding the remedy applied to both. For a child is corrected by being restrained, and when one resists desire, one is likewise brought back to the proper mean of virtue. And so, as a child needs to live according to the command of his or her tutor, so also the concupiscible power needs to be consonant with reason.

3. Is cowardice a greater sin than intemperance?[11]

We can compare one sin to another in two ways: in one way, regarding the subject matter or object of each; in a second way, regarding the sinner. And intemperance is a more serious sin than cowardice in both ways. First, it is more serious regarding the subject matter. For cowardice avoids mortal dangers, and the pressing necessity of preserving one's life induces one to avoid them. But intemperance concerns pleasures of the senses,

---

[10]Ibid., A. 2.   [11]Ibid., A. 3.

and the desire for these pleasures is not so necessary to preserve life, since intemperance concerns added rather than natural pleasures or desires of the senses.[12] But the more necessary the movement to sin seems to be, the less serious the sin is. And so intemperance is a more serious sin than cowardice regarding the object or subject matter causing one to sin.

Similarly, intemperance is more serious regarding the sinner. And this is for three reasons. First, the more sound of mind the sinner is, the more serious the sin is, for which reason we do not impute sins to the insane. And grave fears and sorrows, especially those in the face of mortal dangers, numb the mind of a human being; but pleasure, which incites to intemperance, does not do this.

Second, the more voluntary a sin is, the more serious it is. And intemperance is more voluntary than cowardice. And this is for two reasons. Intemperance is more voluntary in one way because things that are done out of fear have their source from an external force, and so they are not absolutely voluntary, but partially voluntary and partially involuntary; while things done for pleasure are absolutely voluntary. Intemperance is more voluntary in a second way because an intemperate person's actions are more voluntary in particular and less voluntary in general. For no one would will to be intemperate. Rather, particular pleasurable things entice human beings and make them intemperate, and so the best remedy to avoid intemperance is for human beings not to delay in considering particular things. But the converse is true about things that belong to cowardice. For particular actions in the face of imminent danger, such as throwing away one's shield and the like, are less voluntary; but the general action, such as saving oneself by flight, is more voluntary. But what is more voluntary in particular actions is without qualification more voluntary. And so intemperance, since it is without qualification more voluntary than cowardice, is a greater sin.

Third, one can more easily use a remedy against intemperance than against cowardice. For the pleasures in foods and sex, which intemperance concerns, happen throughout life, and a human being can without danger be trained to be temperate; but mortal dangers happen more rarely, and one is trained to avoid fear in their regard at greater peril. And so intemperance is, without qualification, a greater sin than cowardice.

---

[12]In the preceding article (*ad* 2), Thomas explains that nature requires only the specific things that preserve human individuals and the human species. Desires for such things are natural in that sense, and the desires can be sinful only by quantitative excess. Human beings devise other things (e.g., delicately prepared foods and finely dressed women). These things especially incite sinful desires for food and sex.

Objection. We censure a sin as being contrary to the goodness of a virtue. But cowardice is contrary to fortitude, which is a more excellent virtue than temperance, and intemperance is contrary to temperance. Therefore, cowardice is a greater sin than intemperance.

Reply Obj. We can consider the excellence of fortitude over temperance in two ways. We can consider the excellence of fortitude over temperance in one way regarding their ends, which belong to the nature of good; namely, that fortitude is more directed to the common good than temperance is. And cowardice exceeds intemperance in that regard; namely, in that some persons desist from defending the common good because of fear.

We can consider the excellence of fortitude over temperance in a second way regarding their difficulty; namely, inasmuch as it is more difficult to undergo mortal dangers than to abstain from pleasures of the senses. And in this respect, cowardice does not necessarily exceed intemperance. For, as it is characteristic of a greater virtue not to succumb to something stronger; so also, conversely, it is characteristic of a lesser sin to succumb to something stronger, and of a greater sin to succumb to something weaker.

4. Is the sin of intemperance most worthy of reproach?[13]

Reproach seems to be contrary to honor and glory. But honor is due to excellence, and glory signifies brilliance. Therefore, intemperance is most worthy of reproach for two reasons. First, it is the most contrary to the excellence of human beings, since it concerns pleasures common to us and to irrational animals. Second, it is most contrary to the brilliance or beauty of human beings; namely, that less light of reason, from which the whole brilliance and beauty of virtue derives, is shown in the pleasures that intemperance regards. And so also we call such pleasures most slavish.

Objection 1. As virtue deserves honor, so sin deserves reproach. But some sins (e.g., homicide, blasphemy, and the like) are more serious than intemperance. Therefore, the sin of intemperance is not the most worthy of reproach.

Reply Obj. 1. Although carnal sins, which are included in intemperance, are less culpable than some other sins, they are nonetheless more dishonorable. For the magnitude of a sin regards the sin's disorder from our end, but dishonor regards baseness, which we most weigh by how unbecoming the sin is for the sinner.

Obj. 2. Temperance and intemperance concern human desires and pleasures. But some desires and pleasure, the ones we call bestial or the

---

[13]ST II-II, Q. 142, A. 4.

product of disease, are more disgraceful than human desires and pleasures. Therefore, intemperance is not the most worthy of reproach.

Reply Obj. 2. We should understand the statement, "Intemperance is most worthy of reproach," in reference to human sins: namely, sins that we consider to regard emotions in some way conformed to human nature. But sins that exceed the ordinary way of human nature are still more worthy of reproach. And yet even such sins seem to be traceable to the genus of intemperance by reason of their excess, as, for example, if a man were to take pleasure in eating human flesh or having sexual intercourse with animals or other men.

Parts

There are two integral, or necessary, conditions of temperance: a sense of shame, which draws one away from base behavior, and an honorable character, which draws one toward the beauty of moderate behavior.

Temperance concerns pleasures of touch, of which there are two kinds: pleasures related to nourishment and pleasures related to reproduction. Regarding pleasures related to nourishment, there are two subjective parts, or subdivisions, of temperance: abstinence regarding food and sobriety regarding alcoholic drink. Regarding pleasures related to reproduction, there are also two subjective parts: chastity regarding sexual intercourse and sexual modesty regarding incidental pleasures (e.g., kisses, touches, embraces).

Virtues that moderate pleasures in other subject matters and restrain other appetites are potential parts of temperance, that is, virtues connected with temperance. Regarding internal movements of the will, continence restrains immoderate desires, humility restrains immoderate hope, and meekness and mercy restrain immoderate anger. Regarding bodily movements and actions, modesty causes good order, proper attire, and gravity in conversation. Regarding external things, parsimony, or self-sufficiency, causes human beings not to demand superfluous things; and moderation, or simplicity, causes human beings not to demand things that are too special.

1. Do we appropriately assign parts of temperance?[14]

There can be three kinds of parts of a cardinal virtue: namely, integral, subjective, and potential parts. We call the conditions necessarily accompanying the virtue **integral parts**, and in this respect, there are two integral parts of temperance: namely, **sense of shame**, whereby one avoids the baseness contrary to temperance, and **honorable character**,

---

[14]ST II-II, Q. 143, A. 1.

whereby one loves the beauty of temperance. For of all the virtues, temperance most lays claim to a decorum, and the sins of intemperance have the most baseness.

We call the species of a virtue its **subjective parts,** and we need to differentiate the species of virtues by their different subject matters or objects. Temperance concerns pleasures of touch, which are divided into two kinds. For some pleasures are ordered to nourishment, and in these pleasures, there is **abstinence** regarding food and **sobriety,** in the strict sense, regarding alcoholic drink; and some pleasures are directed to the power of reproduction. In the latter pleasures, there is **chastity** regarding the chief pleasure of sexual intercourse itself, and we consider **sexual modesty** regarding incidental pleasures (e.g., the pleasures in kisses, touches, and embraces).

We call secondary virtues the **potential parts** of a chief virtue. Secondary virtues deal with certain other, less difficult subject matters in the same way that a chief virtue deals with the chief subject matter. But it belongs to temperance to moderate pleasures of touch, and it is most difficult to moderate such pleasures. And so we can hold that any virtue that effects a moderation in a particular subject matter and restraint of an appetite tending toward something is part of temperance as a virtue connected with it. This happens in three ways. It happens in one way in internal movements of the soul, in a second way in external movements and bodily acts, and in a third way in external things.

Contrary to movements of desire, which temperance moderates and restrains, there are three movements in the soul toward things. The first is the movement of the will under the influence of an emotional impulse, and **continence,** which causes the will not to succumb even though the human being is being subjected to immoderate desires, restrains this movement. The second kind of internal movement tending toward something is the movement of hope and the resulting boldness, and **humility** moderates and restrains this movement. The third kind of movement is one of anger tending toward revenge, and **meekness** and **mercy** restrain this movement.

Regarding bodily movements and actions, **modesty** causes moderation and restraint, and modesty is divided into three parts. It belongs to the first part to discern what one should do and what one should not do, and in what order one should do something, and to stand firm in this; and we posit **good order** in this regard. The second part is that human beings observe decorum in what they do, and we posit **proper attire** in this regard. And the third part regards conversations or any other things between friends, and we posit **gravity** in this regard.

Regarding external things, we should practice two kinds of moderation. First, human beings should not demand superfluous things, and we posit **parsimony**, or **self-sufficiency**, in this regard. Second, human beings should not demand too choice things, and we posit **moderation**, or **simplicity**, in this regard.[15]

Integral Parts

Broadly speaking, shame, which is fear of disgrace, is sometimes praiseworthy. Shame chiefly concerns reproach on account of sin. We feel greater shame from close associates, who know our deeds better and can help or hurt us more. Even the virtuous have a sense of shame hypothetically, that is, they are so disposed that they would feel shame if there were anything disgraceful in them.

The honorable refers to the same thing as virtue, and virtue is the same thing as beauty, which is the radiance of well-proportioned reason. The honorable and the useful and the pleasurable coincide in the same subject. But they differ conceptually, since we call something honorable insofar as it has an excellence worthy of honor because of its spiritual beauty; and pleasurable insofar as it satisfies a befitting desire; and useful insofar as it is related to something else; namely, happiness. We reckon honorable character under the special aspect of temperance as a precondition of it and so an integral part.

1. Is shame a virtue?[16]

We understand shame in two ways: namely, properly speaking and broadly speaking. Properly speaking, virtue is a perfection; and so anything contrary to perfection, even if it be good, falls short of the character of virtue. And shame is repugnant to perfection, since shame is fear of something base; namely, something disgraceful. And as hope concerns a possible good that is difficult to obtain, so also fear concerns a possible evil difficult to avoid. But a person perfected by habitual virtue does not regard anything disgraceful and base as possible to be done or difficult to avoid, and does nothing base to cause fear of disgrace. And so shame, properly speaking, is not a virtue, since it falls short of perfect virtue. But generally speaking, we call anything good and praiseworthy in human acts and emotions a virtue. And in this regard, we sometimes call the sense of shame a virtue, since it is sometimes a praiseworthy emotion.

---

[15]Thomas explains in detail the potential virtues of temperance and the contrary sins in ST II-II, QQ. 155–162, 166–70.   [16]ST II-II, Q. 144, A. 1.

2. Does shame concern disgraceful action?[17]

Properly speaking, fear concerns an evil difficult to avoid. And there are two kinds of disgrace. One is sinful: namely, the kind that consists of the deformity of a voluntary act. And properly speaking, this does not have the character of an evil difficult to avoid. And since it consists only of the will, it does not seem to be difficult or beyond the power of human beings to avoid. And for that reason, we do not understand it as something to be feared, and so there is no fear of such evils.

The second kind of disgrace is penal, as it were, and it consists of reproaching someone, as the brightness of glory consists of honoring someone. And since such reproach has the character of an evil difficult to avoid, as honor has the character of a good difficult to obtain, shame (i.e., fear of disgrace) first and chiefly concerns reproach (i.e., censure). And because such reproach, properly speaking, is due to sin as honor is to virtue, so also such shame concerns disgrace due to sin. And so human beings are less ashamed of failings that are not the product of their wrongdoing.

And shame concerns wrongdoing in two ways. In one way, shame concerns wrongdoing such that one ceases to do sinful things out of fear of reproach. In a second way, shame concerns wrongdoing such that human beings, out of fear of reproach, avoid public knowledge of their wicked deeds. And the first way belongs to embarrassment, the second to shame. And so one who is ashamed hides his deeds, and one who is embarrassed is afraid of falling into dishonor.

3. Do human beings feel greater shame from close associates?[18]

Since reproach is contrary to honor, just as honor signifies a testimonial to a person's excellence, especially the excellence regarding virtue, so also reproach, the fear of which is shame, signifies a testimonial to a person's failure, especially regarding some wrongdoing. And so the more a person esteems another's testimonial, the greater the shame that one fears from the other.

A person can more esteem another's testimonial either because of the certainty of its truth or because of its effect. Another's testimonial is certain in two ways. It is certain in one way because of the other's right judgment, as is evident in the case of judgment by the wise and the virtuous, from whom a person both desires more to be honored and feels greater shame. And so no one feels shame from children and irrational animals, since they lack right judgment. Another's testimony is certain in a second

---

[17]Ibid., A. 2.   [18]Ibid., A. 3.

way because of the other's knowledge of the things attested, since each person judges rightly about what the person knows. And so we feel greater shame from close associates, who know our deeds better. But we do not feel any shame from strangers and those completely unacquainted with us, who do not know our deeds.

A testimonial has greater weight from its effect because of the advantage or harm it produces. And so human beings more desire to be honored by those who can help them, and feel greater shame from those who can harm them. And so also we feel greater shame about something from close associates, with whom we are always in close contact, as if this contact should entail continual harm to us, whereas the harm from strangers and casual acquaintances rather quickly evaporates.

4. Do even virtuous human beings have a sense of shame?[19]

Shame is fear of a disgrace, and we may not fear an evil in two ways: in one way because we do not reckon something to be an evil, and in the other way because we do not reckon it as possible or difficult to avoid. Accordingly, one lacks shame about something in two ways. One lacks shame about something in one way because one does not understand embarrassing things as disgraceful, and human beings steeped in sins, boasting of the sins rather than being displeased by them, lack shame in this way. Human beings lack shame about something in a second way because they do not understand disgrace as possible for them or difficult, as it were, to avoid. And the elderly and the virtuous lack shame in this way. But these are so disposed that they would feel shame if there were anything disgraceful in them. And so shame belongs to the diligent hypothetically.

5. Is the honorable the same as virtue?[20]

We call worthiness an honorable condition, as it were, and so we seem to call something honorable if it is worthy of honor. But honor is due to excellence, and we most judge the excellence of human beings by their virtue, since one who is perfect is disposed toward the best. And so, properly speaking, the honorable refers to the same thing as virtue.

6. Is the honorable the same as the beautiful?[21]

The nature of beauty, or decorum, combines both radiance and due proportion. And so bodily beauty consists of a human being having well-proportioned limbs and a properly ruddy radiance. Likewise, spiritual

---

[19]Ibid., A. 4.   [20]ST II-II, Q. 145, A. 1.   [21]Ibid., A. 2.

beauty consists of a human being's social intercourse or actions being rightly proportioned by the spiritual radiance of reason. But this belongs to the nature of the honorable, which is the same as virtue, and virtue moderates all human affairs according to reason. And so the honorable is the same as spiritual beauty.

7. Does the honorable differ from the useful and the pleasurable?[22]

The honorable and the useful and the pleasurable combine in the same subject, but the honorable differs conceptually from the useful and the pleasurable. For we call something honorable because of its decorum from the order of reason, and anything directed by reason naturally befits a human being. But anything naturally takes pleasure in what befits it. And so the honorable is by nature pleasurable for human beings. (But not everything pleasurable is honorable, since something can be suitable according to the senses and unsuitable according to reason, and such pleasurable things are contrary to human reason, which perfects human nature.) And virtue itself, which is as such honorable, is related to something else as its end; namely, happiness.

And accordingly, the honorable and the useful and the pleasurable are the same for the subject but differ conceptually. For we call something honorable insofar as it has an excellence worthy of honor because of its spiritual beauty, and pleasurable insofar as it satisfies desire, and useful insofar as it is related to something else. But the pleasurable is in more things than the useful and the honorable are, since everything useful and honorable is somehow pleasurable, but not the converse.

8. Should we posit honorable character as part of temperance?[23]

Honorable character is a spiritual beauty. But the disgraceful is contrary to the beautiful, and contraries most manifest each another. And so honorable character seems to belong especially to temperance, which repels what is most disgraceful and unbecoming for a human being: namely, the lustful pleasures of irrational animals. And so we most understand the good of reason, to which moderating and tempering wicked sense desires belongs, in the very word *temperance*. Therefore, we reckon honorable character, which we ascribe to temperance by a special aspect, as an integral part of it in the form of a precondition, not as a subjective part of it or a connected virtue.

---

[22]Ibid., A. 3.   [23]Ibid., A. 4.

Subjective Parts Concerning Food and Drink

Abstinence is restraint in the consumption of food. Insofar as reason governs such restraint, abstinence is a moral virtue. Abstinence concerns restraint in the desire for the pleasures of food. Gluttony is an inordinate desire to eat and drink, and so a sin. It is a mortal sin if human beings seek gluttonous pleasures as their end, for the sake of which they are willing to act contrary to God's commands. It is a venial sin if human beings seek gluttonous pleasures as a means to be happy, not as something contrary to the laws of God. Gluttony is a serious sin insofar as it occasions other kinds of sin but less serious than other sins (e.g., sins against God), and the glutton is less culpable because of the need for food and the indeterminacy of what moderation in the consumption of food requires. We can consider the disorder of desire in gluttony in two ways. Regarding the substance or kind of food, a glutton seeks grand food or delicately prepared food or too much food. Regarding the consumption of food, a glutton seeks to eat too fast or rapaciously. Gluttony incites human beings to other sins: dullness of the senses necessary for the use of reason, unseemly joy, garrulousness, buffoonery, and bodily impurity.

Sobriety is a special virtue preserving reason from the impediment caused by intoxicating drink. Drinking alcoholic beverages is morally permissible unless one is in no fit condition to drink or has vowed not to drink, or the amount drunk is excessive, or the drinking scandalizes others. Sobriety is more necessary for youth, women, the elderly, clerics, and rulers. Drunkenness is a sin if the drinker immoderately desires or consumes alcohol, or the drinker becomes drunk out of negligence. Drunkenness is a venial sin if one knows that one's drinking is excessive but underestimates its power. Drunkenness is a mortal sin if one knows that one's drinking is excessive and overpowering but chooses to get drunk. Sins contrary to God are more serious than drunkenness. If the prior act of the will causing drunkenness is culpable, that act renders subsequent evil acts sinful, although the latter acts are less voluntary because of ignorance.

1. Is abstinence a virtue?[24]

The word *abstinence* signifies restraint in the consumption of food. Therefore, we can understand the word in two ways. We understand the word in one way insofar as it simply signifies abstaining from food, and abstinence in this way signifies something morally indifferent and neither a virtue nor a virtuous act. We can understand the word in a second way insofar as reason governs abstinence, and then the word signifies a virtuous habit or act.

---

[24]ST II-II, Q. 146, A. 1.

2. Is abstinence a special virtue?[25]

A moral virtue preserves the good of reason against the force of emotions, and so there needs to be a special virtue where there is a special aspect by which an emotion draws one away from the good of reason. But pleasures in food are of such a nature as to draw human beings away from the good of reason, both because the pleasures are great and because human beings need food to sustain their lives, which they most of all desire. And so abstinence is a special virtue.

3. Is gluttony a sin?[26]

Gluttony denotes an inordinate, not any, desire to eat and drink. But we call a desire inordinate because it withdraws one from the order of reason, of which the good of moral virtue consists; and we call anything contrary to a virtue a sin. And so gluttony is evidently a sin.

4. Is gluttony a mortal sin?[27]

Properly speaking, gluttony consists of inordinate sense desire. But the order of reason governing sense desire can be removed in two ways. The order of reason can be removed in one way regarding means to the end; namely, as the means are not so commensurate as to be proportioned to the end. The order of reason can be removed in a second way regarding the end itself; namely, as sense desire turns human beings away from their proper end. Therefore, if we understand the disorder of sense desire in gluttony as turning away from the ultimate end, then gluttony will be a mortal sin. And this happens when human beings adhere to gluttonous pleasure as the end for the sake of which they contemn God; namely, being prepared to act contrary to God's commands in order to obtain such pleasures. But if we understand the disorder of sense desire in the sin of gluttony only regarding means to the end, as in human beings excessively desiring the pleasures of food but not so that they would do something contrary to the law of God, gluttony is a venial sin.

5. Is gluttony the greatest sin?[28]

We can consider the gravity of a sin in three ways. First and chiefly, we can consider the gravity of a sin regarding the matter in which there is sin, and in this respect, sins regarding divine things are the greatest. And so the vice of gluttony will not be the greatest in this respect. Second, we can understand the gravity of a sin regarding the sinner, and the sin of gluttony is less rather than more serious in this respect. This is both because

---

[25]Ibid., A. 2.   [26]ST II-II, Q. 148, A. 1.   [27]Ibid., A. 2.   [28]Ibid., A. 3.

human beings need to consume food and because it is difficult to discern and regulate what is proper in consuming food. Third, we can consider the gravity of a sin regarding the effect resulting from the sin, and in this respect, the sin of gluttony is serious, since it occasions other kinds of sin.

6. Do we suitably distinguish the species of gluttony?[29]

Gluttony signifies an inordinate desire to consume food. But we consider two things in eating: namely, the food eaten and the eating of the food. Therefore, we can consider the disorder of desire in gluttony in two ways. We consider the disorder in one way regarding the food consumed. And then, regarding the substance or kind of food, one seeks grand—that is, costly—food; and regarding the quality of food, one seeks finely—that is, overzealously—prepared food; and regarding quantity, one exceeds the norm by eating too much. And we consider the disorder of desire in gluttony in a second way regarding the consumption of the food, either because one cuts short the proper length of time for eating, which is eating too hastily, or because one does not observe the proper way in eating, which is eating rapaciously.

7. Is gluttony a capital sin?[30]

A capital sin is one from which other sins arise by reason of its end; namely, inasmuch as the sin has such a strongly desired end that it incites human beings to sin in many ways. And an end is rendered very desirable because it has one of the conditions of happiness, which we by nature desire. But pleasure belongs to the nature of happiness. And so, because the sin of gluttony concerns pleasures of touch, which are the foremost pleasures, we appropriately posit gluttony as a capital sin.

8. Do we appropriately assign five effects of gluttony?[31]

Properly speaking, gluttony consists of intemperate pleasure in food and drink. And so we reckon the sins resulting from intemperate pleasure in food and drink as effects of gluttony, and we can understand such resulting sins regarding the soul or the body.

Four regard the soul. First, regarding reason, intemperate consumption of food or drink dulls keen wit, and we in this regard posit as a daughter of gluttony the dullness of the senses connected with understanding, since the vapors of foods disturb the brain. (Similarly but conversely, abstinence contributes to the perceptiveness of wisdom.) Second,

---

[29]Ibid., A. 4.   [30]Ibid., A. 5.   [31]Ibid., A. 6. Thomas, following Gregory the Great, calls these effects "daughters."

regarding the will, intemperate consumption of food and drink disorders it in many ways, as though the rule of reason has been lulled to sleep; and we in this regard posit unseemly joy, since all other inordinate emotions are directed to joy and sadness. Third, regarding inordinate speech, we posit garrulousness.

Fourth, regarding inordinate action, we posit buffoonery; that is, a jocularity resulting from lack of reason, which power can no more restrain the glutton's external gestures than it can restrain the glutton's speech. But we can relate both garrulousness and buffoonery to the speech in which there may be sin, either because of its superfluity, which belongs to garrulousness, or because of its dishonorable character, which belongs to buffoonery.

And regarding the body, we posit impurity, which we can consider regarding the inordinate discharge of any excess fluids or, specifically, the emission of semen.

9. Is intoxicating drink the proper matter of sobriety?[32]

Virtues designated by a general condition of virtue lay special claim to that matter in which it is most difficult and most virtuous to observe such a condition. For example, fortitude lays special claim to mortal dangers, and temperance to pleasures of touch. But we derive the word *sobriety* from measure, since we call someone sober who observes the *bria* (i.e., measure). And so sobriety lays special claim to matter in which observing the proper measure is most praiseworthy. But intoxicating drink is such a matter. For moderate consumption of intoxicating drink is very beneficial, and immoderate consumption very harmful, since the latter prevents the use of reason even more than excess of food does. And so we particularly consider sobriety about drink that is, by reason of its alcoholic content, of such a nature as to disturb the brain (e.g., wine or anything intoxicating), not about any kind of drink. But generally speaking, we can speak of sobriety regarding any matter.

10. Is sobriety as such a special virtue?[33]

It belongs to moral virtue to preserve the good of reason against things that can prevent reason. And so, where there is a special impediment to reason, there needs to be a special virtue to remove the impediment. But intoxicating drink has a special aspect of preventing the use of reason; namely, insofar as its alcoholic content disturbs the brain. And so a special virtue (i.e., sobriety) is necessary to remove this impediment to reason.

---

[32]ST II-II, Q. 149, A. 1.   [33]Ibid., A. 2.

11. Is consumption of wine completely unlawful?[34]

No food or drink, as such, is unlawful; and so drinking wine, absolutely speaking, is not unlawful, but it can be rendered such incidentally. This sometimes happens from the condition of the drinker, whom wine easily harms, or who is bound by a special vow to abstain from wine. And it sometimes happens from the mode of drinking; namely, in that one exceeds the measure in drinking. And it sometimes happens in relation to others, whom the drinking scandalizes.

12. Is sobriety more necessary in persons of greater importance?[35]

A virtue is related to two things: one, the contrary sins it excludes, and the desires it restrains; the second, the end to which it leads. Therefore, a virtue is more necessary in some persons for two reasons. The first reason is because some persons are more prone to the desires that the virtue needs to restrain, and to the sins that the virtue removes. And in this respect, sobriety is most necessary in youths and women, since the desire for pleasure of the senses is strong in youths because of their youthful ardor, and women do not have enough strength of mind to resist such desires. The second reason is because sobriety is more necessary for some persons for their proper activity. But intemperate consumption of wine especially prevents the use of reason. And so sobriety is especially appointed for the elderly, in whom reason should be strong in order to instruct others; and for bishops or any ministers of the church, who should fulfill their spiritual duties with a devout mind; and for kings, who should govern their subjects with wisdom.

13. Is drunkenness a sin?[36]

We can understand drunkenness in two ways. We understand it in one way to signify the very defect of a human being that results when one has drunk much wine and thereby become bereft of reason. And drunkenness in this respect designates the penal defect that results from a sin, not the sin. In a second way, drunkenness can designate the act whereby one falls into this defect, and the act can cause drunkenness in two ways. The act can cause drunkenness in one way by the wine being too strong, beyond the drinker's expectation; and then drunkenness may also happen without sin, especially if it should happen without negligence on the drinker's part. The act can cause drunkenness in a second way because of the drinker's inordinate desire and consumption of wine; and then we hold drunkenness to be a sin, a sin included in gluttony as one of its species.

---

[34]Ibid., A. 3.   [35]Ibid., A. 4.   [36]ST II-II, Q. 150, A. 1.

14. Is drunkenness a mortal sin?[37]

The sin of drunkenness consists of the immoderate consumption and desire of wine. But drunkenness happens in three ways. It happens in one way such that one does not know that one's drinking is excessive and powerful enough to make one drunk, and then we can understand the drunkenness to be without sin. It happens in a second way such that one perceives that one's drinking is excessive but does not think the drink is powerful enough to make one drunk, and then the drunkenness can be venially sinful. It can happen in a third way that one well knows that one's drinking is excessive and intoxicating, but prefers to get drunk rather than to abstain from drinking. And properly speaking, we call such a person a drunkard, since moral things get their species from what one intrinsically intends, not from things that result incidentally beyond one's intention. In such a case, drunkenness is a mortal sin. Because one in this regard knowingly and willingly deprives oneself of the use of reason, by which one acts virtuously and avoids sins, one sins mortally in committing oneself to the danger of sinning. And so drunkenness in the strict sense is a mortal sin.

Objection. One should never commit a mortal sin for a medicinal purpose. But some drink excessively on a doctor's advice in order to induce purgative vomiting, and drunkenness results from this excessive drinking. Therefore, drunkenness is not a mortal sin.

Reply Obj. We should moderate food and drink as they befit the body's health. And so, as it sometimes happens that the food and drink that are moderate for a healthy person are excessive for a sick person, so also, conversely, it can happen that the food and drink excessive for a healthy person are moderate for a sick person. Accordingly, we should not consider food or drink excessive if one eats or drinks a great deal on a doctor's advice in order to induce vomiting. (But it is not necessary that drinking should be intoxicating in order to induce vomiting, since even drinking warm water causes vomiting, and so one is not for this reason excused from drunkenness.)

15. Is drunkenness the most serious sin?[38]

Anything that takes away good is evil, and so the greater the good the evil takes away, the more serious the evil is. But the divine good is clearly greater than the human good. And so sins directly contrary to God are more serious than the sin of drunkenness, which is directly contrary to the good of human reason.

---

[37]Ibid., A. 2.   [38]Ibid., A. 3.

16. Does drunkenness excuse one from sin?[39]

We consider two things in drunkenness: namely, the resulting defect and the prior act. Regarding the resulting defect, in which the use of reason is fettered, drunkenness has the power to excuse one from sin, since drunkenness causes things to be involuntary because of one's ignorance. But it seems that we should distinguish regarding the prior act, since, if drunkenness has resulted from the prior act without sin, the subsequent sin is completely blameless. On the other hand, if the prior act was culpable, then one is not completely excused from the subsequent sin, which is rendered voluntary because one wills the prior act; namely, because a person engaged in something unlawful falls into the subsequent sin. Still, the subsequent sin is lessened, just as the voluntary character of the act is lessened.

Subjective Parts Concerning Sex

Chastity is a special virtue that restrains desires for sexual pleasure. Human beings are most ashamed of sexual intercourse, even marital intercourse, and external signs of sexual desire (e.g., lewd looks, kisses, and touches). But the signs are more likely to be witnessed, and so modesty regards them more than sexual intercourse itself.

Virginity is a special virtue and signifies that a woman is free of desire for sexual pleasure. The unbroken seal of virginity is incidentally related, the absence of sexual pleasure is materially related, and the intention to forego sexual pleasure is formally and perfectly related, to the moral disposition of the virgin. It is in accord with right reason for human beings to abstain from bodily pleasure in order to be freer to contemplate truth, and it is praiseworthy for religious virgins to abstain from all sexual pleasure in order to be freer to contemplate God. Virginity is more excellent than marriage because the divine good, which religious virgins contemplate, is more important than the human good, because the good of the soul is preferable to the good of the body, and because the good of the contemplative life is preferable to the good of the practical life. Virginity is the most excellent virtue in the genus of chastity, but the theological virtues (faith, hope, and charity) and acts of religion are preferable to virginity.

1. Is chastity a virtue?[40]

We derive the word *chastity* from the fact that reason chastises desire, which, like a child, needs to be restrained. But the nature of human virtue

---

[39]Ibid., A. 4.   [40]ST II-II, Q. 151, A. 1.

in this regard consists of things being moderated by reason. And so chastity is evidently a virtue.

2. Is chastity a virtue distinct from abstinence?[41]

Properly speaking, temperance concerns desires of pleasures of touch. And so different virtues need to be included in temperance where there are different kinds of pleasure. But pleasures are related to the actions of which they are the perfections. And actions related to the consumption of food, which preserves the nature of an individual, and actions related to the enjoyment of sex, which preserves the nature of the species, are clearly different kinds of action. And so chastity, which concerns sexual pleasures, is a virtue distinct from abstinence, which concerns the pleasures of food.

3. Does modesty belong especially to chastity?[42]

Properly speaking, modesty concerns things about which human beings are more ashamed. But human beings are most ashamed of sexual acts, so much so that even marital intercourse, which the honorable character of marriage adorns, is not without a sense of shame. And this is so because movements of the genital organs, unlike the movements of other external bodily members, are not subject to the command of reason. And human beings are ashamed about both sexual intercourse and any signs of it. And so, properly speaking, modesty concerns sexual matters and especially such signs of sex as lewd looks, kisses, and touches. And since we are more likely to see the latter things, sexual modesty more regards such external signs, while chastity more regards sexual intercourse itself. And so sexual modesty is directed to chastity as a virtue expressing a condition of chastity, not as a virtue distinct from it. But we sometimes posit the one for the other.

4. Does virginity consist of integrity of the flesh?[43]

We seem to derive the word *virginity* from greenness. And as we say that growth not parched by excessive heat retains its greenness, so also virginity signifies that a virgin is free from the heat of desire, which seems to be in the consummation of the greatest bodily pleasure: that is, the pleasure in sex. And so virginal chastity is integrity free of sexual contact.

And we need to consider three things regarding the pleasure in sex. One concerns the body; namely, breaking the seal of virginity. The second consists of the conjunction of what belongs to the soul and what belongs to the body; namely, the release of semen, which causes sense pleasure. And

---

[41]Ibid., A. 3.　　[42]Ibid., A. 4.　　[43]ST II-II, Q. 152, A. 1.

the third concerns only the soul; namely, the intention to achieve such pleasure. The first is incidentally related to the moral act, which we consider as such only by things that belong to the soul. The second is materially related to the moral act, since sensory emotions are the subject matter of moral acts. And the third is formally and perfectly related to the moral act, since the nature of morals is perfected in what belongs to reason.

Therefore, since we designate virginity by the aforementioned unbroken seal, integrity of the bodily member is incidentally related to virginity. And freedom from the pleasure that consists of the release of semen is materially related to virginity. And the intention always to abstain from such pleasure is related formally and perfectly to virginity.

5. Is virginity unlawful?[44]

Anything in human acts that is contrary to right reason is sinful. But right reason requires that one use means to an end in the measure that they are in accord with the end, and there are three kinds of human good. One consists of external things (e.g., riches); the second consists of bodily goods; and the third consists of goods of the soul, and goods of the theoretical life are still more important than goods of the practical life. And external goods are directed to bodily goods, and bodily goods to goods of the soul. Moreover, goods of the practical life are directed to goods of the theoretical life. Therefore, it belongs to right reason that one use external goods in the measure that they are proper for the body, and so forth. And so if one, for the sake of bodily health or contemplating truth, should abstain from possessing certain things, which it would otherwise be good to possess, this would be in accord with right reason and not sinful. Likewise, if one should abstain from bodily pleasures in order to be freer to contemplate truth, this belongs to right reason; and religious virginity abstains from all sexual pleasure in order to be freer for divine contemplation. And so virginity is worthy of praise rather than something contrary to virtue.

Objection. Everything contrary to a precept of the natural law is unlawful. But as there is a precept of the natural law for the preservation of the individual, so also there is a precept of the natural law for the preservation of the species. Therefore, as one who were to abstain from all food would sin by acting contrary to the good of the individual, so also one who completely abstains from the act of reproduction sins by acting contrary to the good of the species.

Reply Obj. A precept has the nature of something required, but something is required in two ways. In one way, an individual should fulfill, and cannot without sin omit, what is required. In the second way, the commu-

---

[44]Ibid., A. 2.

nity should fulfill what is required. And not every human being is obliged to fulfill such a duty, since one individual does not suffice to fulfill many things necessary for the community, and the community fulfills them when one individual does this and another does that.

Therefore, individual human beings need to fulfill the precept of the natural law laid down for them about eating, since an individual could not otherwise be preserved. But the precept laid down about reproduction concerns the whole human community, for which it is necessary that it both increase materially and progress spiritually. And so it is sufficiently provided for the human community if some persons should devote themselves to carnal reproduction, and some persons, abstaining from such activity, should be free to contemplate divine things for the adornment and welfare of the whole human race. Just so, some soldiers guard the camp, some bear the army's standards, and some fight, but all of these things are required for the army as a corps, and no one unit of the army can fulfill all of the requirements.

6. Is virginity a virtue?[45]

The formal and perfect element, as it were, in virginity is the intention always to abstain from sexual pleasure; and the end of virginity—namely, as undertaken to be free for divine things—renders this intention praiseworthy. The material element in virginity is the integrity of the flesh without any experience of sexual pleasure. But it is clear that there is a special character of virtue where there is a special subject matter that has a special excellence. This is clear, for example, in magnificence, which consists of wealthy citizens' funding of great public events and so constitutes a special virtue distinct from generosity, which governs the use of money in general. And preserving oneself free of the experience of sexual pleasure is more praiseworthy than preserving oneself free of disordered sexual pleasure. And so virginity is a special virtue that is related to chastity as magnificence is to generosity.

7. Is virginity more excellent than marriage?[46]

Virginity is a greater good than marriage because the divine good is more important than the human good, because the good of the soul is preferable to the good of the body, and because the good of the theoretical life is preferable to the good of the practical life. And virginity is directed to the good of the soul regarding the theoretical life, that is, contemplation of divine things; while the good of spouses is directed to the good of the body, that is, the material increase of the human race. But the latter belongs to the

---

[45]Ibid., A. 3.   [46]Ibid., A. 4.

practical life, since husbands and wives need to think about worldly things. And so virginity should undoubtedly be preferred to marital moderation.

Objection. Praise of a virtuous person depends on the person's virtue. Therefore, if virginity were preferable to marital moderation, it seems that every virgin would then be more praiseworthy than any spouse. But this conclusion is false. Therefore, virginity is not preferable to marriage.

Reply Obj. Although virginity is better than marital moderation, a spouse may nonetheless be better than a virgin. This is so for two reasons. First, a spouse may be better than a virgin regarding chastity itself; namely, if the spouse should have a more ready mind to preserve virginity, if it were needed, than one who is actually a virgin does. Second, a spouse may be better than a virgin because one who is not a virgin perhaps has a more excellent virtue.

8. Is virginity the greatest virtue?[47]

We can call something most excellent in two ways. We call something most excellent in one way generically. And virginity is the most excellent virtue in this way; namely, in the genus of chastity, since virginity is more excellent than the chastity of both widows and spouses. And because we attribute beauty to chastity by synecdoche, we attribute the most excellent beauty to virginity.

In a second way, we can call something most excellent absolutely. And virginity is not the most excellent virtue in this way. For an end always surpasses the means to the end, and the more efficaciously something is directed to the end, the better it is. But the end that renders virginity praiseworthy is a person's freedom for divine things. And so the theological virtues themselves and the virtue of religion, whose acts consist of the very occupation with divine things, are preferable to virginity.

Likewise, martyrs, who discount their lives in order to cling to God, and monks and nuns, who discount their will and all possible possessions in order to cling to God, work more energetically for that end than do virgins, who discount sexual pleasures for that end. And so virginity is not the absolutely greatest virtue.

Sexual Lust

We most consider lust regarding wanton sexual pleasure. One can use sex without sin if one does so in the proper way and order, as suitable for human reproduction. Anything in the use of sex done contrary to the order of reason is

---

[47]Ibid., A. 5.

sinful, and so sexual lust is a sin. Sexual lust is a capital sin because many sins arise from it. There are six species of sexual lust: sins contrary to nature and simple fornication, which are contrary to the end of the sex act, and incest, adultery, seduction of a virgin, and rape, which are contrary to the proper relation to other persons.

Simple fornication is a mortal sin because it tends to harm the life of an offspring by depriving the offspring of its father's care. Fornication is a more serious sin than one against property (e.g., theft) but a lesser sin than one against the life of an existing human being (homicide). Touches and kisses are mortal sins only if unmarried people touch and kiss for the sake of sexual pleasure.

Nocturnal emission is not sinful unless it is the product of the person's prior carnal thoughts.

Seduction of a virgin is a distinct species of sexual lust both because it causes the woman to lose her reputation, and because it lacks respect for her father.

Rape is a distinct species of sexual lust because it involves the use of force against a virgin or her father (if she is abducted from his house), or both.

Adultery is a distinct species of sexual lust regarding both the man and the married woman committing adultery. The man prevents the good of an offspring's upbringing and hinders the good of the woman's legitimate children. The woman sins against her husband by creating doubt about who is the father of the offspring and against the good of her legitimate offspring.

Incest is a distinct species of sexual lust for several reasons. First, blood relatives closely trace their origin to the same parents, to whom human beings owe respect, and human beings are ashamed of sexual acts between blood relatives. Second, if sexual union of blood relatives were permissible, there would be too much opportunity for it, and sexual lust would sap the participants' minds. Third, such unions would prevent human beings from having the broad range of friends that one's wife' s blood relatives offer. Fourth, such unions would be too ardent and incite sexual lust.

Sacrilege can be a distinct species of sexual lust insofar as sexual lust violates something belonging to the worship of God (e.g., sexual union with one who has vowed to observe virginity).

Sins contrary to nature are a distinct species of sexual lust because they are contrary to the natural order of the sex act proper to human beings. This happens in four ways: emission of semen without intercourse (impurity with oneself); intercourse with animals (bestiality); intercourse with the same sex (sodomy); and use of an improper instrument or other beastly ways of copulating.

Human beings in sexual sins contrary to nature transgress what nature prescribes about the use of sex, and so such sins are the most serious sexual sins. Incest is the next most serious because it is contrary to the respect one owes to one's relatives. The next most serious sexual sins involve injury to another (adultery, seduction of a virgin, and rape). Simple fornication is the least species of sexual lust.

1. Does the subject matter of lust consist only of sexual desires and pleasures?[48]

A lustful person is dissolute in pleasures. But sexual pleasures most dissolve the minds of human beings. And so we most consider lust regarding sexual pleasures.

Objection. We call lust the desire of wanton pleasure. But there is wanton pleasure in sex and many other things. Therefore, lust does not concern only sexual desires and pleasures.

Reply Obj. Although we speak of wanton pleasure regarding other matters than sex, sexual pleasures lay special claim to being such, and we particularly speak of lust in this regard.

2. Can a sexual act be sinless?[49]

Sin in human acts is anything contrary to the order of reason. But the order of reason consists of suitably directing each thing to its end. And so there is no sin if human beings, through reason, use particular things in a fitting manner and order for the end for which they exist, provided that the end is something truly good. But as it is truly good that an individual's bodily nature be preserved, so also it is a worthy good that the nature of the human species be preserved. And as the use of food is directed to preserving the life of an individual human being, so also the use of sex is directed to preserving the whole human race. And so, as one can use food without sin if done in the proper way and order, as proper for the welfare of the body, so also one can use sex without any sin if one does so in the proper way and order, as suitable for the end of human reproduction.

3. Can sexual lust be a sin?[50]

The more necessary something is, the more necessary it is that one should observe the order of reason regarding it, and so the more sinful it is if one were to neglect the order of reason. But the use of sex is very necessary for the common good, that is, the preservation of the human race; and so we should most consider the order of reason regarding it. And so anything in this regard done contrary to the order of reason will be sinful. But it belongs to the nature of sexual lust to exceed the order and measure of reason regarding sex. And so sexual lust is undoubtedly a sin.

---

[48]ST II–II, Q. 153, A. 1.   [49]Ibid., A. 2.   [50]Ibid., A. 3.

4. Is sexual lust a capital sin?[51]

A capital sin is one that has a very desirable end, so that human beings by such desire go on to commit many sins, which we say arise from that sin as their source. But the end of sexual lust is sexual pleasure, which is the greatest pleasure. And so such pleasure is most desirable regarding sense appetite, both because of the force of the desire and because of the compatibility of the desire with nature. And so sexual lust is clearly a capital sin.

5. Do we appropriately designate six species of sexual lust?[52]

The sin of sexual lust consists of one's enjoyment of sexual pleasure contrary to right reason. And this happens in two ways: in one way, regarding the matter in which one seeks such pleasure; in a second way, as one does not observe other proper conditions when the matter is proper. Because circumstances as such do not specify moral acts, and we understand the species of the acts from their object, which is their matter, we need to designate the species of sexual lust regarding the matter or object.

The matter may not conform to right reason in two ways. It may not conform in one way because it is contrary to the end of the sexual act. And so, insofar as the generation of offspring is prevented, there is a sin against nature in every sex act from which the generation of offspring cannot result. And there is a sin of simple fornication in the case of sexual intercourse between an unmarried man and an unmarried woman, since such intercourse prevents the proper upbringing and development of offspring.

In a second way, the matter in which one performs the sexual act can be contrary to right reason in its relation to other persons, and this happens in two ways. It happens in one way regarding the woman with whom a man has intercourse, since the man does not observe proper respect for her. And so there is a sin of incest, which consists of the abuse of women related by blood or marriage. It happens in a second way regarding the man who has custody over the woman. If the woman is subject to her husband, there is a sin of adultery; and if the woman is subject to her father, there is a sin of seduction of a virgin if there is no use of force, and a sin of rape if there is. These species differ regarding the woman rather than the man, since a woman is disposed as the passive and material party, and a man as the active party, and we designate the aforementioned species by their different matter.

---

[51]Ibid., A. 4. [52]ST II-II, Q. 154, A. 1.

6. Is simple fornication a mortal sin?[53]

We should undoubtedly hold that simple fornication is a mortal sin. To prove this, we should consider that every sin committed directly against the life of a human being is a mortal sin, and simple fornication signifies a disorder that tends to harm the life of the offspring to be born of this union. For we perceive that in all animals in which the upbringing of the offspring requires care by the male and the female (e.g., all birds), there is a sexual union of a male with a definite female, whether one or several, and not a casual sexual union. But it is otherwise in animals in which the female alone suffices for the upbringing of the offspring (e.g., dogs and like animals), and these animals form casual sexual unions.

And it is clear that the upbringing of human beings requires both care by the mother, who feeds the offspring, and, much more, care by the father, who needs to guide and guard the offspring and advance the offspring in both internal and external goods. And so it is contrary to the nature of human beings to have a casual sexual union. Rather, there needs to be a sexual union of a man with a definite woman, with whom the man remains for a long time or even for the whole of life, not for a short period of time. And so males of the human species naturally have concern to ascertain their fatherhood of the offspring, since the upbringing of the offspring falls on them; and this certitude would be removed if there were to be a casual sexual union.

We call this determination of union with a definite woman marriage, and so we say that it belongs to the natural law. But since sexual union is directed to the common good of the whole human race, and common goods fall within determination by law, laws determine the union of men and women, which we call marriage. And so fornication, since it is a casual sexual union outside marriage, is contrary to the good of the offspring to be brought up, and so it is a mortal sin.

Nor does it matter if an individual who fornicates with a woman should sufficiently provide for the offspring regarding its upbringing. This is because we judge what falls within the determination of law by what generally happens, not by what can happen in a particular case.

Objection. Sexual union is to the welfare of the race what food is to the welfare of the body. But not every inordinate use of food is a mortal sin. Therefore, neither is every inordinate sexual union. And this seems most true about simple fornication, which is the least species of sexual lust.

Reply Obj. One sexual union can beget a human being. And so an inordinate sexual union, which prevents the good of the offspring who is to be

---

[53]Ibid., A. 2.

born, is a mortal sin because of the nature of the act and not only because of inordinate desire. But one meal does not prevent the good of a human being's whole life, and so a gluttonous act is not by its nature a mortal sin. But a gluttonous act would be if one were knowingly to eat food that would alter the whole condition of one's life, as was the case with Adam. Nor is fornication the least sin included under sexual lust, since sexual union with one's wife out of lust is a lesser sin than fornication.

7. Is fornication the most serious sin?[54]

We can note the seriousness of sin in two ways: in one way in itself; in a second way as incidental. We note the seriousness of a sin in itself by reason of its species, which we consider by the good of which the sin is the contrary. But fornication is contrary to the good of the human being who is to be born. And so it is specifically a more serious sin than sins contrary to external goods, sins such as theft and the like; but less serious than sins directly contrary to God and sins contrary to the life of an existing human being, such as the sin of homicide.

Objection. The more a sin results from greater wanton desire, the more serious the sin seems to be. But the greatest wanton desire is in fornication, since the wanton passion in sexual lust is the greatest. Therefore, it seems that fornication is the most serious sin.

Reply Obj. The wanton desire making a sin more serious consists of the inclination of the will. But the wanton desire in sense appetites makes a sin less serious, since the greater the emotion that impels one to sin is, the less serious the sin is. And the wanton desire in fornication is the greatest in this respect.

8. Is there mortal sin in touches and kisses?[55]

We call something a mortal sin in two ways. We call something a mortal sin in one way specifically; and kisses, embraces, and touches do not by their nature designate mortal sin in this way. For one can do these things without lust, whether because of the customs of one's country or because of a duty or reasonable cause.

In a second way, we call something a mortal sin by reason of its motive, as, for example, one who gives alms to induce another to heresy sins mortally because of one's evil intention. And consent to the pleasure in a mortal sin, and not only consent to a sinful act, is a mortal sin. And so, since fornication is a mortal sin, and much more the other species of sexual lust, consent to the pleasure in such sins—and not only consent to the sinful

---

[54]Ibid., A. 3.   [55]Ibid., A. 4.

acts—is a mortal sin. And so, if one should engage in kissing, embracing, and the like for the sake of such pleasure, these acts are mortal sins. Only then do we call them lustful. And so such acts, insofar as they are lustful, are mortal sins.

Objection. We call fornication a mortal sin because it prevents the good of the offspring to be begotten and brought up. But kisses and touches, or embraces, do nothing to prevent that good. Therefore, there is no mortal sin in these things.

Reply Obj. Kisses and touches, although they do not in themselves prevent the good of a human offspring, result from lust, which is the cause that prevents that good. And so they have the character of mortal sin.

9. Is nocturnal emission a mortal sin?[56]

We can consider nocturnal emission in two ways. We can consider it in one way in itself, and then it does not have the character of sin. For every sin rests on a judgment of reason, since even the first movement of a sense appetite is sinful only insofar as a judgment of reason can stop the movement. And so the character of sin is taken away when the judgment of reason is taken away. But one does not have free judgment while sleeping, since sleepers attend to particular imaginary representations as real things. And so we do not impute to a human being as sin what a human being does while asleep without the free judgment of reason, just as we do not impute to a human being what a lunatic or imbecile does.

We can, in a second way, consider nocturnal emission in relation to its cause. And there can be three kinds of causes. One is material. For if there should be overabundant seminal fluid, or if the fluid should be released, whether because of overabundant heat in the body or because of any other disturbance, the sleeper would dream about things belonging to the emission of the overabundant or released fluid. The like happens when any other superfluity burdens nature, so that the imagination sometimes forms sense images related to the emission of such superfluities. Therefore, if the overabundance of such fluid is due to a culpable cause (e.g., too much food or drink), then nocturnal emission has the character of wrongdoing by reason of its cause. But if the overabundance or release of such fluid is not due to any culpable cause, then nocturnal emission is not culpable, neither in itself nor in its cause.

A second cause of nocturnal emission can be immaterial and internal (e.g., when a prior thought causes a sleeper to have a nocturnal emission). A prior thought when the sleeper was awake is sometimes purely theoretical (e.g., when one, for the sake of discussion, thinks about carnal sins),

---

[56]Ibid., A. 5.

and sometimes with a feeling of desire or repugnance. But nocturnal emission happens more from thought about carnal sins that was accompanied by the desire for such pleasures. This is so because a vestige and inclination in the soul from this abide, so that a sleeper is more easily led in imagination to assent to the acts from which emission results. And then nocturnal emission evidently has the character of sin regarding its cause. And nocturnal emission during sleep may also sometimes result from prior theoretical thought about carnal acts, even if the thought should be repugnant. And then nocturnal emission does not have the character of sin, neither in itself nor in its cause.

The third cause of nocturnal emission is immaterial and external (e.g., when the activity of the devil disturbs the sense images of the sleeper in order to produce such an effect). And this may sometimes be in conjunction with a prior sin; namely, negligence in preparing oneself against his illusions. But this is sometimes entirely due to the wickedness of the devil and without any sin by a human being.

Therefore, it is clear that nocturnal emission is never a sin, but is sometimes the consequence of a prior sin.

10. Should we posit seduction of a virgin as a species of sexual lust?[57]

There should be a distinct species of sin when there is a special deformity regarding the matter of a sin. But sexual lust concerns sexual matters, and there is a special deformity if a virgin in the custody of her father is violated. There is a special deformity regarding the maiden, who is prevented from acquiring a lawful marriage as a result of being violated outside the bond of marriage and led down the road to a wanton life, from which the fear of losing the seal of virginity would restrain her. There is also a special deformity regarding her father, who has custodial care over her. And so it is clear that seduction of a virgin, which signifies the unlawful violation of virgins under the care of their parents, is a fixed species of sexual lust.

11. Is rape a distinct species of sexual lust?[58]

Rape, as we are now speaking about it, is a species of sexual lust. Rape sometimes coincides with and sometimes occurs without seduction, and seduction sometimes occurs without rape. They coincide when a man uses force to violate a virgin unlawfully. And a man sometimes uses force against both the virgin herself and her father, and sometimes against the father but not the virgin—as, for example, if the virgin herself consents to

---

[57]Ibid., A. 6. [58]Ibid., A. 7.

being forcibly abducted from her father's house. The force used in rape varies in a second way, since a maiden is sometimes forcibly abducted from her parents' house and forcibly violated; and sometimes, although forcibly abducted, not forcibly violated but willingly corrupted. (There can be rape in both fornication and marital intercourse, since the nature of rape remains howsoever force is used.)

And there is rape without seduction of a virgin, as, for example, if a man rapes a widow or a maiden no longer a virgin.

And there is seduction of a virgin without rape when a man unlawfully violates a virgin without the use of force.

12. Is adultery a distinct species of sexual lust?[59]

To commit adultery is to enter the marriage bed of another. And in so doing, a man sins against chastity and the good of human generation in two ways. First, he so sins because he enters a woman not united to him in marriage, such union being necessary for the good of bringing up his off-spring. He sins in a second way because he enters a woman united to another man in marriage, and so he hinders the good of the other man's offspring. The argument is the same regarding the married woman whom adultery corrupts. And so a woman who commits adultery sins against the law of God, against her husband by creating doubt about who is the father of the offspring, and against the good of her legitimate children by begetting offspring from another man. Sinning against the law of God is common to all mortal sins, but the other two things belong particularly to the deformity of adultery. And so adultery, as having a special deformity regarding sexual acts, is clearly a fixed species of sexual lust.

13. Is incest a distinct species of sexual lust?[60]

There needs to be a distinct species of sexual lust when there is something contrary to the proper use of sex. But there is something improper about having sexual union with women related by blood or marriage, for three reasons. First, such intercourse is improper because human beings naturally owe respect to their parents and so to other blood relatives, who closely trace their origin to the same parents. But human beings are ashamed of sexual acts with blood relatives. And so it is improper that there be a sexual union with such persons.

The second reason is because blood relatives need to live together in close association with one another. And so, if they were not barred from sexual union, they would be offered too much opportunity for it, and then sexual lust would sap their minds too much.

---

[59]Ibid., A. 8.   [60]Ibid., A. 9.

The third reason is because such union would prevent human beings from having a broad range of friends. For when a man weds a woman unrelated by blood, all the wife's blood relatives are joined to him in a special bond of friendship, as if the wife's relatives were his own.

And there is a fourth reason. Since a man naturally loves a woman who is a blood relative, there would be too ardent love and the greatest incentive of sexual lust, which is contrary to chastity, if the love from sexual union were to be added.

And so incest is clearly a fixed species of sexual lust.

Objection. Whatever does not of itself signify a deformity does not constitute a distinct species of sin. But to enter women related by blood or marriage is not in itself deformed. Otherwise, it would have never been lawful [as in the Old Testament]. Therefore, incest is not a distinct species of sexual lust.

Reply Obj. There is something in itself unbecoming and contrary to natural reason in the sexual union of some blood relatives (e.g., sexual union between parents and their children, who are directly and immediately related). For children naturally owe respect to their parents. But other persons related through relationship to their parents, not immediately, do not of themselves have such unsuitability for sexual union. Rather, becomingness and unbecomingness in this regard vary according to custom and human or divine law. This is because the use of sex is ordered to the common good and so subject to law.

14. Can sacrilege be a species of sexual lust?[61]

The act of one virtue or vice directed to the end of another virtue or vice assumes the species of the latter. For example, a theft committed for the sake of adultery passes into the species of adultery, and observance of chastity as directed to the worship of God (e.g., by those who vow and observe virginity) is clearly an act of religion. And so it is clear that sexual lust, insofar as it violates something belonging to the worship of God, likewise belongs to the species of sacrilege. And so we can posit sacrilege as a species of sexual lust in this regard.

15. Is a sexual sin contrary to nature a species of sexual lust?[62]

There is a distinct species of sexual lust when there is a special character of deformity that makes the sexual act unbecoming. And this can be such in two ways. It happens in one way because the sexual act is contrary to right reason, which is common to every sin of sexual lust. It happens in

---

[61]Ibid., A. 10.   [62]Ibid., A. 11.

a second way because the sexual act is also contrary to the natural order of the sexual act proper to the human species, and we call this a sin contrary to nature. And this can happen in several ways.

It happens in one way if one should procure the emission of semen for the sake of sexual pleasure without any intercourse, and this belongs to the sin of impurity with oneself, which some call effeminacy.

It happens in a second way if one copulates with something not of the human species, and we call this the sin of bestiality.

It happens in a third way if one copulates with the improper sex (e.g., a man with a man, or a woman with a woman), and we call this the sin of sodomy.

It happens in a fourth way if one does not observe the natural way of copulating, whether as to the use of an improper means or as to other monstrous and beastly ways of copulating.

16. Is a sexual sin contrary to nature the greatest sin of the species of sexual lust?[63]

The worst corruption in any genus is the corruption of the genus' source, on which other things in the genus depend. But the first principles of reason are things in accord with nature, since reason, with the things determined by nature presupposed, disposes other things insofar as the disposition is fitting. And this is clear in both theoretical and practical matters. And so, as the most serious and most shameful error in theoretical matters concerns things that nature endows human beings to know, so the most serious and shameful thing in practical matters is to act contrary to things determined by nature. Therefore, since human beings in sexual sins contrary to nature transgress what nature determines regarding the use of sex, the sins are the most serious sins regarding such subject matter. The next most serious sin is incest, which is contrary to the natural respect that one owes to one's relatives.

And other species of sexual lust omit only something determined by right reason, although they presuppose the natural first principles. But it is more contrary to reason that one use sex both contrary to what befits the offspring to be generated, and with injury to another. And so simple fornication, which one commits without injury to another person, is the least species of sexual lust.

And it is a greater wrong if one should abuse a woman subject to the power of another with respect to sexual intercourse than if one should abuse a woman only with respect to her custody. And so adultery is more

---

[63]Ibid., A. 12.

serious than seduction of a virgin. And the use of force makes both more serious. Therefore, rape of a virgin is more serious than her seduction, and rape of a married woman more serious than adultery. And the aspect of sacrilege makes all of these things more serious.

Objection 1. The more contrary to charity a sin is, the more serious the sin is. But adultery, seduction of a virgin, and rape, which tend toward injury of neighbor, seem more contrary to love of neighbor than sexual sins contrary to nature, which injure no one else. Therefore, sexual sins contrary to nature are not the greatest species of sexual lust.

Reply Obj. 1. As the order of right reason is from human beings, so the order of nature is from God himself. And so, in sexual sins contrary to nature, in which one violates the very order of nature, there is a wrong against God himself, who establishes the order of nature.

Obj. 2. If sexual sins contrary to nature are the most serious sexual sins, it seems that the more a sin is contrary to nature, the more serious the sin is. But the sin of impurity with oneself, or effeminacy, seems to be most contrary to nature, since it seems to be most in accord with nature that different things are active and passive. Therefore, impurity with one-self is, in this respect, the most serious sexual sin contrary to nature. But this conclusion is false. Therefore, there are sexual sins contrary to nature that are not the most serious sins of sexual lust.

Reply Obj. 2. We note the gravity of a sin by the abuse of something, rather than by the omission of the thing's proper use. And so the sin of impurity with oneself, which consists merely of the omission of copulating with another, holds the lowest rank of sexual sins contrary to nature. The sin of bestiality, in which one does not observe the proper species, is the most serious sexual sin contrary to nature. The sin of sodomy, in which one does not observe the proper sex, is the second most serious sexual sin contrary to nature. And the sin of not observing the proper way of copulating is the third most serious sexual sin contrary to nature, and more serious if one should use an improper means than if the disorder should regard any other things belonging to the way of copulating.

Glossary

Action: *activity.* There are two basic kinds of activity. One kind, transitive activity, produces an effect in something else. The other kind, immanent activity, is a perfection of the very being that acts. Immanent action produces effects in living finite beings. Plants have the immanent activities of nutrition, growth, and reproduction. Animals have, in addition, the immanent activities of sense perception and sense appetites. Human beings have, in addition, the immanent activities of intellection and willing. *See* Cause.

Appetite *the desire or striving of finite beings for some good.* Nonliving material beings have only so-called natural appetites. Plants have, in addition, vegetative appetites of nutrition, growth, and reproduction. Animals have, in addition, sense appetites. Human beings have, in addition, an intellectual (rational) appetite, the will. *See* Concupiscible, Irascible, Will.

Beatific Vision: *the intellectual intuition of God's essence.* This is the ultimate end of human beings. *See* Happiness.

Cause: *something that contributes to the being or the coming-to-be of something else.* The term refers primarily to an efficient cause; that is, a cause that, by its activity, produces an effect. For example, a builder and those who work under the builder are efficient causes of the house they construct. A final cause is the end for the sake of which an efficient cause acts. For example, a builder builds a house to provide a dwelling suitable for human habitation (objective end) and to make money if the house is to be sold (subjective end). An exemplary cause is the idea or model of a desired effect in the mind of an intellectual efficient cause that preconceives the effect. Efficient, final, and exemplary causes are extrinsic to the effects they produce. In addition, form, which makes an effect to be what it is, and matter, which receives the form, are correlative intrinsic causes. For example, houses are composed of bricks and mortar (the matter), which are given a structure or shape (the form). *See* End, Form, Matter.

Charity: *the infused supernatural virtue that characteristically disposes human beings to love God above all things and to love all other things for his sake. See* Virtue.

Concupiscence: *the inclination of human beings' sense appetites toward actions contrary to reason. The inclination is not completely subject to reason.* Concupiscence is not to be identified with the concupiscible appetites as such. *See* Concupiscible, Will.

Concupiscible: *a sense appetite for something pleasant.* Love and hate, desire and aversion, joy and sorrow are emotions of concupiscible appetites. *See* Appetite, Irascible.

Conscience: *the dictate of reason that one should or should not do something. See Synderesis.*

Emotions: *movements of sense appetites.* Emotions may be ordinate (in accord with right reason) or inordinate (contrary to right reason). Emotions involve either desire for pleasant things or repugnance regarding difficult things. *See* Concupiscible, Irascible, Moral Virtues.

End: *the object for the sake of which something acts.* The end may be intrinsic or extrinsic. The end is intrinsic if it belongs to the nature of an active thing. The end is extrinsic if it is the conscious object of a rational being's action. *See* Cause, Intention.

Equity: *fundamental fairness, or natural justice, in human relations.* Human laws cannot anticipate all contingencies, and it is sometimes contrary to justice and the common good to observe the laws (e.g., laws requiring the return of property to its owner in the case of a sword to an owner who is out of his mind). Therefore, one should sometimes follow what justice and the common good require, not the letter of the law. *See* Law.

Essence: *that which makes things what they substantially are.* For example, the human essence makes human beings to be what they are as substances; namely, rational animals. The essence of a being, when considered as the ultimate source of the being's activities and development, is called the being's nature. For example, human nature is the ultimate source of specifically human activities (activities of reason and activities according to reason). *See* Form, Property (2).

Form: *that which determines things to be the specific kind of thing they are or to possess additional attributes.* For example, the human form (the human soul) makes human beings human, and other forms make them so tall and so heavy. Form constitutes the essence of all finite immaterial things, but matter needs to individuate form to constitute the essence of material things. *See* Essence, Matter, Species.

Fortitude (Courage): *the moral virtue consisting of the right characteristic disposition to withstand and resist fear of the greatest difficulties, namely, mortal dangers, that hinder the will from acting in accord with right reason.* Fortitude involves endurance and moderate boldness in attacking the cause of such fear. Secondary virtues related to fortitude concern fear of lesser difficulties (e.g., patience and perseverance in physically, psychologically, or morally difficult situations). *See* Moral Virtues, Virtue.

Genus: *See* Species.

Habit: *characteristic human disposition.* Habits concern being or acting in a certain way and belong chiefly to faculties of the soul; namely, the intellect and the will. Habits may be innate or acquired, natural or supernatural, good or bad. For example, the habit of logical argumentation belongs to the intellect; the habit of justice belongs to the will; the habits of the first principles of theoretical and practical reason are innate; the habit of cleanliness is acquired; the habit of courage is natural; the habit of faith is supernatural; the habit of generosity is good; the habit of stinginess is bad. Habits belong secondarily to the body, as the latter is disposed or made apt to be readily at the service of the soul's activities. *See* Virtue.

Happiness: *the perfect attainment of the ultimate good, that is, the end, for which human beings by nature desire and strive.* Happiness as such is an objective state of perfection, not a subjective state of euphoria, although human beings possessing the state of perfection will experience joy and satisfaction. For Aristotle, human beings become happy—that is, achieve the state of perfection—by engaging in activities of reason and living in accord with right reason. For Aquinas, human beings can only be perfectly happy when they behold God as he is in himself, although activities of reason and activities in accord with right reason bring human beings to a state of imperfect happiness in this life. *See* Beatific Vision, End.

Intellect: *the human faculty of understanding, judging, and reasoning.* Aquinas, following Aristotle, holds that each human being has two intellectual powers: one active and the other passive. The active intellect causes the passive—that is, potential—intellect to understand the essence of material things, to form judgments, and to reason deductively. *See* Reason.

Intellectual Virtues: *virtues consisting of the right characteristic disposition of the intellect toward truth.* Theoretical intellectual virtues concern first principles, scientific knowledge, and theoretical wisdom. Practical intellectual virtues concern prudence and skills. *See* Principle, Prudence, Science, Theoretical Wisdom.

Intention: *an act of the will tending toward something.* The human will necessarily tends toward the human end (happiness) and freely toward means to the end, which are only imperfectly good and so subject to choice. Human beings are morally responsible for the evil they intend or fail to take reasonable care to avoid. *See* End, Happiness, Will.

Irascible: *a sense appetite for a useful object, and one can obtain the object only by overcoming opposition.* Fear and anger are emotions of irascible appetites. Unlike the objects of concupiscible appetites, the objects of irascible appetites do not seem pleasant. *See* Appetite, Concupiscible.

Justice: *the moral virtue consisting of the right characteristic disposition of the will to render to others what one owes them.* This is the special virtue of justice, and there are two particular kinds. One kind, commutative justice, concerns the duties of individuals and groups to other individuals and groups (including the community as a corporate entity). The other kind, distributive justice, concerns the duties of the community to insure that individuals and groups receive a share of the community's goods proportional to the individuals' and the groups' contributions to the community. But justice in general is moral virtue in general, insofar as all moral virtues can be directed to the common good. Aquinas and Aristotle call such justice legal justice because the laws of the political community prescribe the moral virtues of citizens. *See* Moral Virtues, Virtues.

Kingly Prudence: *the archetype of political prudence; that is, prudence in governance.* *See* Political Prudence, Prudence.

Law: *an order of reason, for the common good, by one with authority, and promulgated.* For Aquinas, the archetypical law is God's plan for the universe and each kind of thing he creates. Aquinas calls this plan the eternal law. Human beings, as rational creatures, can understand God's plan for them as human beings and can judge what behavior it requires of them. Aquinas calls this participation in the eternal law the natural law. The general (primary) precepts of the natural law are that human beings should preserve their lives, mate and raise offspring, seek truth, and live in communion with other human beings. Human laws either adopt conclusions from the general precepts (e.g., *do not commit murder*) or further specify the precepts (e.g., *drive on the right side of the road*). He calls those human laws that are proximate conclusions from the general precepts of the natural law, the common law of peoples (*jus gentium*); and those human laws that are more remote conclusions from, or further specifications of, the general precepts, civil laws. There is, in addition, divine law: the Old Law for the Jewish people before the coming of Christ, and the New Law after his coming. *See* Political Community.

Matter: *the stuff or subject matter out of which things are constituted.* *See* Cause, Form.

Moral Virtues: *virtues consisting of the right characteristic disposition of the will toward the ends that reason prescribes for human actions: namely, that* *they be just, courageous, and moderate.* Reason directs moral virtues: theoretical reason by understanding their ends, and prudence (practical wisdom) by choosing means to the ends. Moral virtues concern the mean between too much and too little. The chief moral virtues are justice, fortitude, and temperance. Justice concerns external things, and fortitude and temperance concern control of emotions. *See* Emotions, Fortitude, Justice, Prudence, Temperance, Virtue.

Nature: *See* Essence.

Political Community: *the organized society in which human beings seek their proper well-being and excellence.* Like Aristotle, Aquinas holds that human beings are by their nature social and political animals. Human beings need to cooperate for self-defense and economic development, but they also and especially need to associate with one another for their full intellectual and moral development. Only an organized community of a certain size can be self-sufficient to achieve these goals. Political community thus differs from the state, which is the supreme agency responsible for organizing the community; and from government, which is the machinery and personnel of the state. Unlike Aristotle, however, Aquinas envisions a supernatural end for human beings beyond their temporal well-being and, by reason of that supernatural end, the membership of Christians in another, divinely established community: the church. The two communities should cooperate to achieve their respective ends. *See* Beatific Vision, End, Happiness, Polity.

Political Prudence: *the intellectual virtue consisting of the right characteristic disposition to reason about matters of governance.* Kingly wisdom is the archetype of political prudence in rulers, and other kinds of rulers share in this prudence in lesser ways. Citizens or subjects of the rulers have another kind of political prudence, one that consists of the right characteristic disposition to obey the rulers' laws. *See* Kingly Prudence, Law, Prudence.

Polity: *the regime or constitution that gives a political community its distinctive form.* For Aquinas, polity also has the meaning of a particular regime or constitution that mixes—that is, combines—features of monarchic rule (rule by one best person), aristocratic rule (rule by the few best persons), and democratic rule (rule by the people). Such a regime includes only limited popular participation. *See* Political Community.

Power: *the active capacity to perform a certain kind of activity.* For example, the intellect and the will are the powers of human beings to perform specific acts.

Glossary | 163

Principle: *the major premise of an argument.* Principles presupposing no other principle, or at least no principle other than the principle of contradiction, are first principles. There are theoretical first principles (e.g., *everything coming to be has a cause*) and practical first principles (e.g., *do good, avoid evil*). *See* Intellectual Virtues, Synderesis.

Property (1): *any material possession.*

Property (2): *a quality or characteristic that necessarily belongs to something but is not a part of the thing's essence or definition.* For example, human beings' ability to use speech to convey their thoughts is a characteristic proper to them, and so one of their properties, but not part of their essence or definition (rational animal).

Prudence (Practical Wisdom): *the intellectual virtue consisting of the right disposition to reason about what human beings should or should not do.* Prudence concerns human action and so differs from theoretical wisdom, which concerns the ultimate causes of things without regard to human action. Theoretical reason understands the ends of moral virtues, and prudence chooses the proper means to achieve those ends. As the most important natural virtue connected with human action, prudence is sometimes listed as a moral virtue. *See* End, Habit, Happiness, Moral Virtues, Political Prudence, Theoretical Wisdom, Virtue.

Reason: *(1) the process of drawing conclusions from principles; (2) the power to draw conclusions from principles; (3) the power of the intellect in general.* Aquinas often uses the term in the third sense. *See* Intellect, Principle.

Regime: *See* Polity.

Right: *the objectively right, that is, just, order of human relations.* Natural law, divine law, and human law determine this order. Aquinas is concerned about the duties that human beings owe to others, not the rights individual human beings possess, although the rights of some human beings are necessarily correlative to the duties that other human beings owe to them. *See* Justice, Law.

Science (Aristotelian): *knowledge about things through knowledge of their causes.* Science studies the efficient, final, material, and formal causes of things. Physical, psychological, and social sciences study the secondary causes of material and human things, and philosophy (metaphysics) studies the first causes of being as such. For Aristotle, philosophy is the highest science. For Aquinas, theology, the study of God in the light of Christian revelation, is the highest science. *See* Cause, Intellect, Intellectual Virtues, Theoretical Wisdom.

Slavery: *involuntary servitude.* In medieval society, war captives became slaves, and their servitude was terminated by ransom or treaty. The feudal institutions of serfdom and vassalage were similar to slavery in that serfs, vassals, and their children were bound to certain lifetime duties to their lords and masters. But serfs and vassals, unlike the slaves of ancient Greece and Rome and those of the antebellum American South, had rights that their lords and masters were in theory bound to observe.

Species: *the substantial identity of material things insofar as that identity is common to many things.* The species concept (e.g., human being) is composed of a genus concept (e.g., animal), which indicates the essence of material things in an incompletely determined way; and a specific difference (e.g., rational), which distinguishes different kinds of things of the same genus. The species concept, or definition, thus expresses the whole substance or essence of a particular kind of material thing. *See* Essence.

Subject (1): *that in which something else inheres.* In the strict sense, subjects are the substances underlying accidental characteristics. For example, human beings are the subjects of their powers and acts. In a broader sense, powers are the subjects of the powers' acts. For example, the intellect is the subject of intellectual acts.

Subject (2): *a human being bound to obey another human being.* For example, British citizens are British subjects—that is, bound to obey British authorities.

Synderesis: *habitual understanding of the first principles governing human action.* This habit is innate. Human beings are disposed by their rational nature to recognize that they should seek the good proper to their human nature and avoid things contrary to it. The human good involves preserving one's life in reasonable ways, mating and raising offspring in reasonable ways, and living cooperatively with others in organized society. Conscience applies these first principles to particular acts. *See* Conscience, Habit, Law, Principle.

Temperance (Moderation): *the moral virtue consisting of the right characteristic disposition to restrain irrational sense appetites for the greatest sense pleasures; namely, food, alcoholic drink, and sex.* See Moral Virtues, Virtue.

Theoretical Wisdom: *the intellectual virtue consisting of the right characteristic disposition to reason about the ultimate causes of things.* See Intellectual Virtues, Virtue.

Virtue: *human excellence.* Virtue is an enduring quality and so a characteristic disposition. Aquinas distinguishes three kinds of virtue: intellectual, moral, and theological (supernatural). Concerning theoretical truth, intellectual virtues comprise understanding first principles, scientific knowledge, and theoretical wisdom. Concerning practical truth, intellectual virtues comprise prudence and skills. Moral virtues consist of characteristic readiness to act in practical matters as prudence dictates. Natural prudence and natural moral virtues are acquired. The theological virtues are faith, hope, and charity. These virtues are infused, and supernatural prudence and supernatural moral virtues are infused with charity. *See* Charity, Habit, Intellectual Virtues, Moral Virtues, Principle, Prudence, Science, Theoretical Wisdom.

Will: *the intellectual (rational) appetite of human beings; the intellectual faculty of desire.* In addition to sense appetites, which are common to all animals, human beings have an intellectual (rational) appetite. Human beings can and do desire things that reason apprehends as good. The will necessarily desires the ultimate human perfection, happiness, but freely desires particular goods, which are only partially good. *See* Happiness, Intention.

Wisdom: *See* Appetite, Kingly Prudence, Political Prudence, Prudence, Theoretical Wisdom.

Select Bibliography

Life and Works of Thomas Aquinas

Torrell, Jean-Pierre. *St. Thomas Aquinas, vol. 1: The Person and His Work.* Robert Royal, trans. Washington: The Catholic University of America Press, 1996.

Tugwell, Simon, ed. "Introduction to St. Thomas." In *Albert and Thomas: Selected Writings,* 201–351. New York: Paulist Press, 1988.

Complete Translations of the Summa Theologica

Summa Theologiae. English Dominican Fathers, trans., with Latin text, introduction, notes, appendices, and glossary. 60 vols. New York: McGraw-Hill, 1964–1966.

Summa Theologica of St. Thomas Aquinas, The. English Dominican Fathers, trans. 3 vols. New York: Benziger, 1947–1948; reprint ed., Allen, TX: Christian Classics, 1981. Available online: <www.newadvent.org/summa>.

Partial Translations of the Summa Theologica

God and Creation. William P. Baumgarth and Richard J. Regan, trans., with introduction. Scranton: University of Scranton Press, 1994.

Human Constitution, The. Richard J. Regan, trans., with introduction. Scranton: University of Scranton Press, 1997.

Law, Morality, and Politics, 2nd ed. William P. Baumgarth and Richard J. Regan, eds. Richard J. Regan, trans., with introduction. Indianapolis: Hackett Publishing Company, 2002.

Summa Theologiae: A Concise Translation. Timothy McDermott, ed., trans. Westminster, MD: Christian Classics, 1989.

Summary of Philosophy, A. Richard J. Regan, ed., trans., with introduction. Indianapolis: Hackett Publishing Company, 2003.

Treatise on Law. Richard J. Regan, trans., with introduction. Indianapolis: Hackett Publishing Company, 2000.

Virtue: Way to Happiness. Richard J. Regan, trans., with introduction. Scranton: University of Scranton Press, 1999.

Translations of Other Works of Thomas Aquinas

Cardinal Virtues, The: Aquinas, Albert, and Philip the Chancellor. R.E. Houser, ed., trans. Toronto: Pontifical Institute of Medieval Studies, 2004.

Commentary on the Nicomachean Ethics. Charles I. Litzenger, trans. Chicago: Regnery, 1963.

"Commentary on the Politics" [selections]. In *Medieval Political Philosophy,* 298–334. Ralph Lerner and Muhsin Mahdi, eds. Ernest L. Fortin and Peter D. O'Neill, trans. New York: Free Press, 1963.

Disputed Questions on Virtue. Ralph McInerny, trans. South Bend: St. Augustine's Press, 1999.

On Evil [De Malo]. Brian Davies, ed., with introduction. Richard J. Regan, trans. New York: Oxford University Press, 2003.

On Kingship, to the King of Cyprus [De regno]. I. Th. Eschmann, ed. Gerald B. Phelan, trans. Toronto: Pontifical Institute of Medieval Studies, 1949.

General Commentaries

Aertsen, Jan. *Nature and Creation: Thomas Aquinas's Way of Thought.* Leiden: Brill, 1988.

Clarke, W. Norris. *The One and the Many: A Contemporary Thomistic Metaphysics.* Notre Dame: University of Notre Dame Press, 2001.

Davies, Brian. *The Thought of Thomas Aquinas.* Oxford: Oxford University Press, 1992.

———*Aquinas.* London: Continuum, 2002.

———ed. *Thomas Aquinas: Contemporary Philosophical Perspectives.* Oxford: Oxford University Press, 2002.

Elders, Leo J. *The Philosophical Theology of St. Thomas Aquinas.* Leiden: Brill, 1990.

Gilson, Etienne. *The Christian Philosophy of St. Thomas Aquinas.* Laurence K. Shook, trans., from the 5th French ed. of *Thomism,* cited below. New York: Random House, 1956.

———*Thomism: The Philosophy of Thomas Aquinas,* 6th [final and substantially revised] ed. Laurence K. Shook and Armand Maurer, trans. Toronto: Pontifical Institute of Medieval Studies, 2002.

Haldane, John, ed. *Mind, Metaphysics, and Value in the Thomistic and Analytic Traditions.* Notre Dame: University of Notre Dame Press, 2002.

Kenny, Anthony. *Aquinas on Being.* New York: Oxford University Press, 2003.

Kretzmann, Norman, and Eleanore Stump. *The Cambridge Companion to Aquinas.* Cambridge: Cambridge University Press, 1993.

McInerny, Ralph. *A First Glance at St. Thomas Aquinas: A Handbook for Peeping Thomists.* Notre Dame: University of Notre Dame Press, 1990.

Pieper, Joseph. *Guide to Thomas Aquinas.* Richard and Clara Winston, trans. New York: Pantheon, 1962

Stump, Eleanore. *Aquinas.* London: Routlege, 2003.

Wippel, John F. *The Metaphysical Thought of Thomas Aquinas.* Washington: The Catholic University of America Press, 2000.

Thomist Ethics in General

Bradley, Denis J.M. *Aquinas on the Twofold Human Good: Reason and Human Happiness in Aquinas's Moral Science.* Washington: The Catholic University of America Press, 1997.

Donegan, Alan. *Human Ends and Human Action: An Exploration in St. Thomas's Treatment*. Milwaukee: Marquette University Press, 1985.

Elders, Leon J. *Lex et Libertas: Freedom and Law According to St. Thomas Aquinas*. Studi tomistici 30. Vatican City: Libreria Editrice Vaticana, 1987.

Elders, Leon J. and K. Hedwig, eds. *The Ethics of St. Thomas Aquinas*. Studi tomistici 25. Vatican City: Libreria Editrice Vaticana, 1984.

Finnis, John M. *Aquinas: Moral, Political, and Legal Theory*. Oxford: Oxford University Press, 1999.

Flannery, Kevin L. *Acts amid Precepts*. Washington: The Catholic University of America Press, 2001.

Lonergan, Bernard. "The Natural Desire to See God." In *Collection*, 2nd ed., 81–91. Frederick E. Crowe and Robert M. Doran, eds. Toronto: University of Toronto Press, 1988.

Mullady, Brian T. *The Meaning of the Term Moral in St. Thomas Aquinas*. Studi tomistici 27. Vatican City: Libreria Editrice Vaticana, 1986.

Pope, Stephen J., ed. *The Ethics of Aquinas*. Washington: Georgetown University Press, 2002.

Powell, Ralph. *Freely Chosen Reality*. Washington: University Press of America, 1983.

Sokolowski, Robert. *Moral Action: A Phenomenological Study*. Bloomington: Indiana University Press, 1985.

Virtue

Geach, Peter. *The Virtues*. Cambridge: Cambridge University Press, 1977.

Hibbs, Thomas. *Virtue's Splendor: Wisdom, Prudence, and the Human Good*. New York: Fordham University Press, 2001.

Hursthouse, Rosalind. *On Virtue Ethics*. Oxford: Oxford University Press, 1999.

Pieper, Joseph. *The Four Cardinal Virtues: Prudence, Justice, Fortitude, and Temperance*. Richard and Clara Winston, trans. New York: Harcourt, Bruce, and World, 1965.

Porter, Jean. *The Recovery of Virtue: The Relevance of Aquinas for Christian Ethics*. Louisville, KY: John Knox Press, 1990.

Westberg, Daniel. *Right Practical Reason: Aristotle, Action, and Prudence in Aquinas*. Oxford: Oxford University Press, 1994.

Natural Law

Armstrong, Ross A. *Primary and Secondary Precepts in Thomistic Natural Law Teaching*. The Hague: Nijhoff, 1966.

George, Robert P. *Natural Law Theory: Contemporary Essays*. Oxford: Oxford University Press, 1992.

Goyette, John, et al. *St. Thomas Aquinas and the Natural Law: Contemporary Perspectives*. Washington: The Catholic University of America Press, 2004.

Hittinger, Russell. *Critique of the New Natural Law Theory*. Notre Dame: University of Notre Dame Press, 1987.

Kaczor, Christopher. *Proportionalism and the Natural Law Tradition*. Washington: The Catholic University of America Press, 2002.

Lee, Patrick. "Permanence of the Ten Commandments: St. Thomas and His Modern Commentators." *Theological Studies* 42 (1981): 422–43.

Lisska, Anthony J. *Aquinas's Theory of Natural Law: An Analytic Reconstruction*. Oxford: Oxford University Press, 1997.

Reilly, James P. *St. Thomas on Law*. Etienne Gilson Series 12. Toronto: Pontifical Institute of Medieval Studies, 1990.

Rhonheimer, Martin. *Natural Law and Practical Reason: A Thomist View of Moral Autonomy*. Gerald Malsbary, trans. New York: Fordham University Press, 1999.

Simon, Yves. *The Tradition of Natural Law: A Philosopher's Reflections*. New York: Fordham University Press, 1965.

Political Philosophy

Bigongiari, Dino. "Introduction." In *The Political Ideas of Saint Thomas Aquinas*, vii–xxxvii. New York: Hafner, 1953.

Fortin, Ernest L. "St. Thomas Aquinas." In *History of Political Philosophy*, 2nd ed., 223–50. Leo Strauss and Joseph Cropsey, eds. Chicago: University of Chicago Press, 1981.

Maritain, Jacques. *Man and the State*. Chicago: University of Chicago, 1951.

Regan, Richard J. "Aquinas on Political Obedience and Disobedience." *Thought* 56 (1981): 77–88.

———"The Human Person in Organized Society: Aquinas." Ch. 2 in *The Moral Dimensions of Politics*, 37–46. New York: Oxford University Press, 1986.

Simon, Yves. *The Philosophy of Democratic Government*. Chicago: University of Chicago Press, 1961.

Recent Bibliography

Davies, Brian. "Bibliography." In *Aquinas*, xiv–xxii. London: Continuum, 2002.

Ingardia, Richard. *Thomas Aquinas: International Bibliography, 1977–1990*. Bowling Green, OH: Philosophical Documentation Center, Bowling Green State University, 1993.

Index